Parades and Promenades

Parades and Promenades

Antrim, New Hampshire
. . . the second hundred years

researched and written by
THE ANTRIM HISTORY COMMITTEE

Dorothy M. Ellison
William A. Gold
Carroll M. Johnson
Donald B. Madden
Isabel Butterfield Nichols
Ralph H. Proctor
Miriam Wadhams Roberts
Arleen Paige White

published for
THE ANTRIM HISTORY COMMITTEE
by
 PHOENIX PUBLISHING
Canaan, New Hampshire

Antrim History Committee.
    Parades and promenades.

    1. Antrim, N.H.—History. I. Ellison, Dorothy M. II.
Title.
F44.A7A57   1977   974.2'8   76-30841
ISBN 0-914016-39-3

Printed in the United States of America
by Courier Printing Company
Binding by New Hampshire Bindery
Design and illustration by A. L. Morris

Contents

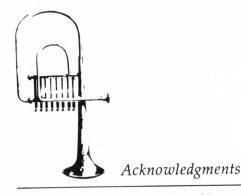

Acknowledgments

This history has been long in the making, and
even longer in the dream stage. It was proposed
as far back as 1896, and reconsidered at various
intervals until 1968, when a committee was
appointed to begin the actual research. Several
of the original members of that committee died
before their efforts reached fruition. We have
used the material they compiled, and hereby
acknowledge our debt to Ellerton Edwards,
Byron Butterfield, and William Hurlin. It is our
hope that they would have been pleased with
this book.

Thanks are also due to William J. Clark, who
researched the chapter on churches, and to
Elizabeth Michael, who typed much of the text
without remuneration.

Antrim is fortunate in having citizens who are so
interested in preserving the town's history that
they have collected priceless pictures of Antrim's
past. We have borrowed freely from them for
our illustrations, and wish to thank Robert
Flanders, Michael Chase, Bernice Robb, Priscilla
Hurlin, Howard Humphrey, and Rose Poor for
the generous loan of their cherished pictures.

We owe special thanks to the Monadnock Paper
Mills and its executive vice president, Richard
Verney, for the gift of all the paper on which
this book is printed.

Finally, we would like to acknowledge our great
debt to the publishers, A. L. Morris and Adrian
A. Paradis, without whose expert help the book
might never have materialized.

Introduction

IN A REVIEW OF THE EVENTS of the past two hundred years, one fact stands out: Antrim was a very social community. The list of clubs, lodges, and kindred organizations is staggering. The Antrim Players, the Antrim Grange, the Antrim Music Club, the Odd Fellows, the Rebekahs, the Woman's Club, the DAR, the Chamber of Commerce, the Women's Relief Corps, the American Legion, the PTA, the Antrim Garden Club, not to mention all the social groups of the various churches, the Boy Scouts, the Girl Scouts, the Cub Scouts, the Brownies, and the 4 H-ers.

Holidays, old Home Days, and some arbitrarily chosen days were celebrated with gusto year after year. May Day breakfasts, Washington Birthday suppers, and town meeting dinners were not to be missed. Nor were the annual church fairs, old school reunions, winter carnivals, Grange harvest suppers, and a variety of Hallowe'en and Christmas parties.

There was an accepted formula for such rituals as the Fourth of July and Memorial Day observances. They were sure to begin with a parade and end with a promenade; the intervening time was given over to Antrim's delight, a double-header baseball game.

The involvement was not always merely social. Everyone had a sense of belonging. If a parade was a symbol of the town's pride, so also was the community effort that produced the Memorial Gymnasium. The annual hospital aid fair is a tribute to the dedicated work of a large percentage of the town's population. The new town beach, sponsored by the Lion's Club, would never have existed had there not been willing volunteers who labored to make the dream a reality.

The soul of a small town finds its expression in these kinds of cooperative ventures; the pride of a small town is mirrored in its celebrations. Parades and promenades. They symbolized the close social structure of Antrim's life throughout most of two centuries. They bound the people together. They were the outward manifestation of Antrim's inner unity.

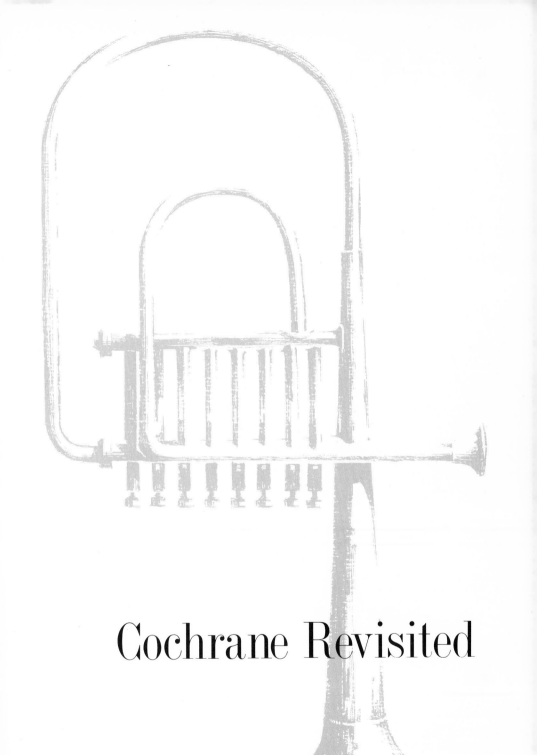

Cochrane Revisited

Antrim
1744-1877

an
examination
of Cochrane's History

It is worthy of remark that a state historian can say what he pleases, and squarely speak of the faults of public men; but a town historian must be blind to many things.[1]

By Way of Introduction

THIS ASSIGNMENT was given to me by my colleagues on the History Committee one evening when I was absent from the monthly meeting. I had, in previous meetings, defended the Reverend W.R. Cochrane and his *History of the Town of Antrim, New Hampshire* from their critics. Simple literary criticism became near calumny when the object was not only the town's principal history, but one written in the Nineteenth Century. As a teacher of Nineteenth Century American literature, I felt almost automatically obliged to rise to Cochrane's defense.

Cochrane's critics claimed that the history was boring and that its language was old-fashioned. I disagreed, a little too vehemently, I suspect, for the committee's response was to assign me the chore of "rewriting Cochrane." Committee minutes do not note whether I was being punished for my impudence or being given a chance to redeem myself by putting my money where my mouth was.

It is the spirit of Cochrane's history that prompted me to his defense, a spirit I thought best exemplified by the lines quoted at the beginning of this chapter, which come from Cochrane's preface to his history. I had recently talked with a book and magazine publisher who, when he learned that I was a member of Antrim's History Committee, lamented the tediousness of town histories. He complained that they were boring because their writers were too timid to record the scandals and crimes of their towns, and what was left was pedantic and dull, a sort of historical public relations effort.

I thought this publisher was, for a New Englander, too naive to believe, for why would anyone intending to remain in the town after the history was published be so foolhardy as to peddle scandal or reopen old wounds? When I read Cochrane's statement that town historians must be blind to many things, I felt a kinship with my fellow historian. . .the bond that unites when one can claim he was proven right. Besides, Cochrane's statement seemed magnificently honest and, if I agreed, then I must be honest, too.

My assignment was vague enough to permit my own interpretation. "To rewrite Cochrane" suggests a *Reader's Digest* condensation, a crime I have no intention of committing. Ideally, I would use Cochrane and others to write a brief history of Antrim's early years, but such a labor would require more time and energy than I could afford. After all, Cochrane spent five years on his history and received $500 from the town. Without such leisure and motivation, my devotion to the job will (understandably, I hope) be briefer. My goal then is to write an essay *about* Cochrane's history, one designed to encourage the reader to dig up a copy of the original and pursue his studies at the source. If I am successful, I will be able to capture a bit of Cochrane's flavor to whet appetites.

> *Of course, it could not be expected that a history of this quiet town would be very romantic or great. We have had no Indian tragedies, no national battles, no men of extensive fame, no mines of wealth, and no very remarkable record in any way. Our town has little that is brilliant; much that is solid, honorable and good. But to those born or bred here, these pages, I think, will be full of interest.*[2]

From Londonderry to Antrim

Cochrane's history of Antrim begins 55 years before the birth of Christ when, in his long "Introductory," he writes of the Roman conquest of England. He begins with the Druids and their "authoritative false religion," and moves on to the Picts and native Scots and the Wall of Severus, a monumental barrier built in 208AD to separate

England and Scotland. For Antrim's ancestors were Scots who migrated across the North Channel of the Irish Sea to Northern Ireland during the reign of James I (1603-1625) to take advantage of better farm land. According to Cochrane, James chose these Scots because they were "exceedingly brave, and industrious and were people of intelligence, reliable in every place." Half of Cochrane's "Introductory" is devoted to the religious oppression these Presbyterians suffered, culminating with their valiant defense of Londonderry, in upper Northern Ireland, one county to the west of County Antrim. This was in 1689 and, drawing heavily from English historian Thomas Macaulay, Cochrane writes in detail of the siege of the city by the French, Irish, and English troops who outnumbered the defenders five to one. "From these unconquerable soldiers who defended Londonderry," Cochrane writes, "descended many of the settlers of Antrim — among them the Dinsmores, Cochrans, and McKeens, and others."

But the Protestants' victory over the Catholics left them little peace, such were taxes, problems with land titles, the monarchy, and the aristocracy, and in 1718 four Scotch ministers petitioned Governor Shute of Massachusetts for "suitable incouragement" to emigrate to the New World.

Three hundred and nineteen men signed the petition, indicating that they represented 1,200 or more with a "sincere and hearty Inclination to Transport our selves to that very excellent and reknown Plantation" of New England.

Governor Shute gave them the encouragement they needed, and four months later they reached Boston harbor in five ships. They split into three groups, one remaining in Boston, another going to Worcester, and a third going to Casco Bay, Maine. The third group spent a winter locked in the ice before sailing south to the Merrimack River and dropping anchor at Haverhill. They heard of a twelve-mile-square tract twenty miles from Haverhill that was available for settling, and there they went, calling their new settlement Londonderry. The first sermon by the Reverend James MacGregor was preached April 23, 1719, under a large oak on the east side of Beaver Pond. His sermon was taken from Isaiah 32:2 —

> Each will be like a hiding place from the wind,
> A covert from the tempest,
> Like streams of water in a dry place,
> Like the shade of a great rock in a weary land.

Five years later, there were 230 church members present at the spring communion and, according to Cochrane, Londonderry was feeling crowded. The early settlers were a restless group. They soon began other settlements in New Boston, Chester, Derryfield, Hudson, Merrimack and, to the west, Cherry Valley, New York, and to the north, Truro, Nova Scotia. Hillsborough was settled in 1741. Three years later Philip Riley cleared the land and established his farm just over the town line in Antrim, but abandoned it when the French and Indian War in Canada threatened Tory and Indian attacks. Cochrane says most of the families fled south to Massachusetts in 1746 and Riley didn't return until 1761.

However, the Pennacook Indians in Antrim were peaceful, and Cochrane tells us there is no record of any attacks.

After Riley's return, others came too, including James Aiken, William Smith, James Duncan, James Hogg, George and James Otterson. They were attracted by an advertisement published by the Masonian Proprietors, who apparently implied that the land was available at no cost. This proved untrue, for the selling price of Antrim real estate in 1766 was nine cents — or half a pistareen — an acre. Although a 160-acre farm could be bought for less than fifteen dollars, these people were poor, Cochrane says, and the physical and economic hardships were severe.

The Masonians had nothing to do with the fraternal order. They were the heirs of Captain John Mason who, in 1621, obtained a grant from King James for land east of the Merrimack. Under it, he and others started settlements in Dover and Strawbery Banke, now Portsmouth. After King James died, Captain Mason obtained a second grant for the lands west of the Merrimack, a triangular piece of territory extending from Conway to Rindge to the Merrimack River, just missing Antrim. Massachusetts, however, had claimed a good portion of southern New Hampshire and by way of exercising jurisdiction made grants to New Boston and New Ipswich in 1736 and Peterborough in 1738. Two years later, George II assumed authority of the land to the Connecticut River and gave it to New Hampshire. Mason's heirs argued in court for years over ownership of the land, and Cochrane covers this litigation in detail in his first chapter.

He also explains that charter dates of towns in this area, if in contention, are based on who had the authority at the time the charter was issued.

Population figures from the 1767 census are, according to Cochrane:

Londonderry	2,389
Bedford	362
New Boston	296
Lyndeboro	272
Greenfield	272
Peterborough	443
Hillsborough	64
Francestown	20
Antrim	12

The state had a population of 52,700, not counting 633 slaves.

Frontier life was not easy, and winters were especially hard. The Aikens lost a child their first winter here, the first death recorded in Antrim. That spring, Mrs. Aiken, Molly, bore the deacon a girl, Polly, the first child born in Antrim. The first male born in Antrim was James Aiken, Jr., in 1772.

The first frame building in Antrim was also Aiken's. It was his barn, built in 1769. The timber was "all got out by hand" near by, but the boards were cut in a Hillsborough saw mill and drawn home on the Contoocook River ice. The nearest road was through West Deering, and presumably the river route was the shortest for Deacon Aiken.

If Riley was the first settler in Antrim and Aiken was the second, then, according to Cochrane, William Smith was the third, Randall Alexander the fourth and, by 1772, the fifth was John Gordon. (From a study of Cochrane's map, presumably accurate at the time it was printed in 1880, Gordon's house was in North Branch, west of the college. I leave the charting of other early settlers' houses and farms to the reader. See Cochrane's map on next page.)

Riley was Gordon's nearest neighbor. One midsummer day, Riley attempted to visit Gordon's cabin in the woods skirting the North Branch. He got lost and was forced to spend the night on the mountain. The next day, he found Gordon's cabin. Gordon, according to Cochrane, when learning that his neighbor had spent the night on the mountain, declared the mountain should be called Riley's Mountain, and to this day it is.

Cochrane tells other good stories, some of which he admits he took from the Reverend John M. Whiton's earlier history. He quotes Whiton when he writes of Major Samuel Gregg of Peterborough deciding to visit his good friend James Aiken in Antrim. It was a cold winter's

Map of Antrim . . . as originally printed in

Cochrane's "History of the Town of Antrim"

This map, names and all, was copied for the most part from the county map. I
be of considera

made some changes and several additions. It is thought to be sufficiently accurate to due to the town.

day and, warmly dressed, Major and Mrs. Gregg walked north on the ice of the Contoocook. But when they got to Antrim they discovered that the Aikens had gone to visit friends in New Boston. They had a cup of tea and some shortcake with Jane, the Aikens' oldest daughter, and returned home, walking on the river ice. Total distance covered that day: twenty-four miles.

By the fall of 1774 there were fifteen families in Antrim. Two lived in East Antrim; six at the Branch or in that vicinity, and seven in what was known in Cochrane's day as South Village and what is now Antrim village. Total population: sixty-two.

The Revolutionary War

The next year, down in Concord, Massachusetts,

> *By the rude bridge that arched the flood,*
> *Their flag to April's breeze unfurled,*[3]

the embattled farmers turned Minute Men fired that shot heard 'round the world. The news didn't take long to reach Antrim. After a brief meeting at Aiken's house, every man in Antrim old enough to carry a gun left immediately for Massachusetts. Every man, that is, except two, John Gordon and William Smith. Gordon left a short time later and Smith, then sixty, followed the next day with provisions. Seventeen men in all answered that first call, and before the end of the war Antrim had contributed 100 percent of its eligible male population to the fight. By that fall there were twenty families in town with a total population of seventy-five.

Antrim now had its first saw mill, and soon there was a second. Lumbering was a brisk business for the next few years, Cochrane says, and 20,000 acres of trees were cut in the next 100 years.

Antedating and anticipating the Declaration of Independence was the Association Test, a document that was circulated throughout the state:

> *We the Subscribers, do hereby solemnly en-*
> *gage, and promise, that we will, to the utmost*
> *of our Power, at the Risque of our Lives, and*
> *Fortunes, with Arms, oppose the Hostile Pro-*
> *ceedings of the British Fleets and Armies*
> *against the United American Colonies.*

All males twenty-one or over, "except Lunatics, idiots and negroes," were asked to sign it. In the whole state, 8,193 signed. Seven hundred and seventy-three refused to sign. Most of these were Quakers, Cochrane says, who were loyal but pacifists, and some were either too old, too sick, or too timid. Cochrane says only a third of the 773 were actually Tories.

In Antrim, twenty-five signed. None refused to sign.

That year papers of incorporation were drawn up and submitted to the legislature at Exeter. On March 22, 1777, the act of incorporation was read for the third time on the floor and the legislature voted in its favor.

The First Fifty Years

Cochrane's "Introductory" and first chapter deal with early history. His next two chapters cover Antrim's first and second fifty-year periods, respectively, up to 1877, the year of the centennial celebration, which he covers in his fourth chapter.

The first town meeting was held May 1, 1777, this late spring date being chosen, Cochrane suggests, because snow had been deep that winter and there were still no roads. They met at John Duncan's house, chose Maurice Lynch as town clerk, voted to pay selectmen twenty-five cents a day for their services, voted forty dollars for highway funds, and taxed residents, "those in the town," a shilling each for the "charge of the Charter."

Cochrane apparently had good access to early records, for he quotes them liberally. They are notable for revealing citizens' concerns about finding the town's geographical center and about clearing land, and for unusual word spelling. (Not all the unique spelling can be credited to Eighteenth Century use of the language.) Cochrane suggests that in choosing the site for the meeting house the selectmen veered from the surveyor's exact town-center stake and chose a site with a good view. It was about a quarter-mile due north of where the Grange is now.

That year the town built a bridge across the Contoocook where, 100 years later, the Baldwin bridge stood. This is apparently the site of the bridge south of town near the Bennington line. The road was cut and cleared from this bridge through Antrim Center over Meeting House Hill and thence to Hillsborough. Cochrane says the road wasn't much . . .barely passable for a single horse. . .but a road, nevertheless, and the first road.

These people were all farmers and since Antrim's site was heavily forested clearing of the land was a primary problem. Many people spent several summers in Antrim clearing their land before eventually building a cabin or house and moving in. They also built stone walls, many of which are still visible.

The next regular town meeting was held in March, 1778, at the house of Richard McAllister. The town voted to raise $32 for preaching and $500 for roads. Pay for road work was to be $3 a day per man, $2 a day per ox. This increase in road appropriation was due, Cochrane says, to the depreciation of paper currency, which was quite rapid and severe. Wages for road workers in the years before had been 50 cents a day.

Currency depreciation continued. In 1779, the town voted $3,000 for roads, and wages were $10 a day. Such was the value of paper money. Cochrane says silver coins had all but disappeared. The Reverend James Miltimore was paid $70 a day for preaching. Seventy dollars, that is, worth $4. Three years later paper depreciation had reached the point where the Reverend Jonathan Barnes of Hillsborough paid a whole year's salary for a four-week-old pig, Boston sailors sewed paper money together to make coats of them for parades, and barbers papered their shops with them. The worth of one thousand paper dollars was one silver dollar.

In 1779, the town's first tithing man was chosen and two years later another town official, the hog reeve, was added to the roster. The tithing man's badge of office was a long stick tipped with brass or pewter. His job was to keep order in religious meetings and to see that the Sabbath was strictly observed. This included policing of the prohibition on Sunday travel.[4]

The hog reeve was a sort of hog catcher. Since there were few fences in Antrim, his job was to round up wandering pigs on complaint, yoke them so they couldn't pass through what fences there were, ring them so they couldn't root up neighbors' vegetables, and collect fines from their owners. Eventually the job lost its importance when fences became the custom, and hog reeves elected at town meetings were usually newly-married people, "on the ground," Cochrane says, "that such people were not capable of discharging any duty."

There was also the office of dog pelter, instituted in 1793. Cochrane says:
The duty of this officer was to sit near the door with a cudgel, and lay it on to every dog which attempted to enter the church. Sometimes these officers

were armed with a long staff having an iron point, or hook, at the end, to be used in severe cases. It is related that one dog-pelter struck the hook into the back of a rebellious cur, and swung him, howling, over his shoulder. This would be very interesting to the audience and helpful to religion, of course. An occasional wake-up in the process of a two-hour sermon would certainly have its uses. As a great many babies were then carried to church, it may be supposed that small noises were not noticed. Perhaps our modern looking round at the step of a slipper, or the rustle of silk, or the snore of some restful saint, may be taken as a mark of our too great fastidiousness as to silence in church.

It will be observed that some of the most responsible men in town were promoted to this office. The salary is not mentioned. But these men were willing to remain in the office year after year, as the annual record is, "Voted to continue the old Dog pelters." The fact that these men's pews were near the doors, may account, in part, for their annual election to this office of trust and honor. Dogs were plenty, every farmer having one or more. They made considerable disturbance in church, with a dog-fight in the aisles at any time possible, and various uncleanly demonstrations at the corners of the pews. To prevent these insupportable trials, dog-pelters were first chosen. But the object of silence was scarcely attained, since often all business had to stop through a tremendous howling, till the officers cleared the aisles. One person remembers seeing Samuel Dinsmore, who sat with a heavy cane leaning over his pew by the west porch, when a big dog came in and proposed to stop a minute at his pew-door, strike him a blow that sent him, with inconceivable yells and howls, clear up to the pulpit. The audience were all waked up!

Cochrane says the winter of 1779 was known as the Hard Winter, and I'll let him tell you about it.

Dr. Whiton tells us that water did not drop from the eaves in any place for six weeks. For most of the winter snow was five feet deep on a level. The only communication was by means of snow-shoes. Roads were out of the question. Boston harbor was frozen hard enough for a sleigh-ride on it, according to report. People could not go to mill, and, after their stock of meal was used up, they lived for weeks on boiled corn and various broths. Wood was drawn on hand-sleds most of the winter, it being impossible to move a team. It is related that one lad and his little sister, their father being in the army, drew wood in this way for the family all winter. Having no boots, they sewed rags round their feet and saturated them with neat's-foot oil to keep from freezing, and then sallied forth into the woods. Old stockings, thus saturated, were called proof against frost. As evidence that *the reports of cold and snow were not greatly exaggerated, the Journal of the New Hampshire Legislature, March 8, 1780, contains a "Resolve to enable the Court of Common Pleas in the County of Hillsborough to take up and finish sundry matters pending at said Court at their next term, the last term being lost by reason of the stormy weather." In some of these deep snows and blows ordinary log houses were entirely covered out of sight. In one place in New Hampshire, nearly a month after a great storm, a flock of one hundred sheep were dug out of a snow-bank that was sixteen feet deep above their backs, most of them being dead, the few alive having subsisted by eating the wool off the dead!*

In such a winter the privation and solitude of these few scattered settlers must have been oppressive. It was a rare thing to see a neighbor's face. Each family was shut up by itself. Even the larger places, like Boston and Portsmouth, were thoroughly blockaded with snow. In those families where the husband and father was in the army, the long winter must have been desolate in the extreme! With all our winter comforts and social enjoyments, we are in no condition to appreciate what was endured by the founders of our institution.

Was there any connection between this severe winter and the following May's Dark Day? Again, Cochrane writes:

Following this severe and long winter came the celebrated "Dark Day," May 19, 1780. I take the liberty to copy such statements about it as have fallen under my eye. For several days previous the air was full of smoky vapors, as if fires had been burning in the woods, the sun and moon appearing red and somewhat obscured. The early morning of May 19 was cloudy and showery and cool, with some thunder and lightning. But about ten o'clock, when the artisans were busy in the shop and mill, the women spinning and weaving, and the farmers hurrying with their spring work in the field, it began to grow dark. The wild birds screamed and flew to their nests, – the hens went to their roosts, – the cattle came up, uttering strange cries, to their stalls, – the sheep, bleating wofully, huddled under the fences, – the buds and small leaves on the trees were colored almost to an indigo blue, – robins and blue-birds flew into the houses as if they sought the protection of man, – the rain that soon followed was full of a substance like burnt vegetable matter, forming a scum, with smell of soot, over everything, collecting on the Merrimack river here and there to the depth of half a foot, – and this strange darkness increased until by noon people had to light candles to eat their dinners by! Lights were seen in every window, and, out-of-doors, people carried torches to light their steps. Everything took a different color from what it had by sunlight, and consequently the strange reflections of the torch-lights were in keeping with the marvelous and changed appearance of everything. Hosts of people believed the end of the world had begun to come; men dropped on their knees to pray in the field; many ran to their neighbors to confess wrongs and ask forgiveness; multitudes rushed in to the meeting-houses in towns where they had such, where pious and aged ministers, pleading repentance, interceded with God in their behalf; and everywhere throughout this day of wonder and alarm, the once careless thought of their sins and of their Maker! At this time the legislature of Connecticut was in session, and when the growing darkness became so deep that at mid-day they could not see each other, most of them were so alarmed as to be unfit for service. At this juncture Mr. Davenport arose and said: –

Mr. Speaker, it is either the day of Judgment or it is not. If it is not, there is no need of adjourning. If it is, I desire to be found doing my duty. I move that candles be brought, and that we proceed to business.

The darkness somewhat increased all day, and before time of sunset was so intense that no object whatever could be distinguished. Anxiously and tremblingly people waited for the full moon to rise at nine o'clock, and even little children with strained eyes sat silently watching for its beautiful beams to appear. But they were disappointed, the darkness being unaffected by the moon. The most feeling prayers ever prayed in Antrim were at the family altars that night. Children never had more tender blessing than these mothers gave them that night. They slept soundly for the most part, but the parents chiefly sat up all night to wait and see if the glorious sun would rise again. Never dawned a lovelier morning than that 20th of May! Never were hearts more thankful on the earth! Even thoughtless people praised God! So much were the whole population affected by this event, that, at the succeeding March meeting, the town voted, March 9, 1781, to keep the next 19th of May as a day of fasting and prayer.

The darkness was greatest in northern Massachusetts and southern New Hampshire. It covered New England more or less, was noticed on the Hudson river, but was not thought of farther south and west. As to causes and explanations of this event, a high authority says: –

The Dark Day in North America was one of those wonderful phenomena of nature which will always be read of with interest, but which philosophy is at a loss to explain.

In 1781, Cornwallis surrendered at Yorktown and two years later a treaty between England and the United States was signed in Paris. The war was over, the soldiers returned, and the town began to grow. The record in 1783 would lead some to believe, however, that Antrim was either not eager to grow or, at least, was selective about its population. This was the "warning out of town," in which public notices were posted, duly signed by selectmen, notifying the public that certain people. . .and they were named. . .were not welcome as inhabitants. Not only were they unwelcome — they were ordered out of town.

Cochrane notes, however, that these warnings were formalities not designed to create exclusivity, but as legal defenses against supporting any newcomers who fell on hard times. Many of these new citizens eventually prospered, Cochrane notes, and became solid citizens.

Not so with Antrim's first settler, Philip Riley. His fortunes suffered and he was forced to depend on the charity of his son-in-law, Michael Cochlan. Cochlan was consequently exempt from taxes. In those days, it was the custom to put the care of paupers out to the lowest bidder, and in 1788 this became Riley's fate when Cochlan's burden became too great. Eventually, he returned to his relatives and finished out his days with them.

By 1834, there were twenty paupers in town, and the system of "selling" off the poor to the lowest bidder came under scrutiny by "more thoughtful people," as Cochrane puts it. Obviously, the old system smacked of a certain inhumanity and, obviously, not all paupers fared well under the care of their hired benefactors, so the town voted to buy Hutchinson Flint's farm, which was, according to Cochrane's map, on Smith road. By 1869, this poor-farm was discontinued because the county too had built one and Antrim's poor had declined in number. But Cochrane notes that the county farm was far from satisfactory. He said he had heard of much criticism of the place — that it was hard and cruel and distasteful — and he suggests a state farm should take over this duty.

Cochrane says that the winter of 1784-1785 was cold and long, and the snow was deep. Settlers were often awakened at night by the howling of wolves at their doors, children were in constant danger, and even armed men feared to travel at night. Town records in 1784 show that a bounty of five dollars was voted in addition to a state bounty for the killing of wolves.

While records do not indicate if any were killed by wolves, the *Village Messenger* of Amherst on September 30, 1800, reported that sixty-two persons had died in Antrim from dysentery. The summer was hot and dry, and children especially were afflicted. The scourge lasted only two months but there were nineteen funerals in a single week in August.

The meeting house, raised in 1785, was said to be the grandest building in town. Cochrane notes that Antrim people were poor, there being only one frame house in town. All the rest were log cabins. It wasn't until 1788 that the first store was opened. Most Antrim shoppers went to Amherst or New Boston (even Peterborough, with its population of 800, had no store). Antrim women thought nothing of riding horseback to New Boston with linen cloth woven at home to exchange for money or other goods and returning the same day. Francestown had a store two years before Ebenezer Kimball opened his in Antrim, and James Wallace followed with a second store the next year. Despite the competition of two stores in town, prices were high, Cochrane reports, and profits were large.

It was about this time (the mid 1780s) that John Duncan, representing Antrim, Deering, and Hancock, was sent to the legislature. Antrim had a population of 289 in 1786, but it wasn't until 1798 that the population was large enough for its own representative.

If there were any slaves in Antrim, Cochrane did not know of them. There were only 657 reported in the state in 1775, and the number decreased steadily to zero by 1810. The constitution in 1784 declared that "all men are born equally free and independent," and any people held as slaves in New Hampshire were not treated as property but as indentured servants, Cochrane reports.

In 1799 a company formed to build a turnpike from Claremont to Amherst asked permission to pass through Antrim. The town voted

First Meeting House . . . 1785

no objection, and the road was cut through the east part of town. Known as the Second New Hampshire Turnpike, it was opened for business in 1801. William Barnes built a three-story tavern on it, and a store opened nearby. The turnpike prospered for twenty-five years. However, Cochrane complains that its route skirted villages and its tolls were burdensome. Cochrane says the gates were closed and locked "at proper bed-time. . .and woe to the young gentleman that was out late with his father's team." Apparently it was designed to carry cargo, not passengers, and when profits declined its owners gave it to the care of the towns through which it passed. Its gates — there were two in Francestown and one in Hillsboro Upper Village — were taken down and its eight-cent toll passed into history.

By the turn of the century, the town's population had doubled within the past decade to 1,059. Although village roads were built to Barnes' tavern, it didn't prosper. It changed hands several times, and after it burned in 1818 it was not rebuilt. The meeting house on the hill began to suffer criticism because, for one thing, it was difficult to reach in winter. A new road was built south of it to go around the west side of the hill and when it was finished in 1822 the meeting house seemed doomed. A committee appointed to select a new site couldn't reach a decision. Eventually, land was bought from Captain Robert Reed at five dollars a rod, and the lower half of the meeting house was moved about a quarter-mile south. The Grange is now there.

The town of Antrim as we now know it was never considered as a likely place for the meeting house. This portion, known as South Antrim, was too far from the center of things.

Coincident with the movement to change the location of the meeting house was another to separate church and state. We know from records that in 1826 the town voted 128-15 to discontinue preaching at the old meeting house and in subsequent meetings voted heartily in favor of no preaching in the new meeting house. The town continued to pay the minister's salary until 1836, when that article was dismissed from the warrant. With that vote, Cochrane notes, "terminated the long-continued connection between town and church." By then, a church had already been built by the Central Society on land next door to the new meeting house. It cost $6,200, excluding the $400 bell which was paid for by subscription.

The topic of the last sermon in the old meeting house was taken from John 4:20:

Our fathers worshipped on this mountain,

from a conversation between Jesus and the woman of Samaria; and the first sermon in the new church was based on Genesis 28:17:

> *"And he was afraid and said, 'How awesome*
> *is this place! This is none other than the house*
> *of God, and this is the gate of heaven.' "*

This was Jacob speaking after he dreamed of the ladder reaching to heaven and his conversation with the Lord.

Thus by 1827, at the end of Antrim's first 50 years, Cochrane reported there were a new meeting house — now called Town Hall — a church, and nine taverns going "full blast." The latter were all licensed to sell no more than a gallon of wine, rum, gin, or other spirits to a person at one time, and Cochrane, at this point, wonders ironically how much progress we made in 50 years.[5]

The Second Fifty Years

Cochrane took fifty-five pages to cover the first fifty years of Antrim's history, fifteen pages to cover the next fifty years. It was less a matter of running out of steam, I suspect, than of running out of material. Early parts of Cochrane's history owe much to Dr. John Milton Whiton's *History of Antrim*, which ends in 1844. After that, apparently, Cochrane was limited in his research to town records and information he could collect from the memories and scrapbooks of older members of the community.

A town history is difficult to write. Town archives offer information, but not a wealth of it. Tales spun around the local stores' hot stoves are always interesting, but sometimes lack accuracy. Contrast, if you will, the material — which includes past histories — available to national historians with that available to local writers. The gulf is wide, and it is little wonder that the local amateur historian suffers scarcity of material. So it was that Cochrane constructed his history the way he did.

His book is nearly 800 pages long but the cumulative history, which attempts to describe the town's past in terms of its politics, society, morals, and mores, is only 113 pages. This is followed by a long chapter on the town's centennial celebration and shorter chapters concerned with churches, the military, schools, societies, roads and bridges, cemeteries, town officers, and mills and manufacturing. He chose not to incorporate such information into the main body of his history.

The last five of his chapters are devoted to:
Old Customs and Habits
Inconveniences the Settlers Had to Contend With
Scotch-Irish Character and Influence
Various Descriptive Items of a Topographical Nature
and then the final catch-all:
Containing Various Scraps and Remnants Worth
Gathering Up and Preserving.

But this brings him only to page 325. The rest of his history is devoted to a standard genealogy with names and dates — a lot of historical information in narrative form.

In 1828 (to return to Cochrane's chronological history), a move failed to divide Antrim. The proposed boundary line would have set apart east and west Antrim. The legislature overwhelmingly rejected the proposition, obviously heeding, Cochrane suggests, the lobbying efforts of the majority who opposed the division. A portion of Antrim to the southwest was eventually lopped off and given to Hancock because there was no road connecting it with Antrim.

Federal aid to Antrim was noted by Cochrane in 1835 when the town debt soared to $9,000. The population was decreasing and taxes were severe. The country being out of debt, Congress passed an act the next year distributing some of the surplus to the states. Antrim got $3,000 to ease its financial burden.

There was a small-pox scare in 1840. One man died in Bennington and Cochrane reports this was enough to stimulate vaccinations in Antrim.

Judge Luke Woodbury brought Antrim its first piano in 1842. Despite this civilizing influence, "it was customary to have no adornments except those of personal beauty, neatness, and virtue, about the house. Even as late as fifty years ago," Cochrane adds, "the walls were as bare of pictures as our barns are now. A few were able to have certain figures painted on the plastering, relics of which, in some old houses, may yet be seen. Hardly a dwelling can now be found in Antrim without its chromo, or engraving of some kind, and neat little ornaments — attractive, even if cheap. But there was nearly nothing of the kind in our ancestors' humble abodes."

There were moves toward temperance in 1846 and 1848, but the town voted them down both times. Cochrane, always optimistic, notes that the sentiment shown by the second vote for temperance, although not a winner, was ever-increasing. Besides, he writes, since

1842 the church had demanded abstinence from its members "except as medicine."

In the eighteenth century Robb Mountain to the west was well populated. About a dozen families, sixty persons in all, lived there with Andrew and Moor Robb, and they were considered prosperous farmers. All lived in log houses, Cochrane writes, and had their own school. But they began to move out, one at a time, and by the early nineteenth century all had gone. Their log houses rotted away. No roads had ever been built to this community and to this day the only routes to the mountain are hiker's trails. One is from the west, from Stoddard, and the other, I'm told, is from the east from Gregg Lake. The eastern trail isn't even marked on a U.S. Geological Survey map. It was 90 years since the Robbs and their neighbors lived there, Cochrane notes, and all traces of them are gone. Cochrane muses on the passage of time and what changes it can make.

When Hillsboro's Franklin Pierce was elected president in 1852, Antrim was proud and pleased. Many people had known him personally and felt a close bond. Especially so, Cochrane notes, when in 1853 his only son was killed in a railroad accident in Andover, Massachusetts. But when Illinois' Senator Steven A. Douglas fathered the Kansas-Nebraska Compromise of 1854, thus permitting slavery north and west of Missouri and, in effect, destroying what the Missouri Compromise had set as the limitations of slavery, "many thoughtful minds here," Cochrane notes, "were slowly alienated." Opening these new territories to slavery "awakened a sullen and deep opposition at the North and multiplied the strength of the anti-slavery party." Cochrane charges Pierce's administration with setting up the forces which clashed in 1861.

In 1860 there was an outbreak of the cattle disease, pleuro-pneumonia. One Antrim man (not born here, Cochrane notes) refused to buy meat out of a butcher's cart because the creature, he feared, had had the "E Pluribus Unum." The disease was severe in some parts of the country, and when it reached New Hampshire the legislature gave towns power to destroy livestock to suppress it.

Suspected cattle were isolated behind double fences, people feared to eat beef and, since cattle were important to the farmers. . ."the hills of Antrim were covered with herds of cattle," Cochrane writes. . .anxiety ran high. When one heifer was suspected of the disease, 250 men "and a crowd of boys" assembled on Holt's Hill to see the animal destroyed and examined. Eventually, less than a dozen animals were destroyed. None was reported to have the disease.

Three weeks after the shelling of Fort Sumter, Antrim called a town meeting to deal with this crisis — the War of the Rebellion, as Cochrane calls it. Antrim's part in the Civil War is covered elsewhere in this history.

Cochrane ends his chronological history with the report that the Baldwin road was raised five feet in 1878 to prepare for the opening of the railroad. Cost: $1,200.

Weather, Disaster, and Disease

Cochrane devotes some of his history to natural phenomena such as weather, disaster, and disease. These were probably the stories told by earlier generations of a New England farm community as examples of how much easier life is today. I once visited a graveyard on Prince Edward Island and noticed that several members of the Sudsbury family were buried there. I mentioned this to Gordon Sudsbury, Sr., on returning to Antrim, and he recalled his boyhood on the island "where the snow was so deep that when we walked to school in the mornings, we guided ourselves by holding on to the telegraph wires."

The Great Frost, or as Cochrane calls it, "a remarkable frost," was May 18, 1794. There was wind from the northwest and severe cold. Water in tubs froze an inch thick, and water thrown out froze as soon as it touched the ground. Wheat, barley, oats, flax, and fruit crops were destroyed. Thankfully, Cochrane notes, the corn had not been planted yet.

The winter of 1804 really began on October 7 with a foot of snow. Although most of it melted in the open fields, thus permitting the harvest to continue, drifts secluded from the sun lay until the next spring. In 1807, the snow was so deep in April that Dr. Nathan Cleaves, in visiting patients, "got his death" by traveling on snowshoes. The snow was so deep that when Dr. Cleaves died it was difficult to get his body to the grave.

The winter of 1812 was severe, too. Not only was there still a foot of snow on the ground in May, but an epidemic of spotted fever as well. Cochrane writes about it:

The first case occurred Feb. 7, 1812, the first subject being a child of Samuel Weeks, then for a short time living on the Dea. Shattuck place. This child recovered. On the following day, Robert Nesmith, child of Dea.

Jonathan, was taken, and lived but a few hours. This first victim died Feb. 9, 1812. Then cases followed rapidly in all parts of the town. Dea. Nesmith's child died on Sunday, and was buried the following day. The next death was that of Mrs. Daniel Paige, sick only a little over half a day. Persons would be taken with a violent headache, or, as in the case of Mrs. Abraham McNiel, with a pain in the little finger, or in some other strange way, and, in severe cases, the victim usually died in less than twelve hours. There were two hundred cases and forty deaths, in two months. Everybody wore mourning till the deaths became so numerous it was impossible to provide mourning apparel. It was hard to find well persons enough to take care of the sick. At many times there were two or three funerals per day, and on one day there were four funerals and four processions up the hard, snowy road to the cemetery on the hill. Sometimes they threw a little snow and dirt over the coffin, and then left the grave unfilled till spring. All ages were taken, from sixty years down to the infant of days. Daniel Nichols, Esq., surveyor, deacon, and nine years selectman, fell a victim. None were attacked by it who were over sixty years of age. The "Cabinet" at Amherst printed reports from Antrim mournful indeed, week after week. These reports bear the mark of Mr. Whiton's hand. For ten weeks all work was suspended except what was absolutely necessary, and people gave their attention to the care of the sick and the burial of the dead. As this was a new disease, physicians did not know how to manage it, and most of them adopted the roasting process. This they carried to such an extreme that many were actually roasted to death. Families held themselves ready to apply the roasting or sweating process, at a moment's warning, night or day. With hot bricks, hot stones, hot blocks of wood, hot rooms, hot drinks, and piles of clothes, the poor creature, burning with fever, was roasted out of the world. But, after many deaths, experience and the "sober second thought" brought about a more merciful and successful treatment. Houses were kept lighted all night, and for more than a month there was one body, or more, awaiting burial all the time. But, as the spring advanced, the disease took a milder form, and entirely ceased about the middle of April. In other towns this scourge was felt. In Acworth there were fifty-three deaths, and many fatal cases occurred far and near. In some towns the disease returned in milder form when cold weather came again, but not here; and it is not known that there has been a case among us since that lamentable winter.

There was a terrible wind in September, 1815, and Clark Hopkins, then a small boy, told Cochrane that he remembers lying in bed that afternoon and seeing the trees go down, one after the other, until they were all gone.

The old timers remember calling 1816 the "Mackerel Year" or the "Poverty Year." It was so cold and frosty the corn would not ripen, and farmers had little to feed their cattle. They were compelled, Cochrane writes, to live mostly on fish.

The summer of 1819 was remarkable for the number of thundershowers that passed over town. Although Antrim was noted as the place "where showers generally went 'round," there were many weeks that summer when there was a thundershower every day.

The "Grasshopper Year" was 1826, and half the hay crop was lost to these insects. "I have heard some of the older farmers tell how they drove the grasshoppers in between the rows of potatoes or corn and then scooped them up by the bushel to feed their hogs," Cochrane writes.

The Centennial Celebration

At the annual March meeting in 1875, the town voted $1,000 toward the cost of celebrating its centennial. A committee was formed and the date of the celebration scheduled for June 27, 1877.

Such was the nature of the occasion and such was its proximity to the publication date of his history that Cochrane writes of the day not so much as an historian but as a newspaper society writer. This is one of the few times in his history that his style and tone changes.

He records the program of the day and prints every speech and poem of which he could get a copy. The oratory that day was awesome.

C.B. Dodge, Esq., read the town charter.

Reed P. Whittemore, Esq., then living on the farm that Philip Riley carved from the forest, gave the Address of Welcome.

Professor James E. Vose, of Ashburnham, Massachusetts, one of the many native sons and daughters who returned for the celebration, gave the Centennial Address. In the program, it was known as the "Oration," and it takes Cochrane ten and a half pages to print it.

Professor J.W. Barker, of Buffalo, New York, read the Centennial Poem, all 230 lines.

The Honorable Charles Adams, Jr., of North Brookfield, Massachusetts, spoke on "Scotch Character — Still Marked by Grit and Grace." His speech covers eleven pages in the history.

Professor Cyrus Baldwin, of Meriden, New Hampshire, spoke of "Rev. John M. Whiton, D.D., — His Life a Gospel of Peace." He limited himself to three and a half pages.

Then the Reverend J.M. Whiton, Ph.D., of Easthampton, Massachusetts, talked on the "Influence of hill-towns on the destiny of our country." Three and a half pages.

Frank Pierce, Esq., of Concord, spoke on "Lawyers of Antrim." The speech was short, eloquent, and interesting, Cochrane says, and he regrets that he could not find a copy of it.

A letter was read from E.A. Wallace, Esq., of Havana, Illinois.

Henry Reed, Esq., of Lowell, Massachusetts, and the Reverend Arthur Little of Chicago could not be present, but their letters were read, too.

"The Clergy of Antrim — May Their Power Always be Felt," was the topic of an address by the Reverend J.L. Felt of Antrim.

There were other speeches, poems, and letters reprinted, and newspaper accounts of the occasion were recorded. Food had been prepared to feed 3,000 people, but the crowd was so large that extra provisions had to be found. There were two cornet bands, no drunkenness, no noise, and no fighting, Cochrane tells us. He reported from an anonymous source that it was a day of "high-toned entertainment." Total cost to the town, exclusive of contributed food and labor, $661.25.

FOOTNOTES

[1] Cochrane, Rev. W.R. *History of the Town of Antrim, New Hampshire, From Its Earliest Settlement to June 27, 1877, With a Brief Genealogical Record of All the Antrim Families.* Published by the Town. Mirror Steam Printing Press, Manchester, N.H. 1880.

[2] Ibid.

[3] From the first stanza of Ralph Waldo Emerson's "Concord Hymn." Sung at the completion of the Battle Monument in Concord, Massachusetts, July 4, 1837.

[4] In his chapter on Old Customs and Habits, Cochrane tells of one tithing man who drove a nail into the end of his long cane, leaving it projecting, and then sharpened it. When a dog entered the church that next Sunday, he buried the nail in the dog's head and dragged the yelping creature out. It died in a few minutes on the church steps. Most of the tithing men he writes about in this chapter were as harsh and unforgiving.

[5] Cochrane's attitude about liquor and drinking is not inflexible. In his chapter on Old Customs and Habits, he writes quite cheerfully about the early settlers' drinking habits. He implies that Eighteenth Century liquor was better than that sold in the Nineteenth Century, that it was less corrosive to the innards. Rum, especially, was a popular drink, no community work ever being attempted without a supply on hand. Thus, barn raisings, butcherings, weddings, burials, and other gatherings were made more sociable by a ready supply of rum. In 1845, for example, Jonathan Carr makes his mark in Antrim history as the first man to raise a house *without* the use of rum. Even children drank, Cochrane says. It was their custom to save their school stove ashes to sell for soap manufacture and to buy rum with the proceeds. A party was held the last day of school.

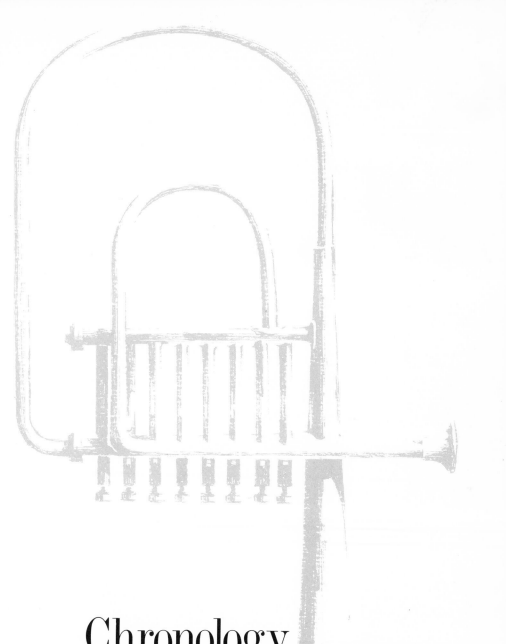

Chronology

Antrim
1877 - 1976

---

a
year to year
chronicle of events

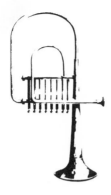

THE WINDS OF CHANGE

A T THE BEGINNING of Antrim's second century, change was in the wind. To be sure, the first century had seen changes. From rude log cabins, people had graduated to more substantial houses, some of them quite large and imposing. From small, one-man business enterprises, industry grew and multiplied along Great Brook and the North Branch river. Schooling was available to all; churches proliferated; roads were built. Certainly life was a great deal easier and more pleasant for the average Antrimite in 1878 than it had been for those early settlers back when the town was first incorporated.

But the pace of change was quickening, and when the Peterborough and Hillsboro railroad opened for business in 1878, the die was cast. It might take a while to show, but no longer would Antrim be an isolated cluster of villages, relatively untouched by outside influences. The iron horse outraced the living animal, shortening the gap between towns, improving mail service, speeding up delivery of goods in and out of town, and providing for the adventurous new and dazzling experiences.

However, the town went about its business as usual, appropriating $1,500 for maintenance of roads and bridges, and $1,200 for support of schools, just as it had done before the railroad came into its life, and as it would do in the succeeding years. There was a motion at town meeting to see if the meeting would be held in South Antrim in 1879, and again in 1880 to see if the town would erect a town house in Clinton Village, but nothing came of either suggestion. Change, though inevitable, was slow at first.

Even Dr. Cochrane's history moved at a snail's pace. Although it had been finished in 1877, it was 1880 before it was published. The selectmen, in conjunction with the centennial committee (left over from 1877), had charge of details. They authorized a printing of 650 copies, to be sold on a sliding scale of $2.50 to $3.25. (They were instructed by our frugal Yankee ancestors "to protect the interest of the voters and inhabitants of the town in the matter of expense, and limit the same to the lowest amount that in their judgment is practicable.")

1880
to
1890

Efforts to establish a high school moved as slowly. The matter was brought up in 1880, and in 1882 the town went as far as appointing a committee to look into it. D.H. Goodell was a member, of course. He, with Henry Chapin, Samuel Sawyer from the Branch, and Dr. Morris Christie, began preparing a report for the town meeting in 1893. Although there was no high school, there were eleven school districts scattered around the various areas in town. Each was close enough to a cluster of houses so that the pupils could walk to school. The buildings were usually of the one-room variety, heated by stoves, and devoid of plumbing. Public exercises were held periodically, and oral examinations conducted by several town dignitaries were annually dreaded events at the end of the school year.

Although school districts were plentiful, they were greatly outnumbered by highway districts. In 1881, there were twenty-eight of them, but this must have been wasteful and inefficient, because in 1887 the number of highway surveyors (road agents) was cut to five. Over the years, a vocal minority has customarily complained about certain things a road agent has or has not done, and these men must really have suffered more than their share of abuse. Paved roads were unheard of, and there was certainly very little that could be done about mud in the spring. There were few snowplows, and much of the drifted snow had to be cleared with shovels in the winter. It is a wonder anyone even wanted the job.

The Fourth Estate

Those who did could have advertised their intentions in the local press. The first such paper, the *Home News,* made its appearance in 1875. Edward J. Thompson was the editor-publisher, but after two years he found he could not keep up with both the job printing and editorial duties, so he chose the former. News had to travel by word of mouth until 1882, when Sumner Ball started *The Antrim Reporter,* a typical small town newspaper consisting of large splashy ads by the local merchants, lurid testimonials to the efficacy of various patent medicines, long and vaporous serials, assorted fillers, and two columns of the "John Doe is entertaining the measles" variety. The format remained much the same over the next sixty years, although ownership changed hands frequently for the first ten of those years (Charles Hutchinson 1887, Amos Brown 1889, George Barron 1892, and Hiram Eldredge from November, 1892, to 1936). Under Mr. Eldredge's long aegis, the paper was blatantly and unabashedly pro-Republican, pro-law and order, pro-temperance, and very careful not to stir up any controversy. He obviously put out a paper which he thought would meet with the approval of the majority of the town's citizens. If he reserved the greatest space for enterprises of which he approved, he also printed letters to the editor in "The People's Column" which must have pained him occasionally, although he rarely struck back.

Sandwiched between the innumerable items of illness, visitors arriving and visitors leaving, runaway horses and lost cows, were a few reports of town, state, and once in a great while national importance. The reader had to be alert to find the national items; the state news frequently had its own column; and the town news generally concerned itself with the annual town meeting, celebrations (both great and small) of important holidays, and church and organizational meetings. Obituaries were fulsome and flowery. All in all, fifty-two issues for a dollar or even a dollar-and-a-half must have seemed a good bargain in those pre-TV days.

Brothers and Sisters

About that time, social organizations began to appear in the town. Few people could have escaped belonging to one or more of them, and the inveterate joiner must have been in seventh heaven. One of the longest-lived was the Grange, which was formally organized with

The Grange Hall . . . before and after

eighteen charter members on December 11, 1883, George Whittum being the first Master. Meetings were held in the homes of various members until 1894, when they purchased the old Center Town Hall for their use. A part of the frame for this building came from the original meeting house on Meeting House Hill, so there is some historical significance attached to it, although it has been known for years simply as Grange Hall.

Another early fraternal society was Ephraim Weston Post #87 of the Grand Army of the Republic, which was started in 1885. As the age of its members advanced, its activities understandably declined, but in the late nineteenth century it played an important part in the life of the town, particularly on those two super-patriotic holidays, Memorial Day and the Fourth of July. Dressed in Union army blue with their peaked hats, GAR men proudly marched in the parades on both days as long as they were able, and when they were no longer up to the long march they were driven at the head of the procession, and seated in places of honor on the platform during the speeches that followed. State and national conventions were called encampments, and the railroads played a vital role, carrying "the boys" to and from these nostalgic reunions.

Waverly Lodge, IOOF, was chartered somewhat earlier, in 1876, and has remained active ever since. The ladies' counterpart, Hand in Hand Rebekah Lodge #29, was instituted ten years later, in 1886. These lodges, and others like them, were a focal point in the social life of the town, and it was a proud moment to have "taken the degrees," or "gone through the chairs." To the outsider, however, their greatest achievements may have been the bounteous collations (as the paper referred to them): the Grange Harvest supper, the mid-day dinners served in Odd Fellows' Hall on town meeting day. The food was good—sometimes mouth-watering—the abundance staggering, and the price dirt cheap. Several sittings were usually mandatory.

No dinner was served on the second Tuesday of March, 1888, however. On that day a storm (the historic blizzard of '88 to which all storms thereafter would be compared) of such proportions raged that no one, not even the town officers, could reach the town house, and the meeting had to be reconvened on March 30. The town hall in that year was still at the Center, of course, which made it even more difficult to reach, so it is odd that when the article "to see what action the town will take in regard to building a new town hall in South Antrim" came up, it was dismissed as usual.

It was a year of calamities. The blizzard in March was pale beside the great fire in May which all but wiped out the center of North Branch (north of Route 9 to the river). Sparks from a defective chimney were fanned into flames that swept twenty-five acres and leveled nine houses, the village store, the post office, seven barns, a saw mill, and numerous outbuildings. In one day, the thriving community was dealt a blow from which it never fully recovered.

News Makers

The biggest event of all in 1888 was perhaps the nomination and election of David H. Goodell as governor of New Hampshire. Antrim became instantly famous, and basked in the reflected glory. Mr. Goodell was nominated for the office in September at the Republican State Convention in Concord. Arriving home by train, he was met at the station by two bands and a huge crowd of enthusiastic fellow citizens, who escorted him to his home in a carriage drawn by four horses.

His campaign, short by today's standards, was successful, and he went on to win the election by a decisive margin. His chief qualifications for the office of governor seem to have been his success-ful record as a business man, and his dedication to the temperance movement, which was almost an obsession with him. He was joined in this feeling by many others of the day: the churches, the YMCA, and the WCTU all stressed the importance of abstinence, and at least once it was proposed that a temperance worker be sent into the schools to get all the children to sign the pledge.

The fervor amounting almost to frenzy with which the temperance

people pursued their goal is hard to appreciate today. Young ladies subscribed earnestly to the maxim, "Lips that touch liquor shall never touch mine." Mothers worried lest their sons take that fateful first drink and be forever lost. Drunken men were called beasts. And the movement which was to save the world snowballed into that unsuccessful experiment called Prohibition.

Not that the principle behind the idea was wrong: it was the rigid lack of understanding that failed. The zeal with which the goal was pursued was often hilarious, as the following two letters, reprinted in their entirety, will show.

Antrim, N.H., June 1, 1892

Mr. Editor:
Will you kindly afford me a little space in your valuable paper to correct an impression which may have gone forth reflecting upon me.
In your last issue, you reported me as having been brought before a special police court and pleading guilty to selling liquor. That I was brought before such a court I do not deny, but that I pleaded guilty I do deny. I pleaded not guilty and I shall stick to it. I am not, neither have I ever been a dispenser of

liquor. I get my living by a more honorable occupation, as everyone who is acquainted with me knows. The facts of the case are these. I was asked by an old neighbor to get him some liquor when I went below. He gave me the money and I did the errand. That is how I am a liquor seller. That he made bad use of it does not reflect on me as a liquor seller. I paid the imposed costs as a matter of expediency, thinking it the best way out of it. That I made a mistake in paying I am now satisfied.

Trusting that this will show to your readers that I am not a dealer in the ardent,

I am yours respectfully,

S.A. Holt

Antrim, N.H. June 5, 1892

Mr. Editor:

As neighbor Holt has informed the public of his transaction in regard to the liquor business, I feel it is my duty to state the positive truth concerning the affair that happened the other day. I refer to the liquor case.

The old neighbor referred to who made bad use of it, is old Captain Dodge, who lives on North Main Street in South Antrim, who works hard and intends to get his living honestly by making and repairing window sash, doors and screens, sharpening saws, or doing anything in the line of joiner work. He being about run down by working in the shop through the winter, exposed to bad air, etc., thought if he had a little new rum to revive the old body, he might saw a pile of hard wood which lay in his dooryard, thinking a little rum and sunshine with good air and exercise would revive him. About that time neighbor Holt came in and wanted to hire a little money, as he was going below to buy some cattle, and the evil spirit told me now is your time to get your rum, and like a fool I approved it, although something told me no don't get it, but I prevailed and received it, feeling quite happy, as I most always treated my dear friends when I had it if they were alright. I have used it carefully all my long life, but of late years have placed little confidence in it.

Feeling tired and heated the other day by sawing wood in the sun, I came into the shop and drank some, as usual, and the first thing I knew after that someone was helping me off the floor into my chair.

I soon recovered, and since I have considered it was a call from the most high to leave all my evil ways and live a true and temperate life.

I have seen at times through all my life, smart likely young men, well qualified for business, commence to drink and go from bad to worse till they

became sots, to fill a drunkard's grave. Thank God I cannot say that of my
children if their father has indulged.
But I have resolved never to use it during the remainder of my life, only for
medicinal purposes, and I would advise kind neighbor Holt to remember his
good, temperate father, and his instructions, and turn from all evil, and live
a pure and spotless life.
If I have done wrong, I will leave it with you and your readers to judge me,
and I ask forgiveness of him "who doeth all things well."

Yours truly,
A. Dodge

(Dodge, a specialist in the repair of chairs, advertised his occupation in rhyme, after the fashion of the day.

"Oh dear me, what shall I do?
This chair is broke and let me through.
Please come quick and help me out
As I cannot get turned about.

"The back is broke, the seat is gone,
I'm sure it was not very strong.
I'll send it to Dodge this very day
And have him seat it right away.")

1890
to
1892

There were, however, more serious pursuits in 1892. E.J. Thompson, something of a mechanical genius, constructed a dynamo at Goodell's which produced 110 volts of electricity, and operated twenty incandescent lights. The company's office was lighted with two bulbs each of thirty-two candle power, which Henry Hurlin pronounced "shed the clearest and steadiest light I have ever seen—better than daylight."

By this time the smaller inter-town railroads had been swallowed up by the Boston & Maine, which had four trains a day in and out of Antrim. Besides providing mobility to the individual, it was a positive boon to the dairy farmer, whose milk could now be transported quickly to the big city markets. All he had to do was haul his forty-quart cans to the station early in the morning, and the railroad did the rest.

In Sickness and in Health

Sometimes in the Winter of 1892 this was hard to do. The roads, thanks to the new snow roller, were usually passable, but often the farmer and his whole family were felled by what was universally referred to in a redundant manner as "the La Grippe." It struck down young and old alike, and the makers of patent medicines capitalized on the opportunity for sales. Dana's sarsaparilla, compounded of beef and iron, Jamaica ginger, celery compound and caffeine, was touted as a sure cure. If that did not work, oranges and lemons were only twenty-five cents a dozen, and perhaps even more efficacious. Haircuts, if anyone cared to risk them in that perilous weather, were also twenty-five cents. N.J. Morse, knight of the razor and brush, sported a new "patent barber chair of the Congress pattern with adjustable back and foot rest of fine design." This luxury was further augmented by a large hanging lamp (the incandescent bulb would come later.)

Those who were not sick enjoyed the grand sleighing in that winter of '92. Huge sleighing parties were organized. On the tenth of February, twenty-nine sleighs—twenty-five single hitches, and four doubles carrying twelve, eleven, ten, and four respectively—took off with a great jingle of bells for Hancock, which they reached in forty minutes. After witnessing an entertainment put on by the Hancock school children, they moved over to the inn for a large supper, and got back to Antrim at one-thirty in the morning. At least half of the old adage, "early to bed and early to rise," was sometimes ignored by our ancestors.

Other sleighing parties took place that winter, one of the most successful happening later in February. Because this was leap year, it was organized by the girls, who not only did the driving (to Henniker) but may also have paid for the supper on the way back (in Hillsboro).

In March, agitation begun earlier for a new town hall in South Antrim increased. It was argued that South Antrim was the "principal village of the town, and has with its near outskirts more than seven hundred population. Here the most important industry is conducted, employing more people than all the other manufactures and mills in town." The theory was that these workers could easily run up to the town hall, if it were handy, and vote during their noon hour. Citizens from the Branch and the Center scoffed at the idea that anyone could vote intelligently and conscientiously in such a short time. Indeed, they considered erecting a town hall in "an extreme corner of the town" incredibly foolish, and suggested that tax money might better

Dedication of the Soldiers' Monument in 1892

be spent reducing the town debt (now $400), or providing town water.

The new town hall was not authorized in 1892. Instead, the town approved $172 for a public library, for which purpose two rooms in the Goodell block were offered for use, free. One room was to be for books, and the other a reading room. And at long last, Antrim was to have a high school. Thirteen hundred dollars was voted to finish off and seat the north room in District #1 school house for a high school.

These two actions represented a giant step in the cultural life of the town. Free libraries are so commonplace now that they are taken for granted. In a day when books were scarce and probably too expensive for the average family, and when newspapers were so limited in their scope, an opportunity to have free access to books of all kinds was an unparalleled chance to increase one's knowledge and enjoyment. Similarly, the fact that there was a high school benefited not only the children of Antrim who wished to further their education, but also children from neighboring towns, who came as tuition students.

While the intellectual needs were being cared for, exercise was not neglected. "The bicycle fever has quite a rage in this town, eighteen or more of these steel horses being owned here." Financially it might have been the modern day equivalent of owning an automobile. Balch's advertised bicycles with solid cushion seats and pneumatic tires, ranging in price from $85 to $115.

Meanwhile, people "from away" were being urged to travel to Antrim via railroad to view for themselves the clean and pleasant town, with its mountain vistas and its clear lakes and streams. Lodging at summer boarding houses was available, with plenty of good, wholesome homecooked food, and such bucolic pleasures as pitching horseshoes and going on hay rides.

The Summer Solstice

Luckily, the summer boarding season had not started when the tornado hit in the vicinity of Thompson's bridge, over East. The temperature was 95° on June 14, and there was a severe thunderstorm accompanied by hail which ruined the young corn crop. Mrs. S.A. Holt picked up eight quarts of hailstones twenty minutes after the storm. Jennie Abbott, who worked in Goodell's office and was so unwise as to answer the telephone during the height of the storm, suffered a

Sartorial splendor for cyclists . . .
Thomas Madden

severe electrical shock, and had to go home and lie down to recover. Meanwhile, tornado force winds ripped the planking off Thompson's bridge, blew down trees, and demolished a barn. The destructive storm was over as suddenly as it began, but it was a topic of conversation for days.

It was replaced as a conversational gambit by the Fourth of July celebration. This very special occasion was marked by dedication of the Soldier's monument on the triangle of the Baptist church lawn. The ceremonies, on another extremely hot day when the thermometer again reached 95°, were the biggest since the centennial anniversary in 1877. The parade was led by members of the GAR, with music provided by Antrim's two bands. Houses along the parade route were lavishly decorated with bunting, and no drunks marred the solemn dedication of the monument, given to the town by the members of the Ephraim Weston Post at a cost of $1,000, forever to keep in memory the soldiers of the Revolution, the War of 1812, the Mexican War, and the War of the Rebellion.

During the summer, weekly festivals were held at Duncan's grove on Clinton Street (across the road from Pashoian's). An area near the brook was lighted with strings of Japanese lanterns, and the Mechanics' Military band furnished the music. Their arch-rivals, the Antrim Brass Band, made it a point to march up the street at the same time, blowing with all their might, which may have disconcerted but more likely titillated the patrons. To provide an added fillip, contests were held to choose 1) the most popular lady, and 2) the laziest man in town. Miss Josie King won the silver cake basket and Henry P. Kimball was awarded a wood saw and a saw horse to encourage him out of his lethargy.

Although the controversy between the Presbyterians in the Center and those in South Village was not definitely settled by the courts until 1896, the village Presbyterians laid the cornerstone of their new church in August, 1892. By then, electricity from Goodell's power plant had been extended north on Main Street as far as the Baptist church. Before the year was over, Balch's store and the post office were lighted by electricity, and this was considered such a wonder that in later reports the exact number of lights was always specified: Harrington and Kibbey's store, nine; Putney and Little's store, nine; Wilson's barbershop, two; the Antrim House (Maplehurst Inn), ten; and Odd Fellow's Hall, two or three.

The power source (Great Brook) of the dynamo was minimal, and the electricity often failed, especially during months when the water was low in the brook. In July, 1893, there was a shutdown of four weeks, and since by that time people were accustomed to the convenience of electric lights, a more dependable plant was set up the next year in Bennington on the Contoocook River.

1893

Furthermore, electricity would also be needed to light the new town hall, which had finally been authorized in the March meeting. South Village had won, and the town purchased from Governor Goodell the land that once belonged to the Woodbury heirs; the barn on the lot was sold to C.R. Jameson for fifteen dollars. Architects from Concord drew up plans for a large brick building with space for the town offices plus some store spaces to rent downstairs, and a large auditorium upstairs. Ground was broken for the foundation late in July, and slowly the building took shape. It was in the very latest Victorian style, of Keene brick, surmounted on the southeast corner by a high rise (75 feet) tower on which stood a handsome weathervane. A coal burning furnace heated the entire building with steam. Including the land, the total cost of the building was just under $16,000. The money may have been hard to come by, for the selectmen advertised in *The Antrim Reporter*, "Money wanted—a few thousand at 4% interest per annum, and interest free from taxes in the town."

Music makers . . . circa 1900

As a matter of fact, this was a recession year, and there were signs that the area was feeling the pinch. Goodell Company curtailed its operation for the first time in its eighteen-year history, and ran only three days a week for a while. When they did go back to a six-day week a few months later, some workers took a cut in pay. Paige's cradle shop shut down entirely for five weeks; payments for goods previously delivered were in arrears. Those who worked at the Bobbin Mill in North Branch had their pay reduced to twenty-five cents a day.

Despite the hard times, the lure of the railroad continued to be difficult to resist, and for those who could dig up the price of a ticket, there were day excursions to Keene and Sunapee. The ticket to the fair at Tilton included not only the transportation but also admission to the fair grounds. The GAR veterans were off to a national encampment in Washington, D.C., and planned a visit to the old battlefield at Fredericksburg on the way. A few long distance travelers were getting up a party to go all the way to the Chicago fair, where Goodell Company had a small exhibit.

The Presbyterians in the village were able to attend services in their new church on February 20, 1893. Those who were left in the Center held their annual meeting, reorganizing, admitting new members, and dismissing those who had followed the church down to the village. Matters were slowly coming to a head between the two factions.

In the summer of 1893, a group of Italian workmen appeared in town, hired to dig the long ditch from Campbell pond to the precinct. The ethnic distinction is interesting: one more example of immigrants being relegated to manual labor that natives knew better than to undertake. The ditch had to be five feet deep, so that when the pipes were laid the water would not freeze, and anyone who has dug more than two feet down in this rocky soil knows what a back-breaking task that was. Half the crew understandably quit before a month was up, but the other half persevered, averaging eighty rods per week, and the grateful citizens of the town gave them a nice farewell banquet when they finished. The pipes were duly laid, and the water was turned on for the first time in October, 1893. Aside from a few leaks which were quickly mended, the convenience of unlimited (except in dry seasons) running water was one more proof that Antrim (or a portion of it, at least) had entered the world of modern technology.

Another modern marvel was the portable steam-operated wood sawing machine. J.W. Bass set one up in his wood lot, and sawed nearly five cords twice in two in sixty-two minutes. The days of the hand-operated woodsaw were numbered.

So were the days of wooden bridges. The Thompson bridge (just *1894* beyond Dave Platt's) which had been damaged by the tornado in 1892 now needed replacing, and it was thought that the high truss iron bridge built in 1894 and financed jointly by Antrim and Bennington would last forever. It was the only high truss bridge in the vicinity, and quite a wonder for its day. It turned out to have a life span of eighty-one years, and today (1976) has been declared unsafe.

The town hall, not having the same wear and tear as the bridge, has lasted longer. It was dedicated in March, 1894, with great fanfare— speeches in the afternoon, and a concert and dance in the evening. The auditorium upstairs added a lot to the life of the community. For years it accommodated high school graduation exercises, basketball games, lyceum speakers, masked balls, concerts, town meetings, and plays. For the latter, the town thoughtfully ordered a drop curtain, and four sets of all-purpose scenery, one each representing a street scene, an open landscape, a kitchen, and a parlor. These, it was thought, would cover any contingency.

Many groups used the town hall for their meetings. One was the newly-formed Antrim Improvement Society, a primitive precursor of the town planning board. Its stated aims were to encourage new industries, to improve highways, to make the town a more desirable place to live for those already here, and to bring in new residents. Its actual accomplishments were not quite so lofty, consisting partly of agitating for the removal of fences around village properties, erecting street signs, preserving shade trees along the roadsides, and placing

The "new" Town Hall

a tablet on the site of the first school house. All residents of Antrim, both male and female, were urged to join, and its projects were financed by membership fees of fifty cents. It almost died a-borning, having been unfortunate in its choice of an outside speaker, who was supposed to give credence to the objectives, but somehow managed to antagonize nearly everyone, including the usually charitable editor of the paper. This was a blow that stunned, but luckily did not kill the embryonic organization, which remained active for twenty-one years.

Two other dedications took place in 1894. One was that of the newly-built Presbyterian church in the village. (The old church at the Center still stood at this time, and the lawsuit between the two erst-while groups of members had yet to be resolved by the courts.) The other was the town bandstand, erected on the piece of land where the Texaco station now stands. The Antrim Brass Band and the Antrim Improvement Society were instrumental in promoting the idea. N.W.C. Jameson, whose house was next door, gave the use of the land for five years. The cost, including the electric lights, was seventy-five dollars, and the whole was to revert to the Antrim Improvement Society if the band ever folded, which it eventually did.

Electricity which was originally turned off from midnight to seven in the morning now began to run all night. By the end of 1894, Clinton Village and Antrim Center had their first street lights. There was even a chance that the telephone might come to Antrim. The Contoocook Valley Telephone Company agreed to extend its lines through Antrim in return for purchase of a thousand dollars worth of stock. The Antrim Improvement Society threw its weight behind this worthy adventure, and by November forty shares had been sold at twenty-five dollars a share. From then on, it was just a matter of waiting for the poles to be set and the lines strung. Gossip, heretofore limited to the neighborhood, soon would expand its boundaries to include the whole town, facilitated by multi-party lines and an all-knowing central.

While that particular form of amusement was in the future, the present offered several choices. The Carter House put in a billiard room—an euphemism for pool hall, a name with less acceptable connotations. More genteel kinds of entertainment, although nonetheless competitive, were the harvest suppers and fairs put on by the Congregational church at the Center (net profit $40), and the Presbyterian church in the village (the winner with $71). A party at B.S. Buckminster's fared less well. All present partook liberally of the delicious vanilla ice cream for dessert, and many became quite ill the next day. The culprit was thought to be the vanilla bean.

One of those stricken was John G. Abbott, who owned and ran Abbott's factory in Clinton Village. Although there probably was no direct connection, it is a coincidence that he died two weeks later, and the cause of death was officially pronounced to be "perverted nutrition." He was only forty years old at the time of his death, and was universally mourned. Sixty business men wearing white gloves marched ahead of the horse-drawn hearse from the corner of North Main and Clinton Streets to the Baptist church, where they were joined by twenty shop workers. At the church door, the company opened ranks to let the chief mourners through. There were more than four hundred present at the service, after which the procession marched in the same order to Maplewood Cemetery for the interment.

The next two years would see the final resolution of the Center church case. Developments in 1895 were these: the law suit, originally scheduled to be heard June 5, was postponed until August to the chagrin of several interested persons from Antrim who had gone to Concord to hear the proceedings. That the whole business was pre-

Center Church and vestry

cipitated and fed by intra-village rivalry is adequately shown in this North Branch news item:

It is with genuine sorrow that the people of this section learn that the old meeting house, in which three generations have worshipped, is, by process of law, to be taken from them and placed in the hands of those whose interests lie in another section of the town. The undeniable intention of the old records was to dedicate the building to the public, but they seem most unhappily to have failed in their objective.

1895   The court case was actually tried late in July, and a verdict handed down in favor of the village people. Eben Bass, et al, from the Center, the defendants, claimed that they had been unlawfully dispossessed by virtue of a vote taken earlier by the whole congregation to sell the property. The court ruled that the right of the society to sell was unquestioned, since the vote (three fourths for, one fourth against) clearly was a majority, and dismissed the case. The Honorable John Flint, who owned much property at the Branch, wrote from Minnesota to deplore the loss of the church, but to no avail. Meanwhile, Eben Bass and his neighbors, who had continued to hold services in the old church, having taken precautions to change the locks, had to move their meetings to Grange Hall after the verdict. The beginning of the end was near.

Other events of that year may have seemed pale by contrast, but life did go on. For some time there had been talk of establishing a creamery in Antrim, a sort of farmers' cooperative. North Branch residents were eager to have it set up in their village, probably because they had little industry left there. Capital was to be raised through the sale of stock, and it was moving slowly. It had been determined that to be successful there would have to be a guarantee of at least two hundred and fifty cows to produce the necessary milk. There seemed to be all kinds of obstacles, and in actuality it was not until 1910 that the creamery got underway, and then only with limited success.

The telephone, so eagerly awaited the previous year, finally appeared, coming from the Branch over the hill to the Center, and ending up with a public booth in the rear of the Antrim Pharmacy (in the town hall building). With awe, the newspaper reported that one could talk with a neighbor in another village and actually recognize his voice! That other utility, electricity, was still supplied to the town from Mr. Goodell's plant, but there was increasing speculation about the advisability of purchasing power from a private source.

The weather in 1895 had its ups and downs, as usual. The winter produced plenty of snow, and sleighing parties were still in fashion. One of the biggest involved fifty sleighs and one hundred and fifty folks who set off for Hillsboro preceded by the Antrim Brass Band. Coming back, they stopped at the Antrim House for supper and then went across the street to the town hall for a promenade. There seemed to be a distinction between a promenade and a dance, the former being in the nature of a grand march (or military drill to music), and the latter strictly a one-to-one relationship.

The year 1896 had its share of trivia. If proof were needed that the mills of the gods grind slowly, consider that this year and for the next several years articles appeared in the town warrant asking that the town authorize and finance an updating of the Cochrane history, an effort only now some eighty years later being realized. Despite eloquent pleas that such a history, besides being a valid objective in its own right, would increase in monetary value over the years, the suggestion was always voted down. 1896

An example of the clouded crystal ball was a bill in Congress proposing that the metric system be the only legal system of weights and measures in this country. When it was defeated, the editor of the paper wrote, "It is claimed that the metric system will obtain in this country inside of the next ten years."

He also had a choice comment regarding the new fire hydrants. There was some fear that they might freeze in the sub-zero winter weather, so woolen jackets were put over them. Perhaps these jackets were homemade, as they were about six inches too short. In the midst of an unusually warm April, Mr. Eldredge noted that "The firewards have done a humane act during the past week in removing the winter clothing from the fire hydrants about town."

People were not at all bashful about airing their grievances in the paper, paying the standard advertising fees for the privilege.

It is very convenient to have tools to loan to a neighbor, but it is more convenient if they will bring them home so that the owner can have them to use once in a while and give him a chance to accommodate the next neighbor

or

I wish to inform the party that took those seed potatoes out of my wagon in my shed on the evening of the 3rd of May that the name of the potatoes is

Freeman. I would also respectfully ask them to have the kindness to return as many as they took in the fall, providing they have a good yield.

However small town all this sounds, there was proof that South Antrim was growing. Seven new streets were named by action of the Antrim Improvement Society, which put on a masked ball in the town hall to raise money for the new street signs. Ninety dollars was sufficient to provide signs for Wallace, Grove, Forest, Summit, Maple, and Water (formerly Factory) Streets, and for the classy sounding Jameson Avenue. This area of the town obviously was the most heavily populated, and perhaps this gave credence to the argument for the new Presbyterian church.

The old brick church at the Center had its last service in August, 1896. One hundred townsfolk were present to hear the sermon preached by Dr. Cochrane. Shortly thereafter, a notice appeared in the paper stating that the property together with the organ, weathervane, fixtures, etc., would be sold at public auction on September 5. There is no more mention of the matter until 1900, when the Reverend Orlando Lord bought the land on which the church had stood and built his house there. The next year he advertised a quantity of used bricks for sale. These could well have been the bricks from the old building. (See chapter on churches.) Thus the story of the old Center church comes to an end. Even those of us who never saw it except in pictures are somehow touched by it.

After this traumatic schism, Antrim needed to get her mind on other things. That business was still something less than booming showed up in several ways. For one thing, there were five vacant tenements in South Village, where earlier the constant cry had been to build more rental housing. For another, a marked spirit of frugality hung over the March town meeting. N.C. Jameson, a Democrat (and everyone knew the Democrats were reckless spenders), actually tried to cut expenses by proposing that some street lights be shut off. But it was agreed this was going too far, and he did not prevail.

1897   It was decided, however, that one way to counteract the recession was to lure more summer people. They were beginning to be an important source of revenue for the whole town as well as for the farmer who, with his big house and kitchen garden, found the summer boarding trade an ideal way to supplement his income. A long poem—Victorians were prone to break into rhyme on almost any occasion—ended with the candid quatrain:

> *Young and old we greet you*
> *Open doors and hearts to all*
> *Hope you will increase our banknotes*
> *And remain with us 'til Fall.*

The natives thought the summer people should be able to get close enough to see the big boulder on Robb mountain. This natural wonder—a caprice of the ice age—weighed several tons and was perched precariously on a much smaller stone. The Antrim Improvement Society promised to check on the feasibility of building a carriage road to the spot.

Meanwhile, a life size, honest-to-goodness burglary finished off the year in a burst of excitement. The front door of the post office, located in the town hall building, was jimmied daringly in the glare of the new electric light, and stamps and money worth $400 were stolen. This was crime on a big scale, and Antrim people were more than a little concerned about it.

No further criminal activity took place during the next several years, although those inclined to break the law might have done so with impunity on the first day of the new year of 1898 when the electricity declared itself a moratorium. But it came on again long before town meeting, in time for the citizens to cast their votes after having listened carefully, it is hoped, to Mr. Eldredge, who implored them editorially to elect the best man for the job regardless of party affiliation. In addition to electing town officers, they voted $150 for a public

1898

Boulder on Robb Mountain
. . . a delicate balance

drinking fountain to be installed in front of the town hall—the precinct graciously agreed to waive the water rent. When the fountain was put in place late in April, it was reputedly fit for use by man, woman, child, cow, horse, or dog. A motley crew.

The week before the meeting there had been a wild snowstorm (the worst since the blizzard of '88, naturally). The stage going to North Branch was unable to get through from Tuesday until Friday. Mr. Brown, taking milk to the railroad station early in the morning, was unable to find his way through the storm, and was forced to wait until daylight to get his bearings. The wind accompanying the storm was so strong that it blew out a window at the new Congregational church.

Another chill wind was also blowing over the land—the wind of war. The battleship Maine had been blown up in February (while on a goodwill tour to Havana) with the loss of 264 men, and Spain and America were heading for a showdown. The reports in the paper were decidedly jingoistic; obviously soldiers were still heroes, and war was still a great adventure. As it happened, it was a short war, and no one from Antrim served in it.

Instead, the young men joined the YMCA, newly established in Antrim. Two rooms were fitted up in the old post office building (the present laundromat)—a reading room and a game room—while downstairs had a furnace, a shower, and "other necessary conveniences." It turned out to be an active organization, mostly of an uplifting nature. Each year it sponsored a lecture course similar to the old Lyceum, it was duly involved with the temperance movement, and in the early 1900s it sent some of its younger members to YMCA camp. There were also a young boys' drill team, and an exercise program involving chest weights and dumbbells. Eventually the leader ran away with the contents of the treasury, effectually dampening everyone's spirits, and it gradually fizzled out.

The temperance movement still flourished outside as well as inside the YMCA, although once in a while one caught a glimpse of a chink in the armor. For instance, the North Branch correspondent asked,

If the governor of New Hampshire had said to the ex-governor what the governor of North Carolina said to the governor of South Carolina, would there have been any ill feelings?

This frivolous comment was effectively quashed by the following novel suggestion:

The bicycle is one of the most effective temperance instrumentalities we

have had in a long time. A drunken man cannot ride a wheel, nor can one partially intoxicated ride it with safety to himself. A clear head is the main requisite for bicycle riding, and the temperance workers should encourage people to ride the wheel.

This suggestion might work in the summer, but what of the winter? *1899* It became standard procedure for each winter to produce "the worst storm since '88," and the people in '99 thought theirs qualified. It was a cinch no bicycle could get far in it. Even the trains were stuck. The snow and high wind persisted for two days. All business was suspended the second day. The wind caused the snow to drift so much and so fast that the horse-drawn plows and snow rollers were virtually useless. There were drifts ten feet high on the road from the Center to the foot of Twiss hill, and it took fourteen men and ten horses to open a path for travel. Maybe the winters are less severe now; certainly we have better means of dealing with big storms.

After one of these winters, people took a good dose of sulphur and molasses and welcomed the summer. August was the big tourist month. The Peterwaugh, a mini-resort at the lake, offered a bowling alley, picnic grounds, swings, croquet, and refreshments, and added for good measure a pavilion eighty **feet** long for social dancing.

The first annual Old Home Week celebration, with festivities and exercises, was held at Kelsea's Grove on the corner of Elm and Concord Streets. Beedle's Military Band provided the music; Miss Gertrude Jameson sang, "My Old New Hampshire Home," and Miss Ethel Muzzey recited, "The Hills Are Home." All without benefit of microphones. Beedle's Band had to be hired because Antrim in 1899 had no band of its own, the two earlier groups having passed out of

The Peterwaugh . . . turn-of-the-century tourist attraction

existence some time earlier. It was a blow to civic pride, having to import talent for home town celebrations, and there was serious talk of forming a new band.

Trials and Tribulations

This eventually was to be in the distant future, however. A more pressing and far more disturbing problem was the high incidence of scarlet fever among the children, particularly worrisome as the nineteenth century gave way to the twentieth. Schools were closed for an unprecedented three months. Whole families were quarantined, an act of civil authority highly resented by some. Books were fumigated, and the library closed.

One has only to read accounts of this and other similar epidemics to realize how far modern medicine has progressed. People living in the early twentieth century were plagued with a whole rash of diseases for which there was no effective prophylaxis or medication once the disease appeared. There were, however, nostrums galore. Weak women could turn to Dr. Shoop's Night Cure or Lydia Pinkham's Vegetable Compound. Worn out men could strengthen their nerves by taking Vitaloids. Both sexes would benefit by doctoring with Dr. Kilmer's Swamproot. Sellers of patent medicines appeared on Antrim's Main Street, and sometimes hired the town hall, where they put on a show, hawking their magic potions up and down the aisles between acts.

Other perils not curable by pills or potions abounded. Transportation powered by horse was often a risky business, especially when combined with poor judgment on the part of the driver. Late in February, Charles Bass broke through the ice at Gregg Lake while drawing a load of logs across with four horses. Horses, sled, logs, and driver all fell into the water—three horses and Mr. Bass got out safely.

No one put the blame for this near-tragedy on the horses, but there were times when the driver seemed absolved from culpability, and horses seemed in need of an equine equivalent of Vitaloids. Not only did they shy at the new-fangled automobile, but a chance-blown paper could produce a wildly exaggerated reaction. Off would go the horse, the driver valiantly and all too often hopelessly trying to regain control, the end result frequently being a broken wheel (the wagon's) or a broken head (the driver's).

Another potential source of danger was the bicycle. Despite a law decreeing a speed limit of five miles per hour and no riding on sidewalks, accidents were numerous. Bicyclists had a tendency to ride in both directions on one side of the street, totally ignoring that law of physics prohibiting two objects from occupying the same space at the same time. Sometimes gangs of boys would line up abreast and advance in a solid phalanx down the street, challenging anything or anybody foolhardy enough to get in their way.

1900

Fortunately, accidents of this sort were rarely fatal. In fact, Antrim's population was gradually increasing, as discovered in the year 1900 by the census taker—A.B. Crombie, who doubled as a school board member, among other things. Citizens were alerted by the newspaper to be prepared for his arrival, and reminded of the type of question he would ask. "Try and remember exactly when and where you were born. It will not be necessary to tell why."

By this time also, the school population had risen, and for the first time there was talk of forming a supervisory union. The state had recently passed a law authorizing state funds to provide half the annual salary for a superintendent who would coordinate the educational systems of two or more towns. Antrim voted $150 for this purpose, and subsequently united with Milford and Wilton, the superintendent spending one day in Antrim and two days each in Wilton and Milford. As with any new venture, its critics were vocal, and in time Antrim resigned from that union and formed a new one with the geographically closer towns of Hillsboro and Henniker.

Another new venture in 1900 was establishment of a town dump just north of the bridge over the Contoocook on Depot Street. It was a sort of do-it-yourself landfill operation: users were requested to cover all putrifying materials. The dump remained in use for the next seventy years until it finally threatened the purity of the river and had to be abandoned.

An innovation in the same year which was even more welcome was establishment of a rural free delivery route serving Clinton Village and Antrim Center, but doing away with the sub-post offices in both these areas. C.D. Sawyer was appointed mail carrier. His route, which he covered with horse and wagon, comprised some twenty miles and accommodated over a hundred families, thereby bringing the news right to their doorsteps. Naturally, the people at the Branch and over East felt neglected, and were delighted when a second route was started within a year, Malcolm French being their first carrier. He too used a horse and wagon, but since an automobile had been seen

RFD mailman . . . "Neither rain nor snow . . ."

passing through Antrim on August 14, 1900, he might have guessed that some day the RFD mailman's lot would improve.

Early mail carriers doubled as expressmen, delivering packages as a sideline, whether out of the goodness of their hearts or for more tangible rewards is not recorded. Nor did they hesitate to pick up and deliver a passenger, particularly if she were pretty. Unfortunately, Uncle Sam did not appreciate this duality of purpose, and in 1904 issued strict regulations making all such activities illegal.

This edict was promulgated by a Republican administration that Antrimites had helped to elect in 1900, when they emphatically favored the McKinley-Roosevelt ticket. All but fifty-eight of the registered voters went to the polls; of these, thirty-one were out of town, so actually only twenty-seven failed to exercise their voting privilege. The results so elated most of those who did vote that the next week they held a victory parade, a grand torchlight affair, featuring mounted cavalry, a brass band, two military companies carrying more than a hundred torches, and Mr. Burnham's barge filled with Republican misses waving banners and blowing tin horns. The line of march covered nearly all of South Antrim, where houses were draped with bunting, the windows were brightly lighted, and trees were festooned with Japanese lanterns. The parade conveniently disbanded in front of the bakery, where the participants were served doughnuts, cheese, and coffee.

1901   The year 1901 began calmly enough, with moderate weather and no legitimate competition to the blizzard of '88. With the spring rains, things began to change, and the annual spring freshet became a lively topic of conversation. The roads were badly washed, guaranteeing plenty of work for the road agents. Great Brook outdid itself, and roared down into the village with such force that it not only moved the foundation of the dam on Summer Street several inches but sent the top of the dam crashing into the stream. Fortunately, enough of the structure remained intact to prevent a flood on the lower end of the brook.

In August, the town water system developed a mysterious ailment. Water from the faucets ran dark and foul smelling. No one wanted to drink it, and the villagers resorted to hauling spring water. Samples of the precinct water were sent to the state for analysis; the problem was diagnosed as an excess of organic matter in Campbell Pond. Two alternatives were proposed—wait a few years to see if it would clear spontaneously, or expend $3,000 to fence cattle from the pond and raise the end of the supply pipe. Impatience won out over frugality. An epidemic of typhoid fever which broke out late in the year was blamed at first on the water supply, but a second analysis disproved this theory.

On September 11, 1901, President McKinley was assassinated by an anarchist. Barely a year before, the people of Antrim had helped elect him, and the news of his death plunged them into gloom. On the national day of mourning, all business was suspended; GAR, YMCA, school, and fire company flags flew at half mast, as did those of Republicans and Democrats alike. Stores and residences on Main Street were draped in mourning. In the afternoon, memorial services were held in the town hall. Six hundred people were present, including 225 school children. The peace of the year was shattered.

The next disquieting development was an uneasy tension that built up and found its outlet in a dispute over who should be postmaster. The incumbent, Albert Clement, was a Democrat, and the Republicans, mindful of the unwritten law that this was a patronage position, wanted one of their own installed. The trouble was that no one could agree on how to go about it. Numerous letters-to-the-editor boiled down to three choices: 1) re-instate the incumbent, who was doing a creditable job; 2) choose a replacement at a Republican caucus; or 3) neither alternative. Since any other solution to the dilemma seemed to lie in the distant future, the congressman from the district bravely stepped in and reappointed Mr. Clement.

From Pestilence to Politics

The typhoid fever epidemic was not so easily disposed of. It continued well into 1902, and a group of men at a logging camp near Gregg Lake were especially hard hit. The Board of Health, fearing that the water of the lake might be polluted, decreed that no ice could be cut from it during the winter of 1901-02. This was a blow to George E. Hutchinson, dealer in ice; with supplies denied him, he was forced to buy elsewhere, with a resulting loss in profit. The Board of Health sympathetically upheld his right to increase his price for the year.

1902

Ice was peddled in a wagon in the summer and a pung in the winter. So also were fish, meat, baked goods, groceries, and tinware. A gypsy lady appeared periodically with notions and laces for sale, which she spread on the floor for her customers' inspection. The convenience of door-to-door delivery is a fond memory of the past—meat on Wednesday, fish on Thursday, and groceries on Friday. For some strange reason, the Antrim Bakery vacillated between Saturday and Sunday delivery dates. Midway in 1902, baked beans and brown bread were delivered on Sunday morning (in time for breakfast, it is hoped), but this apparently was not satisfactory, for by November the rounds were made on Saturday again.

It was still the horse and buggy age in 1902, but there were signs of change. At the same time Antrim selectmen were being petitioned to place hitching posts in front of the town hall for the convenience of those using the post office and stores, the state legislature was considering enacting laws to regulate operation of automobiles. In a declaration of equal rights, *The Antrim Reporter* stated, "The auto has come to stay, but a horse has the right to half the road."

This kind of ambivalence evinced itself in other ways. Antrim High School acquired a new science laboratory in 1902, a step into the modern age. Its graduating class of seventeen was the biggest ever. Some of them may have taken part in the old-fashioned Fourth of July celebration a few weeks later. Definitely not planned by the town authorities, it was pure horse-and-buggy hi-jinks: bells ringing, firecrackers popping, drums thundering, and signs moving mysteriously from home base to strange repositories. Considerable indignation was felt over wanton destruction of property—windows and fences were broken, woodpiles tipped over—and the owners demanded damages if the culprits were found.

Probably they were not, and neither were those responsible for burning down the Antrim railroad station the night of June 25. The fire was thought to have been started by some "Weary Willies," tramps using the station as an overnight hotel. It was totally destroyed, but was rebuilt promptly, and in business again by September.

The station fire seemed to start a crime wave, for soon after this case of suspected arson, the post office was burglarized. The thieves, who left a whole set of clues behind but did manage to escape, had planned the whole operation carefully. First they stole several drills and a sledge hammer from D.P. Bryer, the blacksmith, and a horse blanket from the Antrim House stables. After midnight they entered the post office through a rear window, threw the wet horse blanket over the safe to deaden the sound, and blew up the safe. Scooping out the contents, they made their way to George Colby's house on Depot Street and stole his horse and wagon. On discovering the loss, Mr. Colby followed the tracks to West Peterborough, where he found his rig safely tied up behind a barn. But the thieves, alas, had taken the train to Winchendon, and there the trail was lost.

There were other things to get excited about, too. Practically all of Antrim went to the Oak Park Fair in Greenfield to see and hear Carrie Nation, the female embodiment of the temperance movement. Even the most partisan member of the WCTU must have viewed her with mixed emotions. Dressed entirely in white, with a white shawl over her shoulders, her face bearing an uncanny resemblence to the souvenir hatchets she sold, she lambasted not only the liquor traffic but all political parties except the Prohibition party. She even dressed down the President, and characterized the Republicans of New Hampshire as a gang of anarchists.

Stop, look and listen at the Antrim crossing

Henry A. Hurlin, nominated as his party's candidate for senator, can hardly have been pleased at her remarks. The race between him and the Democrat Marvin of Alstead was hard fought, and the results close, but Marvin was declared the winner by 200 votes. C.R. Jameson of Antrim, a perennial contender for public office, ran for county commissioner and was also the loser in a close race. The Antrim town ticket split about even for a change.

The Demon Rum

Beginning with 1903, Antrim voters were asked to express their preference on the question of whether the town should grant a liquor license. It was handily defeated the first time it came up by a margin of 193 to 85. But the next year was different, and the change could be attributed to ex-Governor Goodell, who finally went too far in his zeal for temperance.

Early in November, 1903, he sent to the barroom of the Valley Hotel in Hillsboro a list of names of men who were not to be served liquor there. This blacklist, as it came to be known, named practically every male voter in town, and because it was so all-inclusive, it did not distinguish between the toper and the teetotaler. Men who were pillars of the church and as abstemious as Goodell himself were incensed. The entire front page of the paper, which rarely carried anything but a few ads and a long serial, was given over to expressions of indignation. An outsize headline screamed "ANTRIM MEN OB-JECT!," followed by

> A very sore feeling exists within the bosom of our people, male and female alike, over the fact that their names appear on a list which is placed in the barroom of the Valley Hotel. To say that we all feel that an injustice has been done is putting it mildly indeed.

A letter of protest was immediately circulated, and was quickly signed by 140 men. The instigators were in such a hurry to send it to the ex-governor that not everyone got a chance to sign it. Goodell defensively stated that he was acting within his prerogative as justice of the peace. In an effort to bolster this claim, he in turn sent a letter to the license commissioners asking them to rule on the legality of his action. The reply was never published.

Obviously he missed the point. It was not the idea of a blacklist that upset the town—a list with only names of known alcoholics would have been tolerated and perhaps applauded—but the indiscriminate posting of everyone's name was an intolerable infringement of liberty.

The Boston papers picked up the story with glee, and Antrim got some free publicity it did not want. *The Boston Post* published a parody on Tennyson's, "Charge of the Light Brigade"—

> *Sad, sullen, savage, sore*
> *Barred from the tavern door*
> *Through street and village roar*
> *Antrim's four hundred.*
>
> *Posted, their names on high,*
> *Theirs not to make reply,*
> *Theirs but to thirst and sigh,*
> *Thirsty four hundred.*

One result which Governor Goodell surely had not anticipated was a flood of offers from liquor firms to send packages of the wet stuff in plain wrappers to any and all Antrim men.

Still he persisted in his efforts to prove he was right. He published statistics showing how small an amount Antrim paid for the support of paupers, claiming that this was directly related to his success in keeping the town temperate. And once more he enraged the citizenry, this time by decreeing that no Antrim man should be allowed in the Valley Hotel barroom for more than two minutes. It seemed they were to be denied even the pleasure of watching others drink.

The North Branch correspondent for the paper had the last word in December. "Are the wells blacklisted too? They're going dry!"

The feelings of outrage persisted into 1904. At the March town meeting, a resolution was passed by unanimous vote that "no citizen ought to have his name placed on a blacklist without his consent except on satisfactory evidence that he is indeed intemperate." After this, things gradually quieted down, although it seems safe to assume that many never forgave Mr. Goodell for his action. In November, when the question of the liquor license again appeared on the ballot, the vote was light, with many voters abstaining, no doubt an ominous result of the hard feelings over the blacklist.

The next year (1905) C.R. Jameson redirected his anger toward the

1904

selectmen, whom he accused of taxing property unfairly. A contentious man, he wrote long and rambling letters to the paper belaboring his point. It was an age-old cry of pain, and not likely ever to be settled to everyone's satisfaction.

1905   Meanwhile, the people "over East" had their own gripe. They had been without telephone service for ten years while the Branch, the Center, Clinton, and South Village kept the party lines buzzing. Sam Thompson's house (near Attridge's) might have been saved from burning had there been a telephone to alert the fire department. As it was, a guest at the Thompson house, Miss Nina Cheney, had to ride to South Village to give the alarm, and by that time it was too late. Telephone rates were eighteen dollars per year, surely a small sum to pay for the utility, comfort, and entertainment it afforded.

Other citizens elsewhere thought the town needed a clock. For some reason funds were not raised in town meeting, but rather gathered in little by little by subscription and by profits from various entertainments. Two potential sites for the clock were debated: the tower of the town hall or the tower of the Presbyterian church.

1906   Early in 1906, the clock was purchased for $600 and installed in the Presbyterian tower. This was thought at the time to be a temporary measure until the town hall tower could be made safer and higher to accommodate it. The clock first struck at three in the afternoon on January 23, 1906, and has recorded the time faithfully for the most part ever since. The voters at the March meeting duly agreed to accept the clock and maintain it, with the privilege of moving it at any time. Yearly appropriations are still made for its maintenance, and it seems to have found its permanent home.

The same March meeting found Charles R. Jameson still furious with the selectmen over what he considered to be the inequality in tax assessments, so he announced his decision to run for selectman. Needless to say, the selectmen were as annoyed with him as he was with them, and since many of the voters sided with the selectmen, he was soundly defeated. Despite all the controversy about him, he seems always to have had the best interests of Antrim at heart, and he certainly was a lively character.

His brother, Nathan C. Jameson, was less controversial, and a highly respected member of the Democratic party. He was a delegate to the national convention, and in 1906 was his party's nominee for governor. (He was the third Antrim man so honored: Luke Woodbury was the Democratic candidate in 1851, but died before the election; David H. Goodell was the successful Republican candidate in 1888.) Jameson's defeat in the popular vote was so narrow that the state legislature had to decide the winner. It goes without saying that Antrim voters overwhelmingly favored Jameson.

There remained only the question of the James A. Tuttle Library to be settled. Nearly everyone had a theory about how Mr. Tuttle's generous bequest should be spent. C.R. Jameson, full of ideas as usual, suggested that it would be cheaper to use the old Methodist church building than to build a new library. Others thought that it would be all right to build a wooden structure that cost no more than $4,000, and use the balance of the money to keep the library open every afternoon and evening. The Reverend William E. Braisted summed it up: "The building should be aesthetically stimulating, and itself a lesson in harmony, good proportions, and adaptability."

TALL TALES 1907-1917

E ARLY IN 1907 the Library Committee called for a special town meeting to consider bids it had received on construction of the James A. Tuttle Library. All prices submitted had been far in excess of the $12,000 originally voted. Even the nearest one, an exorbitant $16,000, was considered outrageous.

1907   The expenditure for the building was limited by the terms of Mr. Tuttle's will, which stipulated that sufficient monies be left over from the cost of the structure to provide for books, care, and maintenance. Since all figures, even the amount of the bequest, were estimates of what the properties might bring, it was obvious that only a town meeting could solve such an indefinite proposition. Even this conclusion was not too rewarding. As soon as the meeting opened it became apparent it was to be the usual battle between the "misers" and the "spenders." Fresh in everyone's mind was the town hall, hilariously voted in by malicious young poll tax payers at the expense of the property owners. The misers felt that at long last here was one project — an outright gift of great benefit — which could be enjoyed without adding to the tax yoke already burdening their weary necks. The spenders argued that no matter what the cost, here was a golden chance for the intelligent people of Antrim to have a library of which the town could be forever proud.

The conflict became a very heated and personal affair in what appeared to be a fairly even division. It was now obvious an impasse was being created of far greater magnitude than the dilemma they had met to solve. It was now up to the town officials to dampen the fury and rescue a worthy venture. The moderator called for a vote.

The result was small, considering the large number of people present, since the women could not vote and many men did not want to be counted in a standing vote. In the intimacy of a small town the open vote often means taking a stand against a friend or an employer rather than a stand upon an issue. This circumstance has often nullified the cherished belief that town meetings are the purest form of democracy.

The vote was thirty to twenty-five in favor of the "tight wads" who clung to the original $12,000 decision. The town fathers waved down the angry protests of the losers, and went into conference. After some minutes they made an announcement. The town would indeed stand by the original $12,000, but the cost of the building must not exceed $13,000.

This Jovian ambiguity was hailed as a victory by both sides. Mollified, the "wastrels" showed their appreciation by joining the winners in unanimously dismissing the three other articles. These were opportunistic pleas slipped in by some sly outer residents who wanted the plank sidewalks extended to cover their muddy foot paths.

Later, in June, the committee announced a contract had been signed. The building, furniture, and grading would be completed for exactly $13,000. Thus Antrim came up with a library of which the town can justly take great pride. A far cry from the ugly town hall, a legacy of long bitterness.

D.H. Goodell, successful local farmer, warns of Brown Tail Moth menace to fruit trees and foliage, and advises action.
D.H. Goodell elected President of Anti-Saloon League in Concord, N.H.
D.H. Goodell buys the Antrim Tavern.
Ex-Governor Goodell and wife married fifty years last Sunday.
Small conflagration in Goodell business block Tuesday morning.

Such repetitious items hint at the amazing abilities of an amazing old man. Suffering lifelong ill health, he was president and treasurer of the Goodell Company with factories in Antrim and Bennington, head of the local power company, active in church and civic affairs, and a zealot regarding temperance. His immense set of farm buildings behind the tree-studded V on North Main Street was an impressive sight. He held innumerable public offices, and was elected governor of New Hampshire in 1888. Due to his poor health, he served only one term. Intolerant, domineering, respected, and detested, he was a history maker.

Coffin Doors

A gruesome double tragedy took place on October 5, 1907, when the large farmhouse of the Amos Colby family on the Hillsboro Road burned to the ground. The chimney was found to be on fire soon after the sudden death of Mrs. Colby that morning. All danger was thought to be over, until about nine that evening upper floors burst into flames. The two sons carried the body of their mother to the nearest neighbors, but on their return they were unable to enter the house or save anything of value. The eighty-five year old house was of brick, and for years had been a tavern for Vermont cattle drivers on their way to Brighton, Massachusetts. A large barn and numerous cattle pens across the roadway remained undamaged.

At this time there were no funeral homes or chapels and, after the embalming, the body of the deceased was returned home to await the funeral. While it rested in the parlor with the shades drawn or the blinds closed, it was customary for some one always to be near the casket, especially during the night. This latter ordeal was frequently spared the family by Charles Eaton, a kindly man who spent endless hours in this self-imposed conception of service to his fellowmen. One reason for this surveillance was the unspoken fear that the family pets might gain entrance to the room, and react in some strange animal manner to the passing of a beloved companion. The studied dark wallpaper, darker woodwork, and message pictures seemed to intensify the sickly sweet smell of the funeral pinks, often serving to associate this room forever with sadness.

Another custom was the attachment of a "crepe" to the frame of the front doors to indicate a death had taken place. The approximate age of the person was shown by the color of the crepe ribbon bow so that a passerby might know which member of the family had passed away. A respectful quiet prevailed in the near neighborhood.

Unnoticed evidence of these home funerals can still be seen in the surprising number of "coffin doors" in many of the older houses. These were narrow double doors, one side used for normal entry, the other generally opened only to allow for the slow dignified passage of a coffin carried by three friends on each side, a much more significant farewell than from commercial establishments.

One sturdy superstition clung to funerals. If a white horse was in the cortege to the cemetery, some person in that carriage would die within a year.

In mentioning the significance of a last departure from the home, it must be remembered that the homestead and its added ells was often the abode of several generations, and that within the many rooms most of the emotions and vital facts of life took place. There were distant hospitals and the poor house or county farm, but these were a matter of last resort. There were no homes for the aged, nursing homes, retirement centers, day care centers, or casual trips to the maternity ward. Weddings, births, deaths, moans, labored breathing, measles, mumps, scarlet fever, pneumonia, midnight crises, parties, dinners, gatherings, Thanksgivings, Christmases, birthdays, homecomings, anniversaries, all took place in "the house," each room a memory of many things.

The senior class joined a thousand other students for a trip to Washington, D.C. One leg of the journey was made on the magnificent new steamboat, the two-million-dollar Commonwealth, largest steamboat in the world. The sea voyage was from Fall River, Massachusetts, to New York City, an overnight trip. Entertainment in the grand salon consisted of doleful chamber music quite out of step with the excited and energetic students, who spent the night racing madly about the open promenades. Many future graduates would experience the same hazardous moments encountered by this class when they too met the open sea and rounded the fearsome Point Judith.

1908

Be sure and take a bottle of Chamberlain's Colic, Cholera, and Diarrhoea Remedy with you when starting on your vacation trip. It cannot be obtained on board trains or steamers.

On May 6, ex-Governor Goodell celebrated his seventy-fourth birthday by issuing a special invitation to each Antrim man seventy years or older to be his guest at a banquet given at the Maplehurst Inn. Thirty-three were present.

Nathan W.C. Jameson passed away on May 12. One of Antrim's oldest, best known, and most highly respected citizens, he lived in the house opposite Wayno's store. He had been one of the guests attending Goodell's birthday banquet a few days earlier.

On June 20 Sutherland's Mill at North Branch burned. Loss was estimated at $1,000.

On June 21, in Clinton, the house and barn of Harlan E. Young, and the house and grocery store of Duane B. Dunham all burned to the ground.

Actually, it was almost impossible to save an out-of-town house or

Goodell's 74th birthday . . . all this and arthritis too!

barn, especially if the fire occurred at night. If the victim had a phone he could call someone near the Baptist church who could ring the bell. Otherwise he would have to drive to a phone or all the way to the church himself. In daytime there were many rigs standing all harnessed, and work teams were around that could be hitched to the "tub" or hand pumper. But in nighttime, it meant harnessing up horses, hitching to the apparatus, galloping all the way to Clinton or North Branch, finding a brook, running the hose, and starting to pump by hand. Once the tub got rocking it could throw mighty streams of water, but by then the house or barn was gone. In the village, equipment could be pulled by hand.

Probably there was nothing quite as thrilling as looking down Main Street and seeing these light emergency rigs coming, their drivers yipping wildly, the horse whips nicking at the horse's shoulders and the gravel flying from the slurring wheels. Then would come the pumper and, if the work horses were young, it too would be in time to help save adjoining buildings.

A new blacksmith, Joe Heritage, of Somerville, Massachusetts, moved into town and took over D.P. Bryer's shop on lower West Street, west of the brook. Opposite him, L.D. Cole had a small shop east of the brook in front of what is now the Legion Hall. He made baskets, filed saws, bottomed chairs, and repaired furniture. He also made fine skis of straight ash for fifty cents a pair. However, the purchaser had to point them and provide his own loose foot straps, which allowed him to abandon skis whenever it appeared he could not avoid a tree or a large rock. Cole wrote poetry for his ads and had quite a following among those who liked poems.

> Yes Cole for years had made his bread
> With saw and plane and hammer.
> Tell him your wants, he'll go ahead
> Without much vocal clamor.
> He'll ask your pardon with a bow
> For truth may not be pleasing,
> But outside jobs are cheaper now
> Than when the pipes are freezing.

Horse and Buggy Days

While Cole's work was a convenience, Heritage's occupation might well have been the most important one in town. Today it is difficult to grasp how essential horses were in the early days, or what a catastrophe it was if a horse went lame because of a poorly fitted shoe, or when broken metal on some vehicle rendered it useless.

In winter the sidewalks were cleared by a horse-drawn plow. The roads were made passable by great six-horse rollers. Cutting ice for summer refrigeration, logging, carrying grain for the stock and cordwood for heat, bringing the doctor, pulling the hearse or the stage to the depot, bringing up freight, taking back manufactured products, trips to Bennington or Hillsboro — all these depended on the horse. In summer there was plowing the land, mowing hay, scooping a cellar hole, hauling lumber for a house, dragging the roads, and pulling barges (huge farm wagons holding many people) to picnics and gatherings. In addition to these were the regular services on certain days: the meatman, the fishman, the iceman, the milkman, the groceryman (who took orders on, say, Wednesday, and delivered the groceries and gossip on Friday, perched precariously on the back legs of a kitchen chair tilted against the dented chair rail). All these visits

Robb's delivery wagon . . . back door bakery service

depended on faithful horses which routinely pulled in to the proper places and promptly fell asleep.

Alas, there was a dreadful threat to this satisfactory way of life. It was the automobile. What once had been an amusing new contraption was now a noisy and smoking vehicle weaving wildly along the same state roads used by horses. While a strong man might keep control of his heavy work team, a woman with a spirited driving horse had no chance as the puffing clattering monster bore down upon them. Frequently the considerate driver would stop or idle the motor, but often this only induced explosive backfiring which sent the frightened horse into a frenzy of backing and rearing, or into a sidewise bolt over walls and ditches.

There were endless shouts, profanity, threats, arguments, fights, injuries, and law suits. The Catholic priest from Hillsboro ran off the road to Antrim and tipped over (which Protestant Antrim thought only fitting), but it did seem to indicate to all that there was not a great deal of celestial sympathy for these infernal machines.

It was not as if autos would ever amount to anything. Strictly seasonal vehicles, there were only a few dry months in the summer when they could be used at all. They were completely helpless in the winter on the hard-rolled icy roads. In wet weather they bogged down in every muddy rut they came to, and some farmers even maintained mud holes for the occasional fee they could charge for dragging a car out of the muck.

While cars were menace enough on the main highways, it was obvious what havoc they could create by roaring down village streets where the service horses stood. Some of these were so well trained that when the order man slipped from one back kitchen door to another, the horse ambled along to each stop by himself. Consequently it was felt that if cars were restricted to the state roads, the normal and necessary routine of small town life could continue.

Then came a devastating decision from a court in Missouri. "The rights in the use of the streets, of the driver of a horse and the operator of an automobile, are equal, and merely running an automobile into a street while horses are driven thereon does not authorize an inference of negligence."

This was a blow similar to what might be felt in later years if some court ruled autos could no longer use roads. It was a situation no man could solve, but another intelligence interceded. It had long been called "horse sense" and the solution was simple. The horses accepted the automobile and lost their fear of them, something humans are still trying to do.

Genius At Work

Back before practical cold storage, evaporated apples were a big industry. Mechanical apple parers were an essential part of the business, and D.H. Goodell decided to have his mechanics invent a machine to compete with those already on the market. Three mechanics worked on the project: Ed Thompson, W.H. Boutelle, and Frank Hunt. The machine they came up with worked and sold well. Some time later, Boutelle left the company and moved to Rochester, New York, where he invented a new parer and started in business for himself. Later on Hunt followed Boutelle into fruit country to locate in Sodus, New York, and he also invented a new parer. Thompson, a shy little man with no interest in success stayed with Goodell and continued to turn out new machines. Goodell was furious with Boutelle's and Hunt's efforts, but did nothing about it. Both Boutelle and Hunt considered their inventions as their own, and saw no reason why they could not compete, but Boutelle, now prosperous, was angered because Hunt had moved into his territory, and sued him for an infringement of a patent. Actually, since all three men had worked together, and parers at best were little more than a roller following a sculptured drum with a few cams thrown in, no doubt all three were similar. Hunt, a talented mechanic, had already invented a thread winder, a raisin seeder, and a knife sharpener, and could easily have remedied the infringement but — enraged by the suit — chose to fight in court. He was crushed by the expense; the business failed, and he died shortly thereafter. Thus three capable men came to hate one another. Boutelle said before he died, "We were all such good friends when we started; to think it came to this, when there was market enough for all of us." The breed has gone, but the machines they made are still around, some here, some there.

Ed Thompson's brother, Old Bussie, who lived where Blackburns do now, was also an inventor, but he had a dreadful weakness for drink, when he could afford it. None too fastidious, when the occasion demanded he chamois-filtered the benzene in which the Goodell workers washed their hands and sipped it.

According to a tracker who once noticed Old Bussie's shuffling footprints in the snow up the Slaughter Barn hill, the effect of this sipping must have been awesome. At the crest of the hill, Bussie apparently envisioned himself face to face with some monstrous apparition beyond belief, for his tracks indicated he turned-tail and with fifteen-foot leaps gained the sanctuary of the Slaughter Barn icehouse in just ten steps. Indeed, Bussie's flight in itself must have been as spectacular as the apparition he saw.

In the shed attached to his house was a fantastic automobile. It had a regular front seat, but the rear seat was round like a large tub with a beautifully upholstered seat following the contour. There was no top, and the only entry to the back seat was from the rear by a step and a small latched door. Once aboard, the four passengers had a choice of riding forward, backward, or sideways. During one gala day, Ed, who owned the vehicle, managed to get it going a short distance in the parade. About that time it was said to have been bought for the Ford museum, and was never seen again.

Bussie's favorite invention was the model of a small boat. In the forward deck were six tilted upright tubes in V formation. These passed down through the bow to join six grooves which ran the length of the hull, which was to be driven by a conventional motor. Bussie's theory was that the forward motion of the boat would draw round air bubbles down into the grooves, and the boat would roll forward on these frictionless ball bearings of air. As the grooves ran the length of the boat, he felt the buoyancy of the trapped air bubbles would lift the hull above the drag of the water with only the sharp edges of the grooves acting as keels. Bussie never had money enough to build the boat, but pushing the model rapidly through the water did stir up a mess of bubbles.

A Sinful Subject

Antrim's attitude in 1909 paralleled that of Bishop Mallalieu of the Methodist Tremont Temple in Boston, who declared,

Dancing in public schools in Boston is responsible for conditions of immorality that are almost as bad as the white slave traffic. There ought to be a state law against dancing. The theatre is a school of vice and a destroyer of morals. Also the vile literature which some journals publish is corrupting the young, lowering the standards of morality among the older people. We ought to lead a relentless warfare to the death against the things that lead to these conditions.

There were a few other things which he did not mention. Sex was sin. Playing cards was sinful. Gambling was sinful. Horse racing was wrong. Drinking was almost as bad as sex. Breaking the Sabbath was not only wrong, but dangerous:

CHAPTER 271 PUBLIC STATUTES
SECT. 4. No person shall, on the Lord's Day, discharge any firearms for sport or in the pursuit of game, nor carry a firearm in any field, highway, or private way, while in the pursuit of game, or with the intent to discharge the same in sport.
SECT. 10. Penalty ten ($10.00) dollars and 30 days imprisonment.
SECT. 11. Any person, upon view of an offense described in this chapter, may apprehend the offender, and bring him before a justice for trial.

As for drunkenness, four men who were intoxicated and used obscene language in front of a lady on Main Street were brought before the local judge. He gave them a choice of punishment: they could go to jail for thirty days or leave Antrim forever. They chose banishment.

Since dancing was not allowed in school affairs and Antrim was a dry community, there was a tendency to look down upon the two neighboring towns, Hillsboro and Bennington. Both permitted school dancing and also were wet, having one or more saloons and legal liquor. Consequently, it was almost instinctive for children growing up here to look with disdain upon any resident from these sinspots, particularly Hillsboro.

Not all local people agreed with the good Bishop's convictions. Many saw no harm in a little dabbling in sin as long as you didn't get into it all over. Antrim put on many plays, and dancing was allowed in the town hall. However, there were some restrictions. Partners had to keep six inches from each other, and such dances as the Bunny Hug and the Turkey Trot were barred. If violations of these orders continued, the janitor was to turn out the lights and lock the doors. This punishment left some doubt as to whose side the selectmen were on.

Possibly there was substance to the attitude toward drinking. Certain individuals, otherwise ordinary citizens, would periodically go on a "bat," a tussle with the devil which might last from one to three weeks. When they surfaced (no one ever saw them or knew where they were), their appearance was such as to strike terror in the stoutest heart. Truly sadder men, but alas never any wiser; in six months or more "John's on a bat" proved to be one more convincing lesson of what a hold drinking could have.

Any casual research into local standards would have disclosed some inconsistencies. While dancing was abhorrent because of its close physical contact, there were no objections to sleigh rides. At the time, these consisted of some farmer with a team spreading a thick mass of hay into a low flatbed sled, and then tossing in all the robes, fur coats, horse blankets and other barn coverings on top of the hay. While the driver took his stance in front, the chaperone covered the rear—to see that no one fell out. In between, couples burrowed into the hay in a sort of boardless bundling that never caught the attention of the arbiters of proper conduct. Thus a sleigh ride was marked only by song and sleigh bells, and was a cherished bucolic event.

Demon rum was evil, but nothing much was ever said about cider. While a barrel was an ordinary measure—even the pantries were designed to hold barrels of flour or sugar—it was amazing how many barrels of cider, destined to be vinegar, were needed in a household. However, here a touch of Satan often intruded. Some cellars, with their damp dirt floors and precise temperatures (natural air conditioning for the rooms above) simply would not turn cider into vinegar. No matter how much "mother" the devout temperance housewife poured into the bunghole, this "beggar's champagne" refused to turn into the sour acid so necessary for a few jars of pickles. Naturally, anyone with such a priceless basement never lacked for friends or customers.

In summing up Antrim's moral standards, it seems the most demanding one was keeping the Sabbath holy. No work, no games, no undue noise, no hilarity, no hunting, no fishing, no sports of any sort. Large dinners, family gatherings, visiting, taking a long walk or a carriage ride—these were permissible. Still, in some of the more devout families, children could not leave their yard unless it was to attend some church service, a great difference from today when the minister's first prayer touches off the chain saws, the power mowers, the bulldozers, and the carpenters!

The Second Annual Poultry Show was held in the town hall, a far more successful effort than the previous one. This time six hundred birds of thirty-four different breeds were shown. There were fifty-three exhibitors, of whom twenty-two were from out of town. While this was helpful to those who kept hens, there was some criticism of using the hall for this purpose. In spite of abundant building paper on the carefully kept hard wood floor, the busy birds had a tendency to scratch the contents of their cages in every direction. The audience aided in spreading the litter, sometimes to the extent of carrying it into their own homes.

Some felt a barn would be more suitable since a telltale chicken odor permeated the hall for a long time after a show, distracting the attention of the assemblies from such worthwhile events as high school debates, commencement speakers, and anti-saloon orators. Despite these objections, the influential Poultry Association persisted in using the hall for some years until a decline in interest finally restored the gathering place to its primary purpose.

On January 15, 1910, the Antrim Board of Trade was formed with one hundred charter members, all men. The purpose of the organization was to make Antrim "Busier, Bigger, and Better." Officers were: President, Wilbert D. Farnham; vice-president, Will E. Cram; secretary, Edmond M. Lane; treasurer, H.W. Eldredge. The directors were B.F. Drake, W.W. Merrill, C.F. Butterfield, S.M. Thompson, W.E. Gibney, Colonel R.C. Goodell.

President Farnham, an "outsider" from Boston, had recently bought Harry Deacon's dry and fancy goods store, renaming it, "A First Class Dry and Fancy Goods Store," sub-titled, "A City Store in a Country Town." This extravagant innovation caused him to be looked upon with some suspicion, but he had come to town with good

Gregg Lake from White Birch Point

references. Besides, people had great confidence that the other trusted local officials would keep an eye on him.

The organization's first initiative established a central business bureau where residents interested in housing summer boarders could present their qualifications in response to inquiries which all hoped would arrive after appropriate brochures and advertising started. Some successful establishments were already operating—the Bass Farm at the Center, the Mountain View House over East, and the Lake House on the road to Gregg Lake. The new approach was to open ordinary residences to less affluent boarders.

As a result of many inquiries, the Board of Trade pronounced the necessity of a local golf links. D.H. Goodell offered the Raymond pasture on reasonable terms, and it was believed the land could be put in excellent condition at comparatively small expense. He also contributed land for single and double tennis courts. Acquisition of these properties led to formation of the Antrim Country Club, directed by the president, E.M. Lane, and the secretary and treasurer, J.C. Hansom. Membership or stock could be acquired from officials.

The Reverend William Hurlin, Antrim's "Grand Old Man," ninety-six years old, passed away on June 28, 1910, the oldest man in town. Born in London, England, on July 31, 1814, he preached his first sermon in that city during March, 1835. In 1840 he was appointed city missionary of London, serving as such for nine years. He immigrated to America in 1848 and settled in Danville, Vermont. In 1866 he came to Antrim where he preached for seven years. It was largely through his efforts that the present Baptist church was built. Although he moved to Plaistow and Goshen, he soon returned to Antrim to spend the rest of his life. He was an extensive writer and held innumerable religious offices. A minister for over seventy years, he officiated at more than 275 funerals, delivered more than 6,400 sermons, and performed uncounted wedding ceremonies.

The Honorable Nathan C. Jameson, one of Antrim's foremost and widely known citizens, passed away August 27, 1910. He had been born May 4, 1849, and attended schools in town as well as Henniker Academy and Phillips Academy, Andover, Massachusetts. He was engaged for twenty years in the wholesale hat business in New York City, but managed to take part in town affairs through frequent visits home. An ardent Democrat, he was often rewarded by offices in his party.

In 1910 the town voted to change the name of Gregg's Pond to Gregg Lake. Already its approach was being referred to as the Lake Road, and Paul Thayer, developer of White Birch Point, maintained that people would be reluctant to build or buy a nice cottage beside or overlooking a mere pond. The innuendo was apparent: there were lily ponds, frog ponds, and mill ponds, none of which compared to this body of water a half mile wide and a mile-and-a-half long.

Charles R. Jameson, developer of the north shore, objected. The place had always been called Gregg's Pond and this name had never affected his properties, one of which was the Peterwaugh, a boarding house. Another was the pavilion, an open air structure all of twenty-one by eighty feet which extended out into the water, resting on the rocks which protrude during low water. Still, regardless of the logic, many habitually used the word *pond*.

As for Jameson, the great dissenter, his role by then was so tiresome that when he did come up with a good idea, the irritated voters cut him down without listening. But he did command something of a loyal following, however, as shown in the one year when he ran for office on an Independent ticket. He made a fairly respectable showing.

Mrs. Hannah J. Goodell, wife of ex-Governor Goodell, died on April 18, 1911. The funeral was held at the Baptist Church, and about one hundred men from Goodell's shop attended in a body. Music was furnished by a double male quartet. The Reverend O.E. Kendall, pastor, directed the services which were largely attended by the townspeople.

1911

On June 7, 1911, Dr. Morris Christie, one of the town's foremost citizens, passed from this life. As a physician he had a wide and extensive practice. Always a man of excellent judgment, his advice was sought by many. He graduated from the University of New York, and was on the medical and surgical staff of Charity Hospital, New York City. He started practice in May, 1860, and continued until ill health forced him to retire.

Antrim's advantages of July 5, 1911

Antrim has:

11 teachers
320 houses
5 saw and grist mills
1 paper box factory
1 approved high school
5 manufacturing plants
1,400 population
4 churches
37,000 acres
90 to 100 miles of good roads
3 inns
5 grocery and dry
*   goods stores*
A cement garage
James A. Tuttle Library

Newspaper and printing plant

A new ice cart
A modern milk wagon

It is 1100 feet above sea level

7 grocery wagons
A good shoe store
A nice bakery
A 5&10c store
A good meat market
A drug store and ice cream
*   parlor*
A town water system
Street lights
300 factory employees
50 in other work

A country club
Concrete sidewalks
It pays for schools the sum
*   of $6,386.13, or 45% of*
*   total taxes.*
It pays for highways, bridges,
*   and sidewalks $3,612, or*
*   26% of total Taxes.*
It is 77 miles from Boston,
*   32 miles from Concord, and*
*   about the same from Nashua*
*   and Keene.*

The Antrim Brass Band gave an open air concert on the bandstand Wednesday night, August 30, 1911. Later the people all gathered at the town hall, where the rest of the evening was spent listening to a musical and literary program. Time was also given during the evening to considerable social intercourse. This proved a very pleasant ending of a most successful observance.

The milk business of G.S. Wheeler & Son has greatly increased since they put on their modern low-down milk wagon, which is on our streets early every morning. It is a wagon of which any town might be proud. Our people can keep this up-to-date milk wagon daily upon our streets for an indefinite period by a generous patronage.

F.T. Graves has been appointed Special Police to look after the contingent which makes a weekly pilgrimage to the thirst quenching town north of us, and make the night hideous on their return.

On September 11, a disastrous fire at the Center destroyed the house, ell, and barn of E.A. Bigelow of Winchester, Massachusetts, treasurer of the E. Howard Clock Company of Boston. The firemen responded but there was no water near at hand. The fire bell sounded at 4:30 A.M. W.E. Cram, auctioneer, will sell what furniture was saved on Saturday morning.

On September 24 a midnight fire burned the farmhouse, ell, sheds, and barn of John C. Butterfield above Clinton on the lake road. The fire department promptly responded, but lack of water rendered their efforts to no avail. The fire was probably set by the ailing eldest son, age forty-five, partially blind, who had always resided at home. His body was found in the barn where he perished.

November 22: A.W. Dudley, civil engineer, is in town surveying for the prospective sewage system. This is in response to the March Precinct meeting when the Water Commissioners were authorized to bring in a report on the matter.

On November 13, 1911, ex-Gov. D.H. Goodell marries Miss Emma S. McCoy, an office worker for Goodell Company for some 26 years.

Stone Walls of Antrim

George A. Cochran, born in 1835, long-time resident of a farm at the intersection of Route 202 and Elm Avenue, came up with an estimate of how many miles of stone walls there were in Antrim. As a 14-year moderator, a 13-year selectman, and the inherited owner of a 200-acre farm, it is probable he was as honest and knowledgeable an authority as could be found at that time. According to authorities, the great wall of China measured 2,000 miles in length, representing an incredible amount of manpower. According to Mr. Cochran's estimates, the stone walls of Antrim measured over a thousand miles and, considering the rise of the population here during the wall-building period, comprised about as impressive a record as the Chinese effort. (No comparison was cited that took into consideration the difference in heights of the Chinese and local walls.)

He based this figure on his own farm's six miles of wall. In addition to the walls, there are the huge piles of boulders found on both working farms and those abandoned farms which were wooded over. All this stone work and many early pictures reveal that at one time most of Antrim was either cleared land or good pasturage.

The heartbreak and discouragement felt by the early settlers when they found they had chosen to clear a land which could not produce consistent crops goes without saying. A short growing season, late or early frosts, summer hail, the inability to raise grain — all served to indicate the necessity of moving on to a more propitious climate.

Yet the lesson has been hard to accept. Again and again, the abandonment of the great barns, the dairy herds, the apple orchards, the chicken houses, truck farms, beef creatures, sheep farms, blueberry acres, and sugar-making have gradually reduced farming efforts to small garden gambling, a sort of vegetable roulette in the back yard where one may win with the tomatoes yet lose all the beans.

Some blame can be placed on a divide near South Lyndeborough, most noticeable during railroad days when the locomotive labored up a southern slope to a crest and then coasted down a long northern grade into Elmwood Junction. On the southern side toward Wilton peaches grow, the snow is less, and frosts are not so frequent.

But still young visionaries come to hack their acre from that persistent foe, the forest, which eases over the walls, creeps into the fields, and springs up in the mowings. Truly, this land must be for the birds — and the woods, and a thousand miles of stones.

The Board of Trade's campaign to encourage more summer boarders met with questionable success. There were many large homes with an abundance of spare rooms which seemed ideal spots for such an endeavor. They were owned by men earning meager wages bolstered by their gardens, berry patches, perhaps a self-perpetuating flock of hens and a pig or two. Any additional money would be welcome. The wives wanted to help but there was little work open to them. Under these circumstances some decided to try a few boarders.

Contact was made by mail and the novice hosts made no effort to misrepresent what they had to offer. There would be plain food, verandas, rocking chairs, a couple of hammocks, and a rural privy.

Happily enough, this was exactly what the urban guests were looking for. The eager applicants seemed to run to two or three females suffering from a bad case of housewives' fatigue, whose only desire was to escape the ailment for a blessed week or two. Unfortunately, their husbands chose to remain in the city, but all they asked was to sleep late, rock on a shady porch, and have someone else get the meals. Most of all they wanted to avoid the large and expensive places which could not offer the peace and quiet of a true country home.

For a couple of days after the visitors' arrival this would work out wonderfully well for all concerned. Then reactions began to turn up which could not really be termed "quaint." After dozing all day in a rocker, the guests obviously couldn't sleep well nights. They blamed the quiet, or the wind in the pines, or the "Whip Poor Wills," or the frogs, or the roosters, or strange noises. What was more, they spoke freely of the bountiful feasts before which country folks said grace, deeply regretting that such a nice custom of giving thanks had naturally died out. But, worst of all, there was nothing to do. In the city you could go to the beach, ride all day in an open street car for only ten cents, or go to an amusement park with seventy-five attractions.

The large places like the Bass Farm countered such plaints with tennis, croquet, horseshoes, whist tables, ego contests, or trips to the lake. Here there were enough people of a like nature to amuse each other. But for a couple of bored city women to move in with a frugal village family was to court a predictable disaster.

Once, in bored desperation, or a concealed urge to get even, one stout female guest insisted she be present at the killing of the daily chicken.

Killing a chicken was usually done by "wringing its neck." This meant grabbing the bird by its head and whirling the body about

Bass Farm in 1904

while the neck bones crunched in a sickening fashion. Another macabre moment came when, after it had been dipped in scalding water, plucked clean and laid on the back porch for dead, its muscular reflexes made it seem to come alive again as it thrashed about until it could be dispatched once and for all. This didn't happen often, but enough to suggest different procedure.

A quicker and more definite method was to chop off its head. But even this, with a two-inch hatchet blade and a crooked and ruffled neck, could still result in a mangling. So the man of the house drove two large spikes into the block just far enough apart to hold the bird's head so the neck could be pulled out straight and thus avoid any near misses.

Consequently, as the determined guest staunchly followed the executioner to the block, she asked what the two spikes were for. Told they were to hold the rooster's head, she hollered, "Oh, my God!" and ran screaming into the house. It took a lot of persuasion to convince her that the spikes were for a merciful purpose and not merely a backyard type of crucifixion.

1912 Probably the biggest social event in Antrim history took place on February 3, 1912, when Isabel Burnham Jameson, only daughter of Mrs. Idabel and the late Honorable Nathan C. Jameson, was married to George Alexander Walker, assistant treasurer of the Pennsylvania Railroad, of Philadelphia. The great interest was due to the wealth and prominence of the bride's family as well as her own popularity and beauty. The auditorium and vestry of the lavishly decorated Presbyterian Church were filled to overflowing. Everyone in town seemed to have been invited and there was a host of guests from out of town. A gala reception for the latter was held in the mansion at the intersection of Main and Summer Streets.

After an extended honeymoon in Palm Beach and Miami, the couple planned to reside in Philadelphia. There was a dreadful irony in the last paragraph of the newspaper report: "A wide circle of friends join with the *Reporter* in wishing the newly married couple health, happiness, and prosperity, and a long life together." Ten months later, on November 28, Thanksgiving evening, Mrs. Walker died in her home in Philadelphia. She had been ill only four days. She was buried in Maplewood cemetery, in the town where she had spent most of her life.

The New Railroad

In February, 1912, great news threw Antrim into an unusual state of excitement. After many vague rumors the Grand Trunk Railroad finally announced definite plans for building new lines through New Hampshire. One of the proposed routes was to run from Claremont to Nashua, and the tracks, if the town gave permission, would pass right through the center of town. At last, the detested Boston and Maine would have some competition.

Immediately, the B.&M. protested. The Board of Trade arranged a public meeting where representatives of both companies presented their arguments. The Grand Trunk promised good service, new equipment, and an intown depot. The B.&M. stressed that the good people of New Hampshire had 39 million dollars of their savings invested in the B.&M., while the G.T. was an alien road owned by foreigners living in luxury in far-away London, England.

Antrim's particular problem relating to railroad service concerned its location. Two main lines served the town. One extended from Concord into Hillsboro and on through Peterborough into Winchendon, Massachusetts. The other line came down from Keene through Hancock into Greenfield and Wilton, and on to Nashua and Boston. If one wanted to go to Manchester, there was a junction at Henniker. Hillsboro, at one time a terminal of the Concord road, had an engine turntable (turned by manpower and innumerable passing kids), and some trains laid over or were made up there.

The line from Keene to Boston crossed the Concord-to-Winchendon tracks at Elmwood Junction. This was about a mile south of Bennington. At present, Route 202 (taking the place of the old road through Hancock to Peterborough) passes close to this barely discernible spot, but in 1912 Y-shaped trackage allowed sections or entire trains to be rerouted there.

Antrim's first problem was having its depot a mile from town, across the river in Bennington. There were conflicting stories concerning this location. One was that Goodell felt a nearer station might be a hangout for drunken idlers. Another was that the town wouldn't donate sufficient money to bring the tracks in to the foot of Carter House hill (Depot Street). Still another was the prohibitive cost to the railroad of building two bridges across the Contoocook. The latter sounds most logical. However, the B.&M. was always blamed even though it seems the earlier roads were small, independent, and were gradually acquired by the B.&M. system.

People finally became accustomed to paying the stage fare to get to the train. Since it was only a mile, one could easily walk, but there was always the matter of luggage. Even a short visit meant a suitcase, a longer one a trunk, and in cold weather there was the added burden of clothes, boots, and possible purchases.

The real grievance was the arrogant air of the B.&M., but since there was no other means of traveling long distances, or of hauling heavy materials such as coal, lumber, or grain, Antrim's public simply had to take it or leave it. Freight service, especially for shipments less than a carload, almost disappeared. This was most true of household goods, and waiting weeks or months for a freight shipment was not unusual.

The most aggravating circumstance was in making connections at the Elmwood Junction. Naturally, trains were scheduled for the most advantageous hours for Keene and Boston and for Concord and Winchendon. Accordingly, their posted passing times at Elmwood often indicated one or two hours' wait. Even this wasn't too bad, but the infuriating moment came when a connecting train took off just as a tardy train was pulling into the station. This then could mean waiting up to four hours. Older residents claimed they had spent more of their life in Elmwood Junction than they had in Antrim!

Not that the goal was too distant. You could walk a mile down the tracks into Bennington and there pick up the highway into town. But what of your trunk or heavy suitcase? If you ever wanted to see them again, it was necessary to ride shotgun on the intricate maneuver of getting them on the train at Elmwood so they could be thrown off at the demolition point in Antrim. The "baggage smashers" of that time were far more dedicated than the parcel post experts of today.

However, generally the service must have been good. The mail and passenger stage listed eight pickups a day. Express service was very expensive but prompt. Excursions were cheap, frequent, and enjoyable. These assets were all stressed at the Board of Trade's meeting, but they bore little weight. The townspeople could hardly wait to welcome the Grand Trunk.

Shortly afterward, one survey was run from Claremont to Nashua to plot the route. The surveying party came down from North Branch, across the Clinton road at about Lowe's, over into Hilton Avenue, between the school and Slaughter Barn Brook, and on toward Bennington. There was great rejoicing by the Board of Trade and everyone else who wanted to see the town grow and progress.

Once it seemed assured that at long last Antrim would have an intown depot on West or Summer Street, a strange reaction set in. Women began to visualize a grimy station, a siding, long dirty coal sheds, coal cars, lumber cars. They pictured the soot, the cinders, the thick soft coal smoke drifting across houses, lawns, clothes lines. Even more awful there would be the noise, the hoboes demanding food, the criminals who beat and robbed lone women. Why, no longer would anyone living on the west side of town be safe, even at noontime! Yes, the B.&M. was bad, but at least it was far enough away so Antrim could continue to live in impoverished peace and clean air.

The Grand Trunk must have sensed the message. Word came through that all plans for building had been canceled. Antrim settled in again to being a backward village, perfectly content to have things stay just the way they always had been.

Very Old History

> On March 2, 1912, Frank Hunt, one of the best known citizens of the town, died after a short illness, at his home on West Street. Mr. Hunt was of an unusually ingenious turn of mind and invented many varieties of machines which were patented and are now in general use throughout the country.

That announcement in the Antrim *Reporter* serves to remind us of the possibilities history offers for amazing coincidences and ramifications in a weaving and meandering trail that can leap suddenly into incidents of the present. It is hard to believe how one interest of this man long dead could possibly have aided a recent Hawthorne graduate in winning a rewarding position in today's tight teachers' market. It is just as difficult to realize that two families could follow such parallel paths for so long a time.

In 1635 a small band of Englishmen led by Peter Bulkley, a nonconformist minister from Odel, Bradfordshire, and Simon Willard, an Indian trader from Kent, landed in Massachusetts and struck inland to settle the town of Concord, Massachusetts. In their group were a George Hayward and a William Hunt, son of Robert Hunt of Halifax, Yorkshire. Hayward died in 1671 and was buried in Concord. Hunt died in 1667 in Marlboro, Massachusetts.

Now, 340 years later, because of the Bicentennial, a woman whose mother is a Hayward and a man whose mother was a Hunt unexpectedly identify each other across a table in the Tuttle library. She — on the Historical Museum Committee, he — on the Town History Committee, only about seventy-five miles from their forebears' original beachhead. It certainly took a long time to get only this far!

Possibly this new association can pool the information needed to determine once and for all which ancestor first set foot on or in the new world. It is of dubious value to assume they jumped ashore in alphabetical order. Or that Hayward lived longer than Hunt. Both Hayward and Hunt had large families. A few of the more hardy ones ventured into New Hampshire, gradually reaching Hancock, by way of Dublin, in the 1700s. There the Haywards became extensive landowners and prominent citizens, taking an active part in civic and church affairs.

Isaac Hunt came in from Dublin about 1800 and subsequently acquired wide land holdings around Nubanusit Lake. A proud patriarch, he had an elevated spot — probably judiciously chosen — where he could boast of owning "all the land as far as the eye can reach." Due to his acquisitions and temperament, Nubanusit was known to the family as Big Hunt Pond, and a smaller body of water nearer the village was Little Hunt Pond. Later on, the large family moved to the latter. The original home (now only a cellar hole) near the boat landing at Nubanusit was abandoned but was always afterward referred to as "The Old Place of All."

Since New Hampshire winters gradually impose their frigid characteristics on proud patriarchs, Frank Hunt ran away from home at an early age and roamed through the deep South. Since there were then no "missing person bureaus" or "tracers," the mother followed the custom of placing a candle in a window so the wanderer could see his way back to home and forgiveness. "Running away" must have been as common then as it is now, since one old song went, "There's a light still burning in the window,/Of the little house upon the hill,/. . .will burn. . .till they return. . .''

Around 1868 Hunt moved to Antrim. Some time previously he had picked up several standard Indian relics — skiver, gouge, battle-ax, arrowheads — found on Charles Hayward's farm in Hancock. For some reason he was fascinated by them and they always held a prominent place on the fireplace mantel in the house which he built here in 1887.

About seventy-eight years later an archeological student named Reid, who was working his way through Hawthorne, was seated next to a Hunt descendant, who was working his way through life. Reid's complaint was he had no material on which to base an original thesis for graduation. The artifacts were mentioned and Reid used them to gain his degree. The relics went back on the mantel and Reid went on to Arkansas where he started a teaching career.

Dropping back to 1889, W.W. Hayward finished writing the Hancock Town History (from which some of this account was taken). In his credits he lists one Lewis Hunt, brother of Frank, as one of the contributors to the cost of publishing the history.

Now, with two more generations of each family aware of one another living within New Hampshire, their mutual paths and contacts can be shared as were their descendants' many years past.

On March 20, 1912, William B. Gove, Antrim postmaster, committed suicide. When the Post Office failed to open in the early morning, a search resulted in his being found hanging from a tree behind the Maplehurst Inn. There never seemed to be any reason for his act; all accounts in the office were in proper order. Only twenty-three years old, he was believed to be the youngest postmaster in New Hampshire. Because of his age and likeable personality, his death was a great shock to everyone.

The Backhouse

When spring came in Antrim, there was one aspect of that cold and dismal season which never inspired a poet to verse. It was time to have the backhouse cleaned out before warm weather set in. This particularly lucrative job was held by one man who, fortunately, lived well into the transition to "water closets" and bathrooms.

The backhouse must not be confused with the outhouse. The latter was, as its name clearly indicates, out and away from other buildings. The backhouse was an integral part of the barn so that, with snow on the ground, a late-night irregular could race through the woodshed and across the splintery barn floor without wasting time to dress or find his boots. Some thoughtful builders occasionally separated the backhouse from the barn by a foot-wide breezeway. This was an advantage since that one step was often just enough to restore regularity, especially on a blustery, cold night when an icy wind came whipping around the corner of the barn.

In the larger houses there were many two-story backhouses and there was even one three-story in town, but this last one can hardly be counted since the ground floor quickly fell into disuse.

For self-evident reasons, most people deliberately avoided this spring backhouse cleaning but were exposed willy-nilly if they met George and his wagon on his way to the burial ground below the river in Bennington. For obvious reasons the selectmen had forced him to throw a few shovels of sawdust over the load. But since this was merely a token, George had buckled on a double length of reins which allowed him to walk some distance to the side, a discretion not available to the poor mule.

The trip down Main and Depot Streets was usually uneventful, but now and then some low character would greet George opposite the Inn. After inquiring about George's health he would ask, "What you got there?" George's response was a bellow that reverberated up and down the whole length of Main Street and left no doubt whatsoever as to what he "had there."

Without question there must have been a veritable tidal surge of genteel shudders all over town, but no one ever admitted having heard that infuriated cry or reported the foul miscreant who had so quickly slipped through the Town Hall doors. Yankee mores had a practical side — who else would take the job?

Modern science has never come up with a village system so economical, so trouble-free, or of such ecological simplicity.

One man held in great esteem by local youngsters gained it in a most passive manner. His legal name was Milan Moses Samuel Dustin John Colton Cooper. All cherished family names, they had a rhythmic spell no child could resist. Probably no alphabet or multiplication table was ever recited so often, so well, or by so many pupils as these seven fascinating words.

The Reverend Warren R. Cochrane, D.D., a Dartmouth graduate, died June 17, 1912. He had accepted a call to the Presbyterian Church in 1868 and preached here for forty years. He was an author of unusual ability, compiling and writing several town histories, among them the outstanding Antrim History for which the town can be forever grateful.

1913   *Antrim Divided*

In January, 1913, Charles R. Jameson announced the introduction of a bill in the Legislature to establish a West Antrim, an area roughly outlined as running west of the old Hancock Road up to the North

Branch River. This new entity would comprise 11,500 acres, compared to the 9,500 acres in the eastern part where the village stood.

The reason for this division was the claim that practically all tax money was being spent around the town, and that the roads, schools, and real estate to the west were being short-changed. Also, it would be of great benefit to the western part if a road should be built on the west side of Gregg's Pond through to the Hancock Road and the Hancock railroad station, a distance of about four miles, the same as the distance to the Antrim depot below the river. The advantage would be that the new road would be on a level grade and a great inducement for people who wished to settle in the more beautiful western area. As it was, the trip from the Antrim depot up to the western and northwestern parts of town amounted to just one long uphill haul after another.

Mr. Jameson hoped that this project would not be treated in the "dishonest and un-Christian way" the Western District was used to, nor that the "dishonest and underhanded tactics employed in defeating his other efforts to help the town" would again occur.

Mr. Jameson, a confessed radical and nominal Democrat, had suggested earlier that the town build its own power plant for local lighting and also, when a nearby desirable business was for sale, that the town buy it, move it in, and run it, using the profits to lower the tax rate. A successful real estate man and energetic politician, he could, when running for office, always depend on the support of those who voted a straight Democratic ticket. However, Mr. Jameson was regarded by the business men and, particularly by the Moderator at Town Meeting, as a damned nuisance.

Antrim needed no newly-planned division. There was already a well established one between the "North End" and the much smaller "South End." The dividing line was the brow of the hill in front of Goodell's office building. Below that point was the disadvantaged part of town.

There were many factors which determined this social curtain. One was the personal appearance of the residents. All the way up Main Street was the Antrim "white collar" class: storekeepers, barbers, doctors, bakers, bookkeepers, and ministers. With possibly one or two exceptions none of this type ever "set up shop" or built residences in the south end of town.

On the east side of Main Street were the homes of the affluent. On higher ground the large buildings were immaculately maintained, the lawns carefully fenced in and the grounds and shrubbery meticulously tended. There was pretense and rivalry. The residence of Nathan C. Jameson, at the intersection of Main and Summer Streets, had its own small ballroom. The residence of N.W.C. Jameson, opposite Wayno's, had five grand pianos for the benefit of two musical daughters. (Conversation heirlooms?)

This buffer of grandeur further isolated the residential north end from the factory section just below Goodell's office building. Here was his "Main" shop, the "Apple Parer," the "Handle" shop, the "sawmill," and the "Coco Bolo" or "Cucumber" shop on Water Street. There was no "white collar" class here. Working on steel, iron, lead, coco bolo, and rosewood, they were every color but white.

In what is now Goodell's lower parking lot was an enclave built up by Melvin D. Poor. He was miller, sawyer, excelsior maker, tanner, and owner of a curry shop, with a large home across the brook and fourteen tenements nearby. The constant repetition of his name stamped every aspect of the section. It was Poor's Hill. One lived in a Poor house. Or in a Poor tenement. Or worked in Poor's mill. And he had five Poor boys. His prosperity spared one of hearing him called poor Poor.

Years before, Goodell had brought in skilled English cutlery workers from Sheffield. A proud, clannish group which settled on a higher part of the south end, they tended to band together. Naturally, the established and provincial Scotch-Irish already here made no effort to break down this barrier, but rather increased it by calling the neighborhood "Englishville."

It was accepted gossip that these people had wild Saturday night parties when they drank great quantities of beer and beat their wives regularly on these festive occasions. Most people in the north end did not approve of such activities and the resulting antagonism lasted for many years.

At the time, Goodell èmployed 175 men in Antrim. A number of them lived orderly and admirable lives amidst the churches and schools of the upper end. But below the dividing line there was a much greater concentration of workers, and many were young transients, irresponsible floaters whose interests were in sports or having a good time.

The available abodes for these folk were the teeming tenements, a few boarding houses or spare rooms, and the two choice spots: the Carter House or Miles' boarding house. Accommodations were better at the former, but while Miles' boarding house was crowded, it had a definite advantage in the presence of his attractive daughter. Miles himself was a peppery little worrier who fretted over offending Goodell, and over the reputation of his boarding house, and over his marriageable daughter, and over his income. There were some grounds for his concern over his daughter since she was getting a bit "long in the tooth," but still he did not want her marrying any of the hoodlums who gravitated to his place.

To digress a little, it is necessary to present the most damning indictment of the "South End." It was within easy walking distance of "wet" Bennington and John Adams' Hotel and Bar. As if that wasn't bad enough, Adams himself was either the best or most horrible advertisement of the establishment he maintained. Described variously as a suave "Sport," a spotless "Dandy," a veritable "Fashion Plate," he had the air and manners of the "Ultimate Sophisticate." He was a fast horseman in a none too flashy country setting, and it was a thrill to hear the oncoming "clip clop, clip clop" of his racing pacer as it came up Main Street, and to watch the slowing of the rhythmic sway as the beautiful animal came to a stop in front of the Jameson Block (Wayno's).

Leaping out, Adams would address the saddest-looking of the porch standees, lift his hat high and say, "Sir, would you hold my horse?" On his return, once again he would lift his hat, pluck a cigar from his breast pocket and say, "Sir, you are a gentleman. I thank you. I do, indeed. Have a cigar on me." Then, as the gorgeous horse felt the regal step behind him, he would lean into a racing turn and, while he picked up his incredible speed on Main Street, to the enraptured standees he might just as well have been racing away over the rooftops.

It was a combination of Adams' barroom and a new boarder at Miles' which created one of the many incidents which gave the south end such a bad name. The new boarder, named Stutz, was following the usual pattern of ingratiating himself with Miles, hoping it would lead to talking with the daughter. Before taking off for Bennington, he commiserated at length with the worried Miles about the weight of snow on the roof and how it might well cave in.

Later that night he returned and stole quietly up the stairs to his gable room where he slipped into bed without lighting a lamp. Getting up in the night, he was struck a tremendous blow on the head. Reaching up to see who had hit him, he found the roof was coming in.

Stepping onto the bed, he thrust his back against the descending ceiling and pushed as hard as he could. The bed collapsed under the great pressure.

Down below, the nervous Miles heard the cracking bed and quickly grasped what had happened. "Out! Everybody out! Out! Out! The roof is coming down!" With this confirmation, Stutz added his voice to the exodus and in seconds everyone was out standing in the snow. It was too dark to see the roof, but the boarders could still hear Stutz being slowly crushed to death; so they went back in the house to free him. Getting a lamp lighted, they went up the stairs to his room. Stutz was not crushed. He was standing on the remains of his bed with his neck and shoulders braced against the sloping ceiling. This position was possible because, due to the crowded conditions, his bed had been pushed back under the eaves. Many previous boarders had nearly fractured their skulls in a similar manner but Stutz had created a sort of double jeopardy by his prior visit to Bennington. And he looked it.

Actually, the episode only bothered Miles and the neighbors because it gave the rest of the boarders a good story to tell at work. For a long time afterwards, at one jovial gathering or another, someone would eventually say, "Did you ever hear the one about Stutz holding up the roof at Miles' boarding house?"

Greystone Lodge

After a great fanfare of meetings, searchings, and discussions, Alford K. Hazzard, president of Birch Farms Company of New York City, made a long awaited announcement: Greystone Lodge, an elite summer hotel, was going to be built on Goodell Hill.

Actually, President Hazzard was the only person in all of Antrim who was in favor of this God-forsaken spot. For years Holt's Hill above Gregg's Pond had been the dream site of every person who had ever picnicked there or driven outsiders up to see the view. Not only was there a good road, but there was cleared farmland. The pond seemed to be at your very feet and there were mountains in every direction. Of all the summits around town, Holt's Hill was the ideal spot for such a project as Greystone Lodge. The Board of Trade, the selectmen, the town's most positive individuals, all begged and pleaded with him to build there.

It was a bad time for the Board of Trade. Nothing was going right.

Someone was suing for falling down the town hall stairs. The cream-ery was about to close. The summer boarder campaign was failing. The Raymond pasture golf links had never progressed beyond building the first tee. Now, with some glorious prosperity at hand, one man's stubbornness was going to doom the brightest project.

Hazzard's defense was that this lodge would be a way station for the wealthy travelers who were now switching from the trains to autos on their way to the White Mountain resorts. They would not be the sort who wanted to fish or swim; they would be going to the coast. His clientele would be exclusive and would prefer isolation.

In February teams began hauling sled loads of building materials up the old woods road on the south side of Goodell Hill. Ads for carpen-ters, masons, and weathered fieldstone appeared in area newspapers. At the March town meeting, voters reluctantly adopted a resolution to build an expensive new road up the north side of the hill. By April the cellar had been excavated and the walls of gray stone were up to the second story. The first floor had been laid. In just ninety days from the first shovelful, the lodge was to have a grand opening—on June 16.

Whatever doubt the town had of Hazzard's judgment, it had to admit he was a brash, flamboyant promoter who got things done and done well. The lodge was a ruggedly attractive structure with a de-lightful interior. He had provided jobs for everyone who wanted to work and he staffed with local help except for a professional chef and housekeeper. This group was wholeheartedly behind him even though he fired and rehired them every few hours. Regardless of this diversion, two hundred people attended the Grand Opening and were enthusiastic over the event and the service.

There were many problems at first. The waitresses, chambermaids,

Greystone Lodge

bellhops, and kitchen help all had to be trained (or broken) to abide by instructions. While Hazzard and silent partner McGee did their best, it was actually the in-and-out stream of alcoholic chefs, waving their razor-sharp butcher knives, who brought out the best in the native talent. Hazzard had not been exaggerating about the clientele. Many were prominent Bostonians and New Yorkers with media-enriched names. They seemed to enjoy the innovations and confidences so generously offered by the local help.

But it was not long before the dire predictions of the townspeople began to be fulfilled. Always the next "week" or the next "weekend" or the next "month" the place would be booked full. But if the guests did show up at all, they often departed the next day. Hazzard was never depressed or discouraged and some few families did stay for long periods. Others, with their uniformed chauffeurs, commuted weekends.

Regardless of approaching failure, there were many lighter moments. Anticipation rippled through the help's quarters when Hazzard announced a honeymoon couple was on its way and would arrive before noon. Nothing was to be too good for them and they were to have the best corner room with the most inspiring view. He wanted everyone to be on his or her toes.

The glamorous couple arrived, blissfully unaware of the admiring and envious glances of the entire work force. They were welcomed on the wide front steps by Hazzard himself. Escorted by two bellhops, they quickly disappeared into their special room. In a moment the groom was back at the desk. He did not want single beds, he wanted a double one! In great distress Hazzard apologized profusely for the oversight and said he would make the change before they retired. The groom shouted he did not want the change when they retired; he wanted it NOW!

The volatile Hazzard was at first infuriated at his *faux pas* and then was so amused he could not resist telling it to the gathered help who were still commenting on the love birds. Instead of loyal laughter, he found sympathy here, especially among the local chambermaids, who had long felt if two people knew each other well enough to stay in the same room, they could well use the same bed instead of dirtying up two sets of linen. Reinfuriated at this disloyalty, Hazzard pounced on the help, sending them running top speed to make the exchange, "NOW! NOW! NOW!"

Since there were no back or service stairs, guests who were gathering for lunch were startled to see two mattresses, two bed springs, and two headboards come flying down the main stairway. No less startling was to see a larger mattress, a larger spring, and a larger headboard go flying up the stairway. As the giggling bearers passed each other in the lobby, they whispered loudly, "NOW! NOW! NOW!"

The guests, too refined to show undue curiosity, were still intrigued by the urgency of the operation, particularly because the beds seemed to indicate a medical emergency. Aware that this was none too professional a staff, some sought out his or her favorite employee to find what was wrong. Their reactions were closely watched by the country help who wanted to see how wealthy city people would respond to such rampant sex. The response indicated a new division. The women turned away with smug, serene smiles, while the men snorted contemptuously and uttered obscenities.

Another complaint came from Main Street and the Antrim *Reporter*. This was about the youth who drove the hotel car down for the mail. He would put the car in low gear in front of the fire station, and aim it. Grabbing his out-going mail, he would run for the post office in the town hall and slap his package through the mail window. Scooping out the contents of the Lodge lock box into a bag, he would tear out of the office and catch the slow-moving auto somewhere in front of the Presbyterian church. The editor said this practice should be brought to the attention of the proper authorities.

Bobcats were a problem. Apparently first attracted by the lunch pail scraps of the builders, they soon learned the kitchen garbage cans were a greater boon. Undeterred by the swinging screen door, their nocturnal visits were frequently marred by the early morning cook. Since their only exit was the same door by which he entered, it often ended in a noisy confrontation. To the man, the escaping cat appeared to be charging him and his only defense was to try to hold the flimsy door shut. The resulting repairs caused the handy maintenance man to advise the cook to let the cat go. This advice was never too well received.

Late at night stragglers coming up from the village were often stalked by one of these animals. Staying just out of sight in the bushes by the road side, the cat walked along as the man walked, and stopped when the man stopped. Occasionally star refraction caused two unblinking eyes to be seen no more than ten or fifteen feet away. The straggler had two choices. He could pick up a stick, face the animal, and back up the hill. Or he could hunch up his shoulders, cover his face with his hands, and walk rapidly.

There was never any attack and the only explanation seemed to be that the animal associated the man with food—but only with expectation that if he followed long enough he would find something to eat. To anyone who pictures a bobcat as merely a wild house cat, let it be noted that one was shot at the foot of the hill weighing thirty-five pounds, and that's a lot of scratching cat.

The following February, just a year from the start of the hotel, the Birch Farms Company sold Greystone Lodge to Robert W. Jameson of Antrim. He planned a new local corporation which would make additions and improvements. The president would be William E. Cram, but Jameson would be treasurer. A professional manager would be brought in from New York City. The Lodge lasted for a great many more years, but no management regime was ever like the first one.

Movies

Movies came to Antrim in October, 1913. Ralph Messer of Bennington was the projectionist. Due to fire insurance regulations, the operator and projectionist were enclosed in a small asbestos room located in the town hall balcony. This was necessary not only for the sake of the building but also for the peace of mind of the audience. If the operator allowed the moving film to slow down, the heat from the projector bulb melted it and the conflagration was magnificently enlarged on the giant screen. Confident that the blaze was contained, the audience waited patiently for the slide reading, "One moment please," to reassure them the show would continue and that the operator was still operating.

Music was provided by Gladys Brooks, who improvised on the piano as she watched the action on the screen. Minor intermissions occurred each time a reel was changed, and there was an official one midway in the show of such duration as to give the customers a full-length performance.

Approaching shows were advertised on posters which stated they were to be shown at the Dreamland Theatre. This meant the town hall, and gave an added importance to scheduled attractions. Actually the shows were rated by the number of reels in the picture. A one-reeler was usually a comedy or of an informative nature. There were no news reels. The main feature was a four-reeler. Now and then a stupendous production would be advertised months in advance. The fact it would be an eight-reeler gave a good indication of its importance. Such shows were *Ben Hur* and *Quo Vadis*. They were of a biblical nature and the latter was of special import since the title was in Latin. This required instant translation for the ignorant—"Whither Goest Thou?"

The ministers and prominent people recommended these shows, which guaranteed a large crowd. The only objection to this temporary enthusiasm was the let-down of going back to four-reelers. The feeling was similar to the doldrums which followed a good hell-and-damnation evangelist.

Mr. Messer had many difficulties. He wanted to hire the town hall for every Wednesday and Friday night, but since he was an outsider from Bennington the selectmen would let him have it only when no one from Antrim wanted it. This happened so often on Friday nights that sometimes he was forced to cancel three movies a month. He claimed it cost him fifty dollars to put on a show and that the cancellations were ruining him. This must have been an exaggeration. Admission was ten and twenty cents and while the balcony was often full, there were never many downstairs.

Of course he had other sources of income. He ran movies and dances in Bennington, operated a small lunchroom, and was also town constable. But he had a formidable adversary in Goodell, who did not approve of dances or movies unless they were religious pictures like *Quo Vadis*. Consequently, there were many dance nights when the electric lights suddenly went off around ten o'clock. At this occurrence, Messer would race to the Bennington power plant (owned by Goodell Electric Company) to see if there was water going over the dam. If there was, this would negate Goodell's oft repeated claim of low water.

As a result, Messer sent a letter to the *Reporter* saying it was dangerous to plunge 200 people into darkness on the second floor of a building which had a winding stairway. It was dangerous to have people lighting matches and lamps trying to find their coats and hats. Such actions might cause a panic and result in law suits. This prompted other customers to complain about their service. At this combined protest, Goodell agreed to flash the lights at ten minutes ahead of a blackout, so lamps could be lighted.

However, there were times when low water did cause prolonged shut-downs and Goodell was subjected to harassment which he did not always deserve. At one church meeting he was confronted by a prominent lady who demanded to know what was wrong. He responded in a loud voice for the benefit of all present: "Madam, I would like to have you fully understand that I cannot make water." At the time, this phrase was one you did not shout in the presence of refined people.

These various problems did not rob Antrim of this sort of entertainment. The movies continued for many years, part of the time under the direction of Burr Eldredge, until he left for World War I.

1914 Social legislation for the protection of workers appeared to be discriminatory. On January 1, 1914, the fifty-five hour work week law for females and minors went into effect. Neither would be allowed to work more than ten and a quarter hours a day, or fifty-five hours a week. Men, it seemed, could take care of themselves.

Social fellowship was enhanced late in February when the Antrim Lodge #1488 of the Loyal Order of Moose was instituted with a good-sized membership from Antrim, Bennington, and Hancock. "The Lodge plans to hold regular meetings in the hall connected with the Carter House."

Harness horse racing on the ice at Gregg Lake was the new sport in town. A quarter mile straightaway was used for Saturday's events. In class A racing, John Adams of Bennington won first place in competition with three other entries, finishing in thirty-three and a half seconds. Class B was won by Frank Bass of Antrim, besting two challengers with a time of thirty-four seconds. The trotting class was scratched, due to insufficient entries.

Barreling Along

Returning home from Hancock with a load of empty barrels, the two horses driven by John Paquet became frightened when one barrel fell from the load on to the pole between the horses, the team then being at the corner of Highland Avenue and Summer Street. The terrified horses ran down Summer Street into Main, and continued their mad race some three miles to their barn in Bennington. At no time did the driver have a chance to remove the barrel which was pushing the horses apart.

Mr. Paquet, a strong man, had some control over the animals, but only enough to guide them. Fortunately, neither of the horses nor the driver was injured. But unfortunately, there is no record of Mr. Paquet's remarks, either during the dash to Bennington or on his return when he picked up his wayward load.

Tramps And Gypsies

During the summer months, both types of wanderers regularly passed through town. The least harmful were the tramps, inarticulate old men who shuffled along the dusty roads in aimless pursuit of they knew not what. Indifferent, stolid, dirty, they would sit in the back of a wagon if invited, but for the most part they were content to plod along the side of the road with their eyes on the ground.

On the highway at meal times they would stop at a farm house to ask for food. The reply was a cliché of the time: "If you want to work for it, I will give you something, but I'm not giving anything to a loafer." This work was the nearby woodpile, but the effort was so pathetic that the farm wife quickly relented, gave out the food, and then, uneasy in the presence of an unconventional person, waved the man on.

Those who arrived in town about dusk would ask for the chief of police. Without preamble, the chief would buy cheese and crackers for them, take them down in the basement of the town hall, and lock them up in the jail cell for the night. Eventually people objected to this because of the danger of fire, and the difficulty of locating the jailer. In the morning there were more cheese and crackers, and more waving on.

This cheese and crackers routine became very tiresome, not to the tramps who never complained, but to the chiefs, who found it easier to send the derelicts to the back door of Maplehurst Inn for a handout. Possibly, this gave rise to the snide opinion that most chiefs were appointed solely to keep the chiefs "off the town."

There were many legends about tramps being ex-bank presidents, demented diplomats, or inept geniuses. True or not, there was no evidence of it in their speech or manners. Another story had it that the mysterious signs found on rocks, bridges, or farm gates were left by tramps. Since they were loners, a more likely explanation would be that these messages were the work of imaginative kids, who always had at least a dozen spirit Indian pals treading close behind.

Gypsies were an entirely different breed. Traveling in ramshackle wagons, they spent nights camped along the roadside, and days preying on unprepared storekeepers. A horse or two trailing behind the wagons gave some substance to the story that the men were horse traders, but otherwise the women appeared to be the providers. Usually the wagons arrived in pairs, but what the relationship was between them no one knew or cared.

Here in town they had a well prepared plan which worked year after year with amazing success. Actually, the old stores were fairly impervious to shop lifting as long as the customer kept his place, which was in front of the small serving counter. Here, he or she would order, and the leisurely clerk would take the requested merchandise from the rear shelves and place it beside the cash register. Valuable items were kept in glass display cases up front, protected by sliding panels.

The gypsies were well aware of these arrangements. Leaving the men and the wagons a few doors below Cram's general store (Edmunds'), two or three women surrounded by a few kids would burst into the store. As the oldest of the women approached the service counter and demanded some article, the rest of the group raced to the back of the store. While she waved a dollar bill and loudly berated the clerk for his stupidity, the youngsters were busy. Darting in and out and under the counters, they constantly circled back to the other women, who slipped the loot into the many folds of their innumerable petticoats.

When the frantic storekeeper finally dashed to the rear, the culprits easily evaded him and worked the front counters before slipping out the front door and into the parked wagons. If the irate man were foolish enough to follow, he was hindered by the older woman, who waved her honest purchase and called down gypsy curses as she explained the matter to the vicious looking men guarding the wagons. Since her indignation was vented in fluent gypsy-ese, there was little the poor shopkeeper could do but suddenly remember there might still be a couple of small bandits back in the store.

Grocerymen had no effective method of restricting this original self-service other than yelling loudly, "Lock the door! Lock the door! Lock the door! Gypsies!" If a cooperative customer happened to be near the door, he slammed it in their faces. With no state police to help, the best the local constabulary could do was escort the pilferers to the town line and warn them never to return.

The "Cucumber Shop"

In case anyone wonders why Goodell's lower shop (on Water Street, where they chunked up the heavy coco bolo logs from Central America) was called the Cucumber Shop, the answer is very simple. It got its name because one henpecked worker asked permission to raise a few of the cucurbits in back of the building. His co-workers understood this strange request, since it was well known that at home he was restricted to the kitchen.

One day at lunch time as Milan was happily munching away on a mill grown cucumber, one disgusted observer sat ruminating on what a home life Milan must have. He finally blurted out (rather considerately), "This ain't no coco bolo shop; it's a damned cucumber factory." The name caught on and thereafter whenever the term was used one immediately envisioned poor Milan at home, sitting in a straight backed chair, his stained hands folded in his lap and his eyes upon his dust encrusted clothes. Whistler's father?

While this was an accepted example of an immaculate wife, occasionally there was a refreshing case where steel met steel. One middle-aged couple moved into a house on West Street. As soon as all their possessions were in and the movers had gone, the wife declared she did not like the place, would not unpack, and wanted to move. Her peace loving husband agreed that she need not unpack, but by God, they were not moving anywhere for a while. The stalemate lasted for years; just the bare necessities of life were taken out and used. A visitor stopping in for a minute to consult with Ed could sit on a barrel, a box, or a rolled up rug. It all depended on how tall he was.

Goodell Dies

On January 20, 1915, Antrim's foremost citizen, ex-Governor David H. Goodell, passed away at his farm home on North Main Street. He was eighty years old. Born in Hillsboro, he had been brought to the farm as an infant, and lived there the rest of his life.

Plagued by constant ill health, his educational and political careers were severely curtailed. Forced to leave Brown University after his freshman year, he was also barely able to complete his first term as governor of New Hampshire. Still, his frail health did not stop him. As has been mentioned, he was involved in practically every phase of the town's life, and dominant in most of them. As president and treasurer of Goodell Company for fifty years, he was canny enough to establish a prosperous business, mainly the manufacture of cutlery, which has endured through the years, including those depression years when many larger concerns failed.

Around 1915, he provided employment for 175 persons in Antrim and 75 in Bennington. Due to economic factors, his employees were more or less obliged to tolerate some domineering treatment. With no transportation, a man worked where he owned a home. And although

Goodell Estate

the pay might have been only two dollars a day, nearly everyone did own his own home. The reason might have been the following:

> For sale — 1½ story house, 7 rooms, barn 36' x 36', shop 16' x 20', hen house, good well, main road. Price $600. Terms: cash $300, low interest rate.

Governor Goodell was certainly controversial: a zealot who was overactive in pursuit of his pet projects, and consequently one who made bitter enemies of those who did not believe as he did. As president of the Anti-Saloon League, he went far out of his way to blacklist a drinker, or condemn a town which voted "wet." Yet he had very little control over a large transient segment of his work force, and conveniently overlooked in them anything that might injure his business.

As a "dry" religious and business man, he had the backing of the churches, the WCTU, the Anti-Saloon League, *The Antrim Reporter*, and some of his fellow businessmen, even if they did not approve of all of his methods. He may only have been a small ripple in the wave of feeling which culminated in Prohibition, but his influence was such that it was thirty-one years after his death, in 1946, before Antrim finally voted "wet" — by ten votes!

Christmas Party

Antrim had its first community Christmas tree in 1915. It was placed in the triangle in front of the Baptist church. The tree, decorations, lights, and labor were all contributed by Goodell Company.

Late in the afternoon, two large sleighs filled with carolers moved about town singing for shut-ins and invalids. Returning to the triangle, they joined in song with the five hundred people present, waiting for Santa Claus. His arrival was greeted with joy by two hundred children for whom he had substantial gifts of candy, horns, knives, dolls, and books. The candy was donated by Cram's general store, and Howard Paige solicited the money for the generous gifts. It was a joyous and memorable evening for all.

Sports   1916

With no television or radio, and few telephones and autos, one can appreciate today how much spare time Antrim's earlier residents had. Of course, a great deal of it was devoted to churches, organizations, and conversations, but for the more violent and noisy Southenders, basketball and baseball provided delightful outlets. Not only were there high school teams, but there were also one or more town teams, depending on how much talent or antagonism existed at the moment. Antrim always had an abundance of exceptional athletes and a following of equally exceptional fans. The result was many a championship, even though the competition was against larger towns.

Basketball in this period (1916) resembled today's hockey rather than the graceful leaps and bounds which now comprise the "pas de cinq" of professional basket-ballet. The only unencumbered shot then was for a foul, and the scores indicate this. They ranged from 20 to 40, and were made under the most adverse conditions. Body checks, knees, elbows, karate chops, tearing the ball from an opponent — all were applauded. About the only foul was for tripping. This had to be called, because of the danger of hitting the exposed cast iron registers which heated the various town halls in which the games were played.

One local problem was protecting the windows. The most popular solution was to string large fish nets in loose V's from the backboards to the side walls. A possible hand-me-down idea from the gladiators, these gave the smaller player a chance to wrap up a more powerful opponent, or divert his shot with a quick yank of the draperies.

Superstars . . . the Cuddihy Basketball Team

The enthusiasm was not limited to Antrim. Every visiting team brought its own backers, and the Carter House was host on many a lively evening to victors and victims alike. An estimated five hundred spectators attended the Southern Interscholastic Basketball Championship held in the neutral Antrim hall. Special trains were run from Wilton and Jaffrey, and each team brought its own band. This dual mob must have reduced the playing court to a narrow stretch of floor space, but all such handicaps were as fair to one team as to the other.

Baseball was the summer sport. Any celebration or special day was built around a game or a double header. There would have been nothing but ridicule or indifference to such "sissy" games as soft ball or soccer, which probably would have been included with the sack races, dashes, and pie eating contests.

The West Street ball grounds provided a standard diamond, but the outfield was not ideal. Most engaging was a point of gray birches protruding into left field which provided a bonus home run for any batter lucky enough to hit a two-bagger into it. Another hand-out was deep right field, which sloped away enough so that a long fly sent ball and fielder out of the sight of both crowd and umpire. These two refuges were so beneficial to batting averages and arguments that no mention was ever made of correcting them.

There was a large grandstand on the home side of the field, while on the other side the visitors could sit on whatever they brought with them. The stand was possibly fifteen feet high and forty or fifty feet long. Without it, the sedentary devotees would have been unable to see over the heads of the more enthusiastic fans who packed the baseline from home plate to first base. It was always surprising that any pitcher could possibly concentrate on the batter with this mob of maniacs shrieking imprecations from a scant twenty feet away.

Strangely enough, instantaneous hate reached its greatest intensity only during games with Hillsboro. Why this was so is inexplicable, because Hillsboro was the focal point for special Saturday night safaris, at which time good fellowship and romance reigned supreme. This sportsmen's animosity was not always just a harmless diversion: on one occasion when the two opposing sides converged on home plate armed with stray bats, Granville Whitney, chief of police, stepped into the center of the potential melee and, pulling his revolver, drove both sides back to their places.

This instance was unusual, but the enthusiasm was not. A crucial game with Marlboro was so important that a special train was provided to bring the supporters to town.

In reporting such a period with so many superb athletes, mention must be made of the Cuddihys. Not only were they great players, they were also great showmen, but such ability was not even recognized at the time. All from the same family, they were spectacular in every effort. They could make an easy catch look impossible, and an impossible play look easy, and as "money" players they could make the big hit which won the game. Andy, Dick, Jim, Matt, and John were as good at basketball as baseball. Up at Gregg Lake they had a green dory with three sets of oars. In the midst of encouraging shouts to each other, they would rush the boat, scramble to their seats, and fairly lift the craft out of the water as they exulted in their strength and muscle. Even without competition, they appeared to be engaged in a desperate race.

Regardless of the sport, one could be assured that if the Cuddihys were playing there would be tremendous thrills, wild excitement, great confrontations, and simulated injuries which were agonizing to behold. And the fans loved it. Three sisters, Anna, Alice, and Mary, were just as able in girl's basketball, but that was before the interest in women's sports.

Automobiles

Several events during the summer months in 1915 seemed to indicate the automobile was here not only to stay, but practically to overrun the countryside. One Sunday observer on the Antrim-Hillsboro road counted, on the Fourth of July week-end, sixty-five cars coming and going during the daylight hours. Some, of course, were just out for a short Sunday afternoon ride, but there must have been enough outsiders to indicate that this road was entitled to a portion of the state highway funds.

Things were getting so crowded locally that H. A. Coolidge, a former minister, built a narrow two-story garage at the foot of Poor's Hill on the thin strip of land between lower Main Street and Depot Street. When asked why he had chosen this particular site, he replied that he wanted the gas pump and repair shop on the busy through road, while the upper floor was for winter storage of automobiles. The location naturally provided entrance for cars at either level, and thus did away with need for ramp or elevator. The only trouble with the lower level arrangement was that if you drove in, you had to back out, and someone always had to stand in the middle of the road to see that the way was clear. Coolidge provided much-needed services, was the agent for Overland cars, and had a telephone connection for emergencies.

There was a great deal of confident expertise about autos. One conclusion was that there would never be a market for the closed car. The rumbling vibration and stuffy air gave everyone but the owner a headache. A deft touch in a closed car was the presence of a small vase for cut flowers. This gave the impression of a dry run in a glass-walled hearse, and was so compared by the village wits.

The proliferation of autos sometimes brought tragedy in its wake. Accidents became more and more frequent. Probably the most horrible occurred in the covered bridge between Antrim and Bennington near the paper mill. A group of young men from Winchendon, Massachusetts, having stayed late in Bennington, were on their way to Antrim at a high rate of speed. One of the youths was crouched down on the right side running board when the car failed to make the sharp turn, crushing him between the car and the bridge.

A portent of the future was the theft of Helen Stanley's brand new Ford touring car from its garage at White Birch Point on Gregg Lake. Happily it was found a week later in a garage in Boston by F.H. Williams of Antrim, who recognized the car because he had recently installed a self-starter in it. Including the trip to Boston, it had been run only three hundred miles.

Naive riders were sometimes betrayed by their limited knowledge of automobiling. Clarence Hanscom, a proper college man in his twenties whose parents lived on Highland Avenue, passed some silly-aged girls on his way up Summer Street. A perfect gentleman, he stopped his car and asked them if he could give them a lift to their homes. This invitation from an older man threw them into a state of confusion, but they could not resist riding in so lovely an auto. However, as no one would ride in front with him, all sat in the back seat. Unable to counter his polite small talk, their only response was to make faces at the back of his head. When he let them out, he told them how much he had enjoyed their company, especially the faces they had been making at him. He then pointed out his rear view mirror. Their reaction was typical: they giggled uncontrollably, and the next day told everyone in town.

North Branch Man Bruised
While M.H. Underwood of Brook's mill was breaking a colt hitched to a pair of wheels, the animal backed off a bank near J.E. Loveren's barn. Mr. Underwood fell over first, then the wheels passed over his chest, and the colt, dropping a distance of seven feet, fell on him. Mr. Underwood was badly bruised, and at this writing is as comfortable as can be expected.

Must have been one of those days!

More About Autos

Ten years after a court ruled that autos had the same right as horses to use public highways, the Ford Motor Company announced it had built and delivered 320,817 cars from August, 1916, to March, 1917. This in spite of the fact that automobiles could not be used in northern climes during the winter months. Possibly the prices — runabout $345, touring car $360 — had something to do with this phenomenal growth.

There were many other makes of cars. The Saxon Six, "a big touring car for five people," advertised that 234 stock cars driven by various drivers under various road conditions averaged 25.9 miles per gallon of gasoline and 175 miles per quart of oil. Modern cars have corrected the oil consumption, but few comfortable vehicles have yet been made which can average 26 mpg on the road. The Saxon was an expensive car — $935 F.O.B. Detroit, Michigan.

1917 *War!!!*

Although World War I was obviously going to embroil the United States, Antrim paid little attention until it was actually declared. Then the town went all out to cooperate.

The First Liberty Loan raised $34,000. The Second had a quota of $43,000, and Antrim "went over the top" for $50,800. Red Cross and YMCA campaigns were oversubscribed.

The Antrim Reporter constantly called for greater efforts in crops and money, and offered prizes for gardens raised by youngsters. One hundred and thirteen school children participated. In addition to back yard gardens, many lawns were plowed and put to beans.

Eighty-seven men registered for the draft, and a good many enlisted before being called. Forty-one special police were appointed. Various committees took over drives and vigilance. Everyone was to do his bit against "the world's and humanity's enemy — Germany! An unprincipled and unscrupulous nation, a crazy bloodthirsty power. Hunt the Hun down!" One Concord man said pro-German things to a patriotic American. He was taken before Judge A. Chester Clark, who sentenced him to three months in jail, suspended.

But all did not go well. Twice frosts wiped out every garden in town. The blackened beans gave rise to some doubt as to just how divine a mission the war effort might be. One woman claimed the very pair of Red Cross socks she had knit were for sale in Cram's store. One soldier swore he knew a civilian who had bought and was wearing a Red Cross sweater. Others said the Liberty Loan Committee was "getting something out of it." Worst of all, a visiting relative of a quiet and harmless German family was arrogant enough to defend the hated Kaiser. These things were idiotic to say in a town whose sons were about to enter the ghastly slaughter of World War I.

In response to these stories, the Antrim Committee of Public Safety placed a thunderous warning in *The Antrim Reporter* addressed to "Traitors and Pro-Germans," relating to "treason and disloyalty . . .

Serve and obey orders . . . or otherwise suitable action will be taken."
This tirade was over the signatures of twelve of the town's most
trusted and respected men!

COASTING ALONG

Saving the World for Democracy

During this year, much community effort and thought was devoted to the war. Antrim had a total of eighty-one men and four women who served in World War I, six of whom died in the service. At home, a "Committee of Public Safety" concerned itself with food production (Victory gardens), vigilance against spies and subversion (a wholly unproductive affair), and organizing the Red Cross drives and Liberty loans. Purchase of War Savings Stamps was urged by the local paper, and Red Cross publicity was given front page prominence. Antrim citizens responded generously: $16,000, the full quota, was quickly subscribed to the Liberty loan.

Fuel conservation was a consideration then as now, the use of wood being urged so that supplies of coal could be diverted to war related industries. It was suggested that the price of wood not exceed one dollar per cord. And speaking of prices, at a "Hoover supper" sponsored by the work committee of the American Red Cross, you could get coffee, baked beans, brown bread, vegetable hash, Parker House rolls, gingerbread, and Indian pudding, all for twenty-five cents!

Cost of living increases, attributable to the war, were in evidence. In one year, the increase was twenty-three percent, food alone increasing forty-eight percent, so it made sense to have a garden. Meanwhile, there were some food shortages. Cram's store advertised that it could only sell one-eighth of a barrel of flour for each family at one time, and then only if an equal amount of flour substitute were purchased—this by government order. Sugar was in short supply, due both to transportation problems and because much was being sent abroad, but the price was held to nine cents a pound. Another form of sweetening available locally, maple syrup, sold for $2.25 per gallon.

In June it was announced that coal and coke would be rationed, each customer being allotted two thirds of the amount used in the previous year.

In September, barrels for the collection of peach and plum stones, as well as hickory and butternut shells, were placed in front of various village stores. It seems that these shells and stones could be converted into a special kind of carbon used in the manufacture of gas masks. On November 11 the war was declared over. Church and school bells started ringing at six-fifteen that morning and continued ringing at intervals during the day until ten that night. In the evening eight hundred citizens gathered in the village to witness a street parade of floats, band and drum corps, boys with banners and torches, marshalls and ladies on horseback, Victory girls carrying a large flag, and a float with a coffin for the Kaiser. The speeches which followed in the town hall may have been an anti-climax.

Fortunately, this celebration occurred after a ban on public meetings due to the epidemic of "Spanish influenza" had been lifted only a week before by the Board of Health. At least two persons died from the disease, and many more were stricken. The public library was closed for six weeks.

1919

The flu epidemic continued unabated into 1919, and early in January the schools and the town hall were closed for two weeks. Not everyone was sick, however, and certain seasonal activities went on as usual. Ice "of good quality and fourteen inches thick" was harvested from the ponds. Tramps made their customary rounds, calling forth the following news item:

> What a surplus of 'knights of the road' we seem to have lately. Chief Heath has had his boarding house patronized almost every night . . . [and] our people, especially the gentle sex, are bothered altogether too much . . .

Fire, an ever present danger, destroyed the wood-working mill operated by W.C. Hills on January 5. Five months too late, on May 28, torrential rains struck. The dam at Caughey's mill on the Great Brook sprang a small leak and the flashboards had to be removed, with the result that the meadows overflowed. Along Cork Plain, the water was over the Hillsboro road from six inches to two feet, and the road to

North Branch over Twiss Hill was closed to travel for a time. Perversely, the autumn was very dry. The water commissioners were worried about the low level of Campbell Pond, and requested users to be sparing with water.

On the bright side, the business outlook seemed good. Goodell's advertised for workers in several departments, raised the pay by ten percent, and insured each employee at the rate of $500 for over three months of service up to a maximum of $1,500. Veterans of World War I got state bonus checks for $70 to add to their purchasing power.

Probably this was just as well, as taxes were going up. The reasons given were 1) a new state education bill, 2) a state tax two and three quarters times greater than the previous year, and 3) the need for better roads and sidewalks. There was, as always, grumbling about this state of affairs, and *The Reporter* commented, "When a farmer has to pay four or five dollars a day for help, it is a pretty hard row for him to hoe and find any potatoes in it."

To make matters worse, electrical rates went up, the minimum rate for big users being ten cents per kilowatt-hour for lights and five cents for cooking. This was bitterly resented because, as a letter to the editor complained, the service was so poor and the power so unsteady.

The memory of World War I was still very strong, and Old Home Day in August was a "welcome home" to all the soldiers, sailors, and nurses. A continuing effect of the war was the rationing of sugar, two pounds per person per month.

Small sidelights on life in Antrim in 1919: George Hunt placed an ad in the paper seeking to trade a five-passenger Cadillac for a cow! Other ads revealed a difference of opinion regarding the sale of fireworks. Goodwin stated he would NOT sell fireworks in *his* store, but Maplehurst Inn countered with a two-day sale of fireworks on its lawn.

Winter Woes

1920   The first three months of 1920 were times that tried men's souls, weather-wise. The winter was a severe one, and the ice so thick at Gregg Lake and in the rivers and brooks that Goodell's shop had to close because there was not enough water to run the wheels and generate electricity. Everyone hoped for a January thaw. On February 4 the temperature plummeted to twenty-eight below zero, and the plumber was busy all day thawing out pipes and replacing those that had burst. That the day happened to be Sunday made no difference: local plumbers did not belong to the union. On Feburary 18, a disgruntled citizen complained that the Campbell Pond road had been impassable for two days, even for the RFD mailman. A frozen crust made all kinds of vehicular traffic impossible. Again, on February 25, the labor of seven men and six horses was required to open a section of the road from M.S. French's to Walter Knapp's. Meanwhile, so much coal and wood had been burned trying to keep the schools warm that they finally ran out of fuel and had to shut down for a week.

March was no better. On March 3, snow drifts were reported to be ten to fifteen feet deep. Then came the crowning blow. On March 5 it rained, followed by snow and high wind the next day, Saturday. Coming on top of previous storms and generally deplorable conditions, the railroad's goose was cooked. No trains were able to reach Antrim from Friday until Wednesday. This meant no newspapers, no news from the outside world, and no supplies, including especially that indispensable item, coal. The editor of *The Antrim Reporter* ran a desperate ad pleading for someone to sell him a ton of coal so that he could keep his office and pressroom warm enough to get out the paper. People went to town meeting via snowshoes. Sheds caved in, roofs leaked, and everyone was miserable. But the town survived. A carload of coal arrived at the railroad station on March 12, the schools reopened after two weeks, and presumably spring finally made a welcome appearance.

It was also 1920 when women were given suffrage. A citizenship class was instituted for women who were interested in learning about town, state, and national government, so that they might better exercise their new voting privilege. Apparently they missed the point, because in July the class was discontinued: some of the ladies complained that too much "politics" was being injected into the meetings. In the September primary, 154 women voted; 232 were registered, of whom 204 were Republicans. In November, the electorate, both male and female, voted overwhelmingly Republican, and the League of Nations was doomed, in Antrim as elsewhere. There were 580 names on the checklist: 500 votes were cast, 226 being straight Republican and 103 straight Democrat.

As in previous years, fire struck again, this time destroying Frank Black's house and barn in Clinton. Every family, especially those in the outlying areas, feared this scourge.

As the year waned, so did the temperature, and on November 17 there were frozen pipes around town again, and presumably busy plumbers. Even the fire whistle felt the cold snap, and when it was blown for the water to be shut off, it stuck and could not be stopped until it had blown itself out.

Late in November, the selectmen passed an ordinance prohibiting the throwing of snowballs on the highways. There is no record of arrests for violation of this ordinance, but it does seem overoptimistic to believe that it could have been unfailingly observed.

At the end of the year, the town treasury had received $920 from auto permits, as compared with $250 in 1919. This reflected a considerable increase in the number of automobiles owned in the town, and the editor of *The Reporter* went out on a limb and predicted even more next year.

News items, verbatim from *The Reporter:*

> The deer hunters are quite plentiful, and a number have been shot in this locality.
> The latest Ford stunt was performed by A.O. Sutherland's car, when it suddenly became violently insane and started for the back of the barn, and, bursting through the boards, looped the loop and landed on its back, where it continued to run until it was gassed. After being righted and led around to the barn, it was found to be practically unhurt.

1921   As yet, no suitable memorial had been voted to honor those from Antrim who served in World War I, but before town meeting there was much discussion on this subject. Some people favored a building to be used variously as a gymnasium, reading room, or general meeting place, but more frugal citizens argued that a new building would cost too much. As an alternative, it was suggested that the historical room on the upper floor of the library be dedicated and used for this purpose. A simple bronze tablet was declared by some to be too gloomy a reminder of war and death.

It took the members of the newly-formed American Legion to resolve the impasse. At town meeting they proposed "a memorial tablet, suitably inscribed, to be placed on a common field stone at a minimum of expense to the town," and this reasonable solution was quickly accepted by the voters.

An appropriate boulder on which the tablet could be placed was located on the Gregg Lake road opposite Caughey's mill. It stood eight feet high and weighed about fifteen tons, and removing it to its site on the library lawn was no simple matter. After two weeks, it had progressed not twelve feet from its original location. At that point, the truck transporting it was adjudged to have such narrow tires that they would cut the road to ribbons, so a different truck had to be found. At long last, with such superhuman effort, grunts, and groans as can only be imagined, it arrived on the library lawn, there to sit naked for a considerable time, awaiting the placement of the plaque, as yet unpurchased.

The condition of the roads, still unpaved, was a subject of much concern to the townspeople. This was especially true in mud season. Three-ton trucks were prohibited from using state roads "from March 21st until further notice." Town scales, purchased for eight hundred dollars and capable of weighing loads up to ten tons, were installed behind the town hall.

Another subject of concern was the fire whistle. Since 1918, a whistle activated by compressed air had been in use. One of its chief drawbacks was that during cold weather the compressed air had to be heated and this was expensive. Never ones to expend money needlessly, the precinct voters authorized the purchase of a new fire whistle, presumably one which did not have to be coddled in the winter.

Electricity seemingly was here to stay, and in June the water power plant in the Antrim-Bennington Electric Light and Power Company was sold to the Monadnock Paper Mill, which was required to furnish seventy-five kilowatts of power to the electric company for ten years.

Non sequitur: On November 30, Liberty Farm offered an eight-week old pig to the student at the North Branch school "who makes the most advancement"—not necessarily the best marks. At the end of the school year, the pig was won by Clifford Sizemore.

The Great Train Wreck

Early in 1922, the greatest excitement was provided by the Boston & Maine Railroad, with which the people of Antrim were not always enamored. For one thing, the railroad clung stubbornly to operating on standard time the year round, regardless of the fact that much of the country, including New Hampshire, had recently adopted daylight saving time in the summer. Antrim's feelings were ambivalent about the new time, so it was adding insult to injury to have to get the mail to and from the depot a whole hour earlier in the morning just because

1922

B & M rolling stock

the railroad clock said seven when the town clock pointed to eight.

For another, the railroad had been guilty (in the eyes of Antrimites) of discontinuing several choice passenger runs, to Concord, for instance, and was even threatening to go into the trucking business rather than persist in what it said were money-losing services to this region.

So although no one thought it was poetic justice when the great train wreck occurred on Washington's birthday, it was exciting, and fortunately no lives were lost. As the train rounded a curve between the paper mill and the Antrim station, the engine stayed on the tracks but several cars broke away and tumbled down a twenty-foot embankment. Two passengers were injured seriously enough to require hospitalization, and three others were rendered first aid on the spot. Two young ladies who had given a musical entertainment earlier were shaken up, and one's hand was hurt, but fortunately their three-thousand dollar harp came through unscathed.

The excitement was enough to keep the town buzzing until town meeting. On that occasion, S.G. Hastings rose to plead for a marker to identify the site of the first log cabin owned by Deacon Aiken. Mr. Hastings, evidently a man with a sense of the importance of preserving history, stated that soon no one would be left who could remember the exact site, since "the boulder against which the cabin was built and which served as part of its chimney was broken up more than thirty years ago, and fragments of it are now part of the Goodell Company's saw mill dam." His words were heeded: the Daughters of the American Revolution has since installed a permanent marker on the site at the head of Depot Street.

Another marker was also taken care of during this year—the much discussed bronze tablet with the names of World War I veterans—and the so-called Soldiers' Monument was formally dedicated on Memorial Day.

The year ended as it began, with the excitement this time being provided by nature. On September 15 a tornado touched down in Antrim, hitting west of Loveren's Mills and cutting a swath of five hundred feet past North Branch cemetery, where it laid flat twenty- six headstones. It continued to the farm of Madison McIlvin, where it created the greatest havoc. His barn was torn apart, with bits and pieces scattered all around. Full grown chickens were blown through the windows of the house into the dining room, and about sixty were killed. The house, which was of brick, was not much injured, although the ell changed location about three feet.

Still full of energy, the tornado continued over the north end of Meeting House Hill and touched down again at the F.C. Henderson place (now Doleac's) and demolished the barn. Strangely enough, the Hendersons did not know until the following morning that their barn was a complete wreck. The storm continued to blow in a southeasterly direction, and did no further damage in Antrim.

In 1923 and for the next several years, there apparently was a shortage of rental housing in Antrim, indicating that most families owned their own homes. The editor of *The Reporter* urged the

The Twisting Terror . . . 1922 tornado

construction of "a tenement building or two," confident that it would be a profitable investment.

He was even more concerned over the condition of the roads, with the era of the automobile an irreversible fact. Roads that had been adequate for horse-drawn transportation were not only inadequate for automobiles—in many cases they were definitely hazardous. "We still build in widths predicated on slow moving vehicles, and we still wind our highways up hill and down dale and around devious curves because it is easier and cheaper to do so. That era is gone!"

Each year seemed to have its own disastrous fire, and 1923 was no exception. In December Goodell's saw mill on Depot Street was entirely destroyed. It had been used for making packing boxes and, being full of wood, was extremely flammable. The building was old but in good repair, having been rebuilt in the early '80s. Barring a fire, things were built to last in those days.

1924   As will be related elsewhere (in the chapter on churches), Antrim seems to have had a plethora of Protestant churches, each with a small congregation required to support a pastor, a building, and all the good offices normally carried on in a church. From time to time there has been talk of uniting two or more of these churches: in 1924, the Presbyterian church being without a pastor, there was a temporary union of the Methodists and Presbyterians. The Baptist church, maintaining its own sovereignty, underwent repairs, culminating in the installation and dedication of a ten-stop Estey organ.

In secular circles, an article in the warrant proposing to add the names of two non-military participants to the War Memorial tablet was vigorously debated. "While consideration of this article was in progress, an hour's adjournment was taken for dinner. Considerable discussion was indulged in before dinner without getting anywhere, but after partaking of a bountiful repast by the Women's Relief Corps at Odd Fellows banquet hall, everybody was happy and indulged almost without limit in oratory, motions and amendments, touching the matter in question as well as almost everything else. After the house had been divided, clouds had dispersed, and the amendments tied to motions as desired, it was found that the meeting had voted the names of Robert W. Jameson and W.J.B. Cannell be added to the Memorial." (Sounds familiar; town meetings were ever thus.)

Just before Christmas, the hotel known as the New Antrim House (formerly the Carter House) on Depot Street burned to the ground. It had been used as a public house since 1876, and at least once had been raided and found to be in violation of the liquor laws. All the guests escaped the fire safely, but lost most of their clothing and personal effects.

Although the transportation situation in Antrim was deteriorating *1925* (the Boston & Maine petitioned to discontinue yet another run, this time between Wilton and Keene) the future of increased electrical power in the area appeared to be improving. A company called the Realty Development Company interested in developing water rights for electrical power along the North Branch River was buying up land, including the property of the late James A. Tuttle and that of Dow Clement. Although they had ambitious plans for a series of dams along the river, they built only one, the Jackman Dam, where the resulting body of water is known today as Pierce Lake.

Campbell Pond, the source of the water supply for the precinct, was also in the news. The State Board of Health issued an order prohibiting further fishing and ice cutting in that pond. It was not always obeyed.

Parties were attempting to do a little fishing at Campbell Pond on Monday, but as their bait was quite plentiful and of a kind to intoxicate—not the fish, but themselves—they did not have much luck catching fish. Officer Tolman caught them, and before Judge Perry in Hillsboro they appeared with some assistance, and paid a fine and costs.

The good news in 1925 was that the tax rate was lowered from $2.90 of the previous year to $1.60. However, since a contract for building

The old Carter House

1.6 miles of gravel road from Munson Cochrane's north toward Hillsboro was awarded for a price of $28,899.92, taxes might well go up in 1926.

Fires often seem to occur in the coldest part of the year. In December, Fred Proctor's barn on the former Governor Goodell estate was totally destroyed. Ten cows, six horses, and three hogs perished.

1926   Fires continued to plague the town in the coldest months. On January 27 the Simonds' house and barn (the former Mary Hopkins' place) at the Branch were totally destroyed, leaving only five families living in the Branch proper.

In Antrim village, there was always the excitement of town meeting to look forward to. Samuel Sawyer, aged ninety, was unable to vote because of illness. This was the first election he had missed since voting for Abraham Lincoln. At least he was spared the anguish of making a decision on the following controversial question which appeared on the 1926 ballot: "Shall a permit be granted to druggists for the sale of liquor in town for medicinal, sacramental, scientific, and mechanical purposes?" The vote was affirmative 124, negative 111. The editor of *The Reporter*, unwilling to believe that the Antrim voters were consciously so depraved, attributed the result to a technicality in marking the ballot.

The electorate also approved the following money-consuming projects: Building and maintaining good roads, purchasing new fire apparatus, purchasing lands adjoining the town water supply, investing in a tractor and snow plow, repairing sidewalks and the town hall, enlarging and remodeling the engine house, plus a liberal appropriation for the support of schools. No wonder the taxes were going up!

1927   The year of the sesquicentennial! This event deserves, and will get, a chapter of its own. Preparations for it were extensive and as the date drew near *The Reporter* devoted more and more space to it.

There were other news items in the paper, also. The snow plow authorized by the voters the previous year was both praised and criticized. A transient stated that Antrim's roads were in the best condition of any in the area. But it was impossible to please all of the people all of the time. Some townspeople complained that the plow removed too much snow and spoiled the sledding.

Sports enthusiasts received a boost when Richard Goodell gave the Robert Shea Athletic Field and the William Cram Grove to the town on the condition "that the town shall keep these properties perpetually for free public use for recreational and educational purposes."

In March, Morton Paige's factory at Clinton burned; the building was a total loss, together with the machinery and all the contents. It had been erected sixteen years earlier, replacing the crib and cradle shop owned by Mr. Paige's father, which also burned. (The site must have a hex on it, because some thirty years later the second reel shop was totally destroyed by fire.) Mr. Paige was the largest manufacturer of wooden reels in New England at the time, and had some of the largest cordage companies as his customers. He planned to rebuild, and did so within a month: six weeks after the fire, he delivered reels made in the new shop. On April 19, many of the citizens of the town—plus the local band—serenaded Mr. Paige, first at his house and then at his new shop.

Also in March, the town clock was illuminated by means of two electric lamps, positioned to throw light on the front dial. They were on a timer which turned them off at midnight. Perhaps the town fathers thought that no self-respecting citizen should be abroad after that hour.

Once again the Boston & Maine Railroad incurred the wrath of the townspeople for discontinuing another train, which meant that the noon train would not arrive, nor would the two o'clock train leave Hillsboro. It was not only an inconvenience to the traveling public, but also a great hardship to local business men. The Boston & Maine called the move "an improved arrangement of passenger trains." This was beyond the comprehension of the general public.

Even so small a town as Antrim was segmented into self-contained communities in the days before transportation was as quick and easy as it would later become. One of these neighborhoods was Clinton . Corner, where a bandstand was erected in the triangle; an annual Fourth of July celebration took place here, complete with fireworks and the customary ball game.

Taxes (like death and the common cold, always with us) went up again in 1927, to $3.50 per one hundred. One cause was the purchase of a new fire truck, but this was not really an extravagance, especially since without it insurance rates would have increased.

Patriotic fervor . . . World War I

Department of utter incredulity:

> One day last week, George Craig sent garden peas by parcel post to
> South Fairlee, Vermont. They left Antrim at 9:30 A.M. and arrived at
> Fairlee in season to be served for supper at 5:30 P.M. the same day.
> Uncle Sam is not so slow!

1928   Travel by auto, both for business and pleasure, was increasing
rapidly. For the convenience of the motorist, auto maps were beginning to be published. One of these new maps, put out by the Geographical Publishing Company, unfortunately did not include the
name of Antrim on its routes. "What is wrong with a town of considerable more than one thousand inhabitants," asks *The Reporter* indig-
nantly, "when that town is not even mentioned, although it is located
on two of the most prominent highways in the state?"

Conversely, travel by train was declining more rapidly, and the
much maligned Boston & Maine threatened to remove still another train
from its schedule. Protesting that this was exceptionally hard to bear
at a time when business was not too good, the Antrim Citizens'
Association sent a letter detailing the hardships to the Boston &

The Glorious Fourth

Maine, and to the Postmaster General, since one of the greatest deprivations was loss of mail service. Persistence paid: the B.&M. was refused a permit to cancel the train by the Public Service Commission.

If train service was an annual occasion for complaint, so also was the tax rate. This year, as in other years, the rate was increased again, to $4.18 on a hundred. We can sympathize with *The Reporter*'s comment: "This is information that always causes a peculiar feeling to course through one's veins, when it is found that for all improvements we must pay."

The Fourth of July celebration was a gala event in 1928. It was estimated that more than two thousand persons witnessed the parade, which featured floats by the local tradesmen with forty dollars given in prizes. There were also two ball games, track and field events, and a band concert and fireworks in the evening. The thermometer stood at eighty degrees and the weather was only briefly marred by an afternoon thunder shower. The storm, coming when it did, may have been a blessing, as the local boys were losing!

The first week in September saw Antrim's version of musical chairs: John W. Thornton moved to Fairview Street; Andrew Fuglestad occupied the house vacated by Mr. Thornton; Guy Hollis moved to the tenement vacated by Mr. Fuglestad; and the house vacated by Mr. Hollis was occupied by Dalton Brooks.

Item of aesthetic importance:

The fire hydrants are much improved by the tops being painted red instead of black.

1929   It seems incredible that so little in the way of news items can be found for this year. The stock market crash and resultant great depression are never once mentioned, as if the town of Antrim were totally insulated from the rest of the world. Perhaps this isolationist attitude is what distinguishes the small town era of the '20s from the world today, a sort of self-contained provinciality with pride in one's town and self-sufficiency being the dominant themes. Whether this is on the whole good or bad is not for speculation.

One sign that times were beginning to change is the recurring frequency of the mention of airplanes. In July, Lyman Tenney at the age of ninety-six rode in an airplane as the guest of the airport proprietors in Keene. "Mr. Tenney was born August 21, 1832, and in his youth the oxcart and the stagecoach, on foot or on horseback were the only means of travel. In the span of his nearly a century of life, he has witnessed the coming of the railroad, the electric car, the automobile and the airplane. He has welcomed the innumerable uses of electricity, and the discovery and invention of the telephone, telegraph, and radio." Had he lived another fifteen years, doubtless he would have become a television addict.

Airplanes had been sighted flying over Antrim, but in October, there was great excitement when a private plane from Keene actually landed in Verto Smith's field on the Hillsboro road. Cars were parked for a quarter of a mile on both sides of the road to witness the event.

One thing that never changed was the attitude of the people toward taxes. This was still, and probably always will be, contentious. It is fitting, therefore, to bring this account of a decade to a close by noting that in 1929, Antrim had the highest tax rate in the state. This is probably a misleading inference, since there was no standard valuation of property, some towns having high valuation and low taxes, while in others, Antrim among them, the opposite was true. Still, there was no getting around the fact that the amount of tax paid had steadily increased over the years, one disgruntled Branchite stating that his (her?) taxes had increased eight hundred percent in twenty years!

HARD TIMES

Main Street, USA

In 1930 Antrim had a population of 1,254 and was pretty much a self-sufficient community. Commercially it had nearly everything a person needed, and with that old standby, the Sears Roebuck catalog, one could live very comfortably without ever going out of town. Goodnow, Derby and Raleigh, the general store in the Odd Fellow's block, was able to supply a full order of groceries (a can of lobster was thirty-nine cents), adequate housewares and tools, some clothing, and a line of notions that would put Woolworth's to shame. For those with a taste for *haute couture,* there was Anna Duncan's Millinery on Main Street, where Wayno's store is now, and Anna Noetzel's Convenience Shoppe on Elm Street. Butterfield's store, now Jackson's, carried a line of men's clothing and shoes for the family, and its principal commodities were newspapers and magazines. Of course, the penny candy counter, just inside the door, was pretty popular after school hours, with Elizabeth Tandy in a black smock waiting on young customers. Sometimes a penny would buy ten pieces of candy.

There were three ice cream parlors on Main Street—Walt Butcher's Main Street Soda Shoppe (which also offered water wings in the summer for thirty-nine cents), sharing what is now the Coffee Shoppe building with the First National Store; the Antrim Drugstore, now the town hall annex, where Mr. Daniels could also fill prescriptions; and the Fruit Store, in the Jameson block, on the site now filled by the Exxon Station and Wayno's. After school a boy's errands might include getting the mail from the post office, now the Little Town Hall, going across the street to Arthur Proctor's big barn for a quart of milk for seven cents, down to Cutter's market (Dodge City) for a pound of hamburg for twenty-five cents, and getting a haircut at Hodges' Barber Shop on Summer Street. (The haircut was probably first on the list, but ended up last in actual performance.)

On Saturday morning you could take a watch for repair to Mr. William Ward on Highland Avenue, and then walk all the way to the north end of Main Street to Mr. Warren's to get shoes fixed, stopping at the corner of Summer and Main Streets to pay the bill at the telephone office, which was really fun because you might have to wait while the operator disentangled the fascinating maze of plugs and cords.

Add to this the icehouse on West Street, Maurice Poor and Don Robinson's Antrim Garage on Goodell's Hill, William Clark's plumbing shop, now Hardwick's Insurance Agency, Al Zabriskie's Garage on West Street, and Sadie Lane's Notions next to the Drug Store, and Antrim's basic needs were well supplied.

The principal industries were Goodell's Cutlery in the Village—and how many mothers said to their offspring, "Come home when the whistle blows!" which it did at 5:00 on weekday afternoons, not to mention 6:00 and 7:00 A.M., 12:00 noon and 1:00 P.M.—and Abbott's shop in Clinton, specializing in baby cribs and playyards. There were other smaller factories, and some men found employment at the Bennington Paper Mill (the popular name for the Monadnock Mill) which really did not seem out of town, since a man could walk to work if he had to.

The five villages were still socially independent to some extent, with Clinton and the Center sharing the same church and grammar school. North Branch had its school and the Chapel, and East Antrim its school, but with the increased use of the automobile, more and more people were finding their way to the Village for social activities, where there was plenty of action. As in all small towns, these activities centered around school and church, but did ever a town support so devotedly so many social and fraternal organizations? There were at least thirteen active groups, not to mention the various societies connected with the five churches.

Local entertainment flourished: in 1930 there were seven plays at the town hall, although some of these were presented by traveling troupes. Harvest suppers at the churches and the Armistice Ball, sponsored by the Legion, were annual events much anticipated and enjoyed.

In February of 1930 a goodly number came from the city to enjoy the winter sports. There was daily train service into town, and Archie Perkins provided livery service by Chevrolet from the depot. (He also rented cars to responsible drivers.) Extensive preparations had been made at both the Waumbek and Maplehurst Inns for the holiday visitors coming on the weekend snow train but mild weather removed the snow so that the visitors had to be content with attending a dance at the Grange Hall and watching two airplanes that flew over from Concord and landed on Gregg Lake.

At town meeting the subject of sidewalks was discussed, with the result that a committee of five was appointed to look into the matter and report back next year with its recommendations as to where new sidewalks were most needed. An article in the school warrant asked for money to improve the toilet facilities at the high school. Quoting from *The Antrim Reporter:* "This matter necessitated considerable explaining and discussion. Estimates of different propositions were given, and the School Board was anxious that something be done. The need is quite apparent to all who have occasion to know anything about it." Thirteen hundred dollars was thereby appropriated, with the implementation put into the hands of the school board, and by September extensive indoor plumbing had been installed in what were known as the boys' and girls' basements.

The American Legion had to be a leading contender for the busiest organization. Supporting a wide range of activities during the year, the men planned and carried out a most effective Memorial Day observance, starting with a parade at the North Branch in the morning. The Village parade formed at the Jameson Block at one o'clock, led by the marshal on horseback, and proceeded to the World War I memorial at the library, the Civil War memorial at the Baptist church, and thence to Maplewood Cemetery. The return march culminated at the town hall with patriotic exercises, and a guest speaker as the main event. With this taxing schedule it was necessary for the school children to present their Memorial Day program on another day.

The Fourth of July, by contrast, was only moderately observed in 1930, but by the middle thirties the celebration achieved staggering proportions. This year, however, the local newspaper reported that the night before the Fourth one heard the ringing of bells and the firing of the cannon, and although no damage was done "different articles that were not nailed down changed locations." A junior ball game was held in the morning, with other sports events in the afternoon. In the evening there was a band concert and fireworks, which were disappointing due to lack of expenditure.

The rest of the summer was filled with the usual activities. The Sunday School picnic, held at Lake Massasecum, was attended by 300. Boy Scouts from the Boston area at Camp Sachem, on the west side of Gregg Lake, and girl campers at Greggmere, on the opposite shore, entered into local activities and invited the natives to their entertainments. White Birch Point continued to have the aura of the summer colonies renowned in more affluent resort areas, while townspeople enjoyed swimming at the small stretch of public beach on the lake. The Waumbek and Maplehurst Inns flourished, with the Harris Tavern, now Herbert Harvey's residence, and Contoocook Manor, at present the home of John McCabe, also taking summer guests. Greystone Lodge opened under new management and served a banquet to 150 area people for $1.25. The menu included Long Island duckling, and afterward the guests were entertained with a magic act, bridge, and dancing.

The new stretch of improved road opened between Stoddard and Antrim the last of August, and on October 15, at 2:00 P.M., dedication exercises were held for the new road, named the Franklin Pierce Highway. Governor Charles Tobey and Mayor Robert Brown of Concord headed a caravan of thirty automobiles of state officials which started in the Capital City and were joined along the route by other cars, making a line of more than a mile. Included in the parade were an open wagon drawn by oxen, and a one-horse shay. More than 250 cars were counted at the Steele Pond Bridge where the exercises were held, with music by the Industrial School Band of Manchester and the Concord Orchestra, and afterward there was a banquet at Greystone Lodge and a dance at the town hall.

Signs of the nationwide depression began to appear locally toward the end of the year. The New Hampshire Unemployment Relief Committee issued a bulletin with suggestions for employers such as "Buy now" and the "stagger system" — employ more workers to work fewer hours, thus providing more wage-earners with a steady, if smaller, income. While business had been so rushing in April that Abbott Company did not close for Fast Day, in September Paige's reel shop was not working full time. Mr. Butcher remodeled his store front, putting in big show windows, and Maurice Poor built his new bungalow-style house at the top of Poor's Hill, but these were the last signs of building and large-scale improvements in the Village for several years.

In March, 1931, Lyman Tenney, Antrim's oldest citizen, at 97 fell down the stairs while getting ready to go to town meeting and died a few days later.

An article in the warrant that year asking to open the road leading from the Forest Road in Hancock to Willard Pond was dismissed, but later in the year the selectmen and 201 petitioners requested that the state rebuild this road, and it was laid out by the state in November. It was also at this time that Elsa Tudor Leland first made an appeal to establish a bird and animal sanctuary at Willard Pond, and she was offered assistance locally by E.E. Smith and his neighbor, Mr. Henderson. The latter had previously voiced the desire for such a haven in his part of Antrim (the area of Smith Road to Elm Avenue) indicating a concern for the preservation of wildlife long before the threatening conditions of the '60s and '70s made conservation a popular issue nationally. Today the Willard Pond Sanctuary provides a great service to our town in the study of wildlife.

Also at town meeting the Sidewalk Committee which had been appointed the previous March made this recommendation:

That the Town adopt a five year program of Sidewalk Construction, building not over 2000 linear feet of walk in any year, providing that the average cost of such walks on any street does not exceed one dollar per linear foot of walk of four foot width, the cost of such walks being borne equally by the Town and the abutters.

The meeting voted to adopt the proposal, and in a month the West Street Sidewalk was in progress. By August the one on Highland Avenue was completed, making an excellent long flat run for roller-skating. But these two were the only sidewalks ever finished, although the committee had recommended sixteen. The five-year plan was extremely shortlived—a casualty of the Great Depression.

After several years of meeting with the Presbyterians, the Methodists decided to go it alone again, and in the spring services were resumed at the Methodist Church (now the Christian Science Society) with Dr. Charles Tilton as pastor. In October, district Presbytery meetings were held at the local church for two days, with local organizations serving suppers to large assemblies. A highlight of the convention was a meeting held at the site of the first Meeting House on the hill. In that same month the Baptists held a surprise party for the Reverend and Mrs. Tibbals on the occasion of their twenty-fifth wedding anniversary. After a day trip to the St. Gaudens museum in

Cornish the couple, with friends, dropped in at the church, ostensibly to view the flower arrangements for Sunday service, and were surprised by many parishioners who provided an evening's entertainment, including a mock wedding. Another church activity during October was the Union Church workers' sponsorship of the appearance of the renowned poet Edwin Markham at the Baptist church, at which time he recited some of his poetry.

Memorial Day events had involved a shorter parade route, and the Glorious Fourth was observed only by baseball games. Later in the season Al Thornton pitched a no-hitter against Weare. In general, summer saw the usual course of events. A mysterious malady which struck down many people immediately after the Sunday School picnic was blamed, for lack of evidence, on the lemonade.

The ninth annual North Branch School reunion was held in July. This yearly event has for many years afforded an opportunity for long-time friends to get together to talk about the good old days.

From Bad to Worse

As always, when the economy declines, crime increases, and Antrim was not exempt. In September Albert Wheeler had his car stolen, but the police recovered it in Wilton before Albert noticed it was gone.

Although there were encouraging reports throughout the year regarding the state's economy, local stores reduced their evening hours to Wednesday and Saturday only, and in December representatives of the local churches formed a committee to meet the needs of the unemployed. They met in the Maplehurst Inn parlor (where Landlord A.J. Kelly did a reasonably thriving business with organizational dinner meetings) and they called themselves the "Antrim Community Employment Committee." The prime objectives were to find employers for the out-of-work and to collect money and clothing for the victims of Hard Times. In just fifteen months Franklin Roosevelt would sail into the White House to the strains of "Happy Days Are Here Again," bringing social reforms that would change so drastically the outlook of the poor, but in 1931 Antrim, in true Yankee style, was prepared to look out for its own.

1932   Nineteen-thirty-two came in with a bang, with a local vaudeville show in the town hall presented by the Washington Bicentennial Committee for the purpose of raising funds to commemorate the two hundredth birthday of the first president. The town hall continued to buzz throughout the month of January, with the Senior Class play, "Charming Pretender," on the fifteenth, followed a few days later by a "Tom Thumb Wedding."

Prior to town meeting a letter to the editor of *The Antrim Reporter* proposed that town employees, including teachers, should take a cut in pay, and a preliminary meeting was held by the taxpayers in February to discuss issues which would require decisions at the March meeting. Items for discussion included schools, salaries, and the hard-topping of Clinton Road to Route 9. Despite this ominous rise of interest in town business, town meeting was reported to have been the best ever, longer than usual, with large cuts, and no fights! An article pertaining to sidewalks was dismissed, as was the black-topping of Clinton Road, but it was voted to give a discount to those property owners who paid their taxes on time. It fell to the selectmen to choose which thirty-three streetlights would be eliminated among the several economies. Although the teachers' salaries were not cut, the tax rate plummeted to $3.09. Town meeting dinner was sponsored by the Senior Class for the first time that year; this event continued to be an annual money-making affair contributing toward the cost of the class trip for as long as Antrim High existed.

Not without criticism, the Memorial Day observance was shortened to the extent that all activities were over by noon, a practice that has been carried out without much change to the present time. The Fourth of July was almost entirely passed over, with a band concert at night in the town hall the only event. Since it rained that day, it was probably just as well that nothing more had been planned. Butcher's sold firecrackers, so at least the young people had something to do to make the day a little different from all the others.

At the request of the Baptist church, the cannon which had been situated on the lawn since 1901 was moved to the Shea Athletic Field (the formal name for the ball grounds) and the church grounds were then graded and generally improved. Subsequently the corner of Main and Concord Streets was widened, all of which altered the appearance of that general area considerably. In the process some shade trees were lost, but the Bicentennial Committee compensated somewhat for the loss by planting several new trees along Main Street in memory of George Washington.

The culmination of the Washington Bicentennial was a pageant, *The Father of His Country*, presented in the town hall to capacity audiences on July 29 and 30. A cast of 114 local people of all ages was directed by J. Lillian Larabee, with Byron Butterfield in the title role and Alice Hurlin as Martha. Ethel Nichols was head of the committee of nine which created the production. Included were orchestra, chorus, solos, dances, and a total of fourteen scenes. The impressive finale, "The Wedding of the Nations," featured thirteen of Antrim's best-looking girls representing the colonies, with Gertrude Thornton as Columbia. The audience of four hundred joined in singing, "America," in this soul-stirring patriotic scene.

Sports activities that summer included golf at the new Mount Crotched Country Club on the Bennington-Francestown Road for a dollar a day, and tennis on a new court back of Leroy Vose's house on Main Street. Of course, there was always croquet in the evening on the lawn between the Harris Tavern and the bandstand.

The Garden Club held the first of several annual Flower Shows in August, and while it was not as extensive as those to follow, the town hall was open from two o'clock in the afternoon until ten at night with a variety of displays, and a one-act play was presented in the evening. There were no dances in the Grange Hall as there had been in previous summers, and no Vacation Church School. In lieu of the latter, thirty-five local children were transported daily to the Deering Community Center for three weeks for an outstanding summer school experience with young people from several surrounding communities. Greystone held its third annual community banquet, "in order to boost morale," but only eighty felt affluent enough to attend.

The curtailment of activities indicated that Antrim was feeling the gloom that permeated the nation the latter part of the year. Although conditions in no way compared with those in large industrial cities — in fact Goodell's was working overtime — nevertheless there was fear that things would continue to get worse. An advertisement in the local paper opened with the words, "Just before the dawn. . .," suggesting that conditions were at their darkest. The Red Cross distributed flour and cotton cloth to the needy, and the Employment Committee augmented its original group to include representatives from other organizations. Crime continued to increase, and a local man was sentenced to five years in the state prison.

The Boy Scouts, reactivated under the enthusiastic leadership of Elof "Vic" Dahl, had a busy and productive year that included a district Court of Honor held in the town hall, and a new building at Camp Caughey, at the south end of Gregg Lake. The boys, along with the rest of the community, received the shock of their young lives when one of their outstanding members, Richard Cuddihy, 16, was killed in a freak hunting accident on Columbus Day. For many years afterward the troop assembled at Dick's grave for "Taps" during Memorial Day services at Maplewood Cemetery.

A special town meeting was held September 13 "to see if the town would accept state money to apply on immediate road building, for the express business of assisting the unemployed." It was agreed to accept a loan of $3,720, without interest, to start work on the road from Clinton Village to the North Branch. Although this move smacked of taking charity, the residents along this three-mile stretch on Route 31 must have received the decision with feelings of relief, since the muddy condition of the road every spring was something more than a mild inconvenience.

Modernization along Main Street appeared when one barber shop expanded to include a Beauty Parlor. The new beautician was Marguerite Howard, who continued her business in various locations in town for nearly thirty-five years. Goodnow, Derby and Raleigh reorganized the general store, with "up to the minute fixtures, modern lighting, etc."

The fad of the moment was jigsaw puzzles (inexpensive and fun to make), which were enjoyed by many through a circulating library. Ines Sawyer (whose delicious doughnuts were on sale fresh every morning at the Fruit Store for a quarter a dozen) took orders for puzzles which she would saw to order for customers to give as Christmas presents.

The presidential election in November brought out over eighty percent of the registered voters, and as in those other Republican strongholds, Maine and Vermont, Herbert Hoover was the victor over Franklin Roosevelt in Antrim, 385-139. Now that the Democratic party was in control again, the repeal of prohibition seemed imminent, and this was strongly opposed by some. In addition to frequent letters to the editor from Fred "Happy" Dunlap elucidating the evils of drink, *The Antrim Reporter* reprinted an anti-wet editorial from another paper which included this prediction:

> . . .they will repeal the whole thing. And then what? Chaos. A national orgy of drunkenness, with all the filth and poverty and lawlessness that goes with it.

All the World's a Stage

Social surveys of the period sometimes include reference to the importance of the Hollywood musical in boosting the morale of the American people, and Antrimites were no exception. Not only did they manage to squeeze out the cost of admission and gas for frequent trips to the Gem Theatre in Peterborough — three changes a week — but 1933 saw no less than three such extravaganzas on the town hall stage. The first, and some think the best, was "Kathleen," presented March 17 and 18 with a cast of 75 — count 'em — 75 local people. It was a package deal, with scripts, music, costumes, and director provided by a remote agency for two weeks. The local committee rounded up the cast and musicians, arranged rehearsals, and canvassed the town for advertising to put in the programs, and then came a flurry of activity building up to two nights of "swell" entertainment for all — those involved and those watching. Although the singing and dancing may not have been any threat to Dick Powell and Fred Astaire, the rapport established between an enthusiastic cast and an appreciative audience of family and friends made "Kathleen" such good escapist fare that it was followed by another lavish production in September, and still another in November. The second one, "The World's All Right," was sponsored by the Citizen's Committee, giving a little respite to the Legion, which produced the other two. "Heads Up," even took the place of the annual Armistice Ball; of course there was dancing after every show to the music of Wes Herrick or Zaza Ludwig.

1933   The last of several heavy snowstorms during the winter of '32-'33 was the famous "blue" snow in April, which deposited thirty inches at forty degrees temperature. The bluish cast on the snow seemingly defied scientific explanation. Needless to say, school was closed, a rather uncommon event up until then, and this met with due appreciation. Extreme cold weather earlier had brought on the usual fires, the worst of which caused the total loss of the Codman house on Summer Street.

Town meeting was heavily attended, and many articles dismissed. Deeming the practice of the previous year a success, it was voted to continue allowing a discount for taxes paid on time. Two articles pertaining to the sidewalk project were dismissed, and that was the end of that project. The completion of Route 31 to the Branch was approved on the strength of anticipated state support. A special meeting later in the year resulted in the state absorbing half of the cost. This easement of a financial burden, although not as much as hoped for, was brought about through the efforts of the local representative to the state legislature, Wyman K. Flint. A complex and wordy article of the annual warrant would allow people to borrow money from the town, with first chance on town labor in order to pay back the loan. Not involving any direct expenditure, the article was so voted.

For a number of years, the town hall had been closed to basketball. As a result of some mild agitation, it was voted to reopen the hall for the benefit of young enthusiasts of the sport, and this continued to be the practice until the Memorial Gymnasium was built in 1953.

Teachers' salaries were cut ten percent for the school year '33-'34, and although the superintendent of schools was to receive four hundred dollars less, this was later rescinded. In spite of all this frugality the tax rate rose to $3.50.

The repeal of prohibition called for decisions to be made at the local level regarding the sale of "3.2" beer. Antrim voted against it, but Hillsboro and Bennington went the other way. Henry Raleigh's Waverly Nook, just over the Bennington line, made the Antrim decision somewhat ineffectual. Some wag left a bottle of the controversial liquid on Happy Dunlap's doorstep the night before the Fourth, but instead of having the desired effect of making Happy unhappy, it gave him the opportunity to respond in his usual manner in his next letter to the editor of *The Antrim Reporter*, thusly: "This article might seem to prove that the bottle of 3.2 beer left on my doorstep the night before the Fourth was intoxicating; however this may be, I was glad to get the bottle and to find out for just how little men are willing to part with fifteen or twenty cents." The whole situation caused a reactivation of the WCTU in town.

In June, Willard Manning died at the age of 79. During his latter years his main contribution to the general good of Antrim was to hold down the steps in front of the Odd Fellow's Hall every day. How fitting that Editor Hiram Eldredge wrote in Willard's obituary: ". . .he was an old member of Waverly Lodge. With this fraternity he was devotedly attached and was constant in his attendance."

The management of the baseball team organized a Glorious Fourth, with a parade of floats ending at the ball grounds, followed by two games with arch-rival Hillsboro. The first three-mile foot race from Bennington became a popular annual event. There was a band concert at the bandstand, followed by a barn dance at the Harris Tavern. Fireworks were left up to private sponsorships.

E.D. Putnam, who had maintained a studio in the Jameson block next to the Fruit Store for the last two years, received national notice when some of his photographs were printed in the magazine *Our Dumb Animals*. He also presented his slide show, "Our Native Wild Flowers," in Washington, D.C., which was quite a step up from his Antrim Town Hall showings.

Summer brought not only lightning storms of alarming severity but also the reinstatement of activities that had been discontinued the previous summer, in the darkest days of the depression. Rock gardens were all the rage — not intended to yield a crop of new rocks, they were artistic arrangements of varying sized rocks with flowers planted cozily in between. Happy Dunlap's comments on the fad concluded with this:

Before I start a rock garden for my beloved wife and daughter, I wish some good lady would write an article telling us men just how long rocks are likely to be an incentive for plants to grow. If the rock garden is to be of the long hair, short hair, or the short skirt, long skirt type of fad, I am going slow on starting one, as moving rocks is hard work, and I would hate to be obliged, in a year or so, to move the rocks back to the old stone wall. There would be less kick in it than there is in the 3.2 variety.

The second annual Flower Show was a huge success, with over 1,000 citizens attending the two-day affair, representing fourteen states and the District of Columbia. Re-creations of gardens and housefronts transformed the town hall into a floral wonderland. The amount of creative energy that went into these annual productions was soon burned out, and after a few such endeavors the Flower Shows were discontinued, never to appear again. One of the most enthusiastic members of the Garden Club was J. Lillian Larabee, who became the first president of the United Garden Clubs of New Hampshire.

The Village school opened in September with several new students, due to the closing of the East Antrim grammar school. Also that month Goodell Company went on a five-day, forty-hour week. No longer did the whistle summon kids home for dinner on Saturday. Another evidence of Roosevelt's New Deal was the formation of the local National Recovery Act's Compliance Board, which requested that any citizen not a member of the NRA submit the reason on a consumer card. Although the town was founded on principles of independence, it seemed to be slipping easily into the ways of national socialism.

October brought a resolution of a court case which had been pending for nearly a year. Road Agent Elmer Merrill had been accused by another local man of wastefulness in his job; Attorney Junius T. Hanchett handled Mr. Merrill's case, which was disposed of in the court, with the road agent receiving a vote of confidence.

October also brought a three-day convention of New Hampshire Baptists to the local church, efficiently organized by Mr. Tibbals. One piece of business was the endorsement of President Roosevelt's recovery program. Meals for the 300 delegates were served by the Maplehurst Inn and local organizations.

In December the Grange celebrated its fiftieth anniversary with a fair and supper. Shrimp wiggle was always a favorite item on Grange menus.

Snow came early, along with cold weather, and the countryside was soon adorned with snow fences which, along with their primary function of preventing drifting, made artistic shadows on the landscape. The IGA general store, now part of the Derby Stores chain, featured a Toyland in the back room where Santa Claus reigned supreme on a December afternoon. The amazing number of 140 kids at one time squeezed in to talk to Santa and receive presents. In addition to the usual Christmas parties, Carl Brooks invited several men who lived alone to his house in Clinton for Christmas dinner.

During the severe winter of 1934, the town kept busy raising money *1934* to send the high school seniors to Washington during the April vacation. Although this had been the practice for many years, the school board had expressed a desire to discontinue it in 1934, as the project necessitated many money-making activities during the year. But a petition led by William Linton and signed by 250 citizens asking that the Class of 1934 not be denied the privilege afforded to all the preceding classes caused the board to relent. However, it stipulated that there could be only three endeavors by the class to finance the trip. The spirit of the townspeople was aroused, as many of them had fond memories of their own Washington trips, and soon there was a flurry of public suppers, all for the benefit of the seniors. So the trip took place after all, and for a week in April all the younger kids in town haunted the Post Office, looking for post cards from their friends in Washington. Judging from personal experience, the memories that linger on are not so much of the wonders of the workings of the government, but more of the adventures in the hotels, but no matter: the Washington trip was an education in life outside the small town.

A heavy, fifteen-hour rain April 11 and 12 caused more damage than did the thirty-inch snowstorm the year before. There were no trains for a day, and no mail in or out of town, and several roads were closed because of washouts. Water came up to the autos' running boards and one driver, whose engine stalled, sat on top of his car until he was rescued. The Depot Street flat was running wild with overflow from the Contoocook, and the residents in that area were forced to move around by rowboat. Probably the only bright note was the closing of school.

A dental clinic, sponsored mainly by the Woman's Club, was held during the closing weeks of the school year, and 146 children were examined. Those needing dental work but whose parents could not afford it were taken care of then and there, as Dr. Harvey Grimes brought his chair and other equipment right into the school.

The ultimate in small-town celebrations had to be Antrim's Fourth of July observance that year. The great day was announced promptly at midnight by the ringing of bells and firing of bombs, and flags were seen waving shortly after sunrise. Providing music for the parade was the Legion-Boy Scout Bugle and Drum Corps, making their first appearance in gleaming uniforms, made up of white ducks, shirts, and sailor hats, all set off by black bow-ties. George DeFoe was the able director of the group, and the icing on the cake was the beautiful majorette, Ida Maxfield.

The 9 A.M. parade was led by another of Antrim's beautiful girls, Isabel Jameson, on horseback, and the stream of floats and "horribles" (walkers dressed in comical costumes) wound its way all through the Village, starting at Pleasant Street and ending at the ball grounds. The baseball game with Hillsboro at 10:30 A.M. was won by the home team, but Hillsboro reciprocated by beating Antrim in the afternoon. The other sports included the three-mile foot race from Bennington. Needless to say, energy was running low by night time, and a 6:30 P.M. band concert was the last event of a gala day.

Although Greystone Inn was closed for the summer, the other inns functioned as usual, camps were open, and annual organizational events were carried out without noticeable change. One of the highlights was the Methodist "Country Fair," planned by the young minister, the Reverend John Brooks. A total of eighty-five dollars was realized for the benefit of the church, and in addition to the booths and tables in the afternoon, an entertainment was held at the town hall in the evening. One of the featured performers was Maydell Eksergian, a summer resident of Bennington, and an accomplished cellist. After a few words of introduction, the charming Miss Eksergian sat down to play, and with her first dramatic stroke, the bow flew out of her hand and barely missed sailing through the open window into the middle of Main Street. With great aplomb, she picked up her bow and continued her recital, but not without having set the young ones in the front row into a fit of giggling. This did not matter much, since the remainder of the entertainment was intended to be high farce, including Jimmy Perkins and his guinea pig in an imitation of Will Rogers and "Blue Boy," from the very popular movie, *State Fair*.

The two-day Garden Club Flower Show had a new feature — prizes for children's home gardens. The club furnished seeds in the spring to all interested young people, and a panel of judges visited the resultant gardens just before the show, so the awards were made when the crowd was there to appreciate them. Although hopes were high in April, enthusiasm waned as the summer months offered more active pursuits. The few stalwarts who stuck with their gardens till show time well deserved their awards.

Other summer events included the Tuttle family reunion held at the foot of Tuttle Mountain. The IGA store underwent another change of management and face-lifting, this time provided by Harold Proctor and Kenneth Hayward, better known as Bub and Bunk. The Grange held a husband-calling and rolling pin-throwing contest, which was won by Hattie Huntington.

A heavy rain in September canceled school for a day. At the North Branch power plant a giant oak fell across the wires, and Ed Grant sent his youngest son Kenny to guard the crossroad until help arrived, in a manner resembling old legends of heroism.

Although prosperity was certainly not running rampant through the town, the total picture was one of contentment, with the mills working full time, places of business maintaining a status quo, and everybody finding money enough to go to Peterborough or Hillsboro to the movies to see Shirley Temple or Will Rogers. The Legion Auxiliary had pledged to make 100 glasses of jelly during the summer for the less fortunate families, and as winter approached an appeal was made for blankets, but these are measures of welfare that might have been taken in a prosperous year, as the poor we have always with us.

"Antrim Boy Makes Good," said *The Antrim Reporter* of Howard Palmer, when he became president of the New York, New Haven and Hartford Railroad. A self-made man, he was the grandson of the Reverend William Hurlin.

The newly formed Men's Music Club, directed by Frank Boyd of Hillsboro, added to the Christmas festivities by driving around town, singing carols out of the car windows with the aid of megaphones, a la Rudy Vallee. Another innovation was the outdoor decorating with colored lights, a practice which grew steadily in Antrim along with the rest of the country, until the energy crisis of the 1970s, when it was deemed wasteful. But in a period when nothing much was new or pretty, it was a thrill to have a lighted tree on your porch every night during the Christmas season.

Sports Spectacular

1935   The winter of 1934-35 was a cold one, but without any incapacitating blizzards. It was a good winter for skating, with the millpond back of the town hall the most popular place for Village youngsters. Each neighborhood had its favorite skating area: Steele Pond at the Branch, Gregg Lake, and back of the Center School Mr. Hanchett made a small rink for the area children. It took a real stalwart to withstand the long periods of sub-zero weather, and clothing styles were not conducive to encouraging a great deal of time outdoors. Nowadays we have thermal socks and underwear, down-filled parkas, and insulated boots and mittens, and nineteenth century sports afficionados were protected by furs and long woolen underskirts. But in the meager winters of the intervening thirties coats were thin, ski pants were expensive, and hands and feet were cold.

A new dimension was added to the basketball schedule with the formation of a girls' team. Although most of the participants were of high school age, the teams were not school supported. Management and coaching were in the hands of willing adult supervisors such as Rupert Wisell. Rupie, a life-long supporter of young people's athletic activities in town, suffered a fatal heart attack in the '60s while working on the back stop for his Little League baseball team.

President Roosevelt's birthday in January was celebrated with a benefit card party at the Maplehurst Inn. Dedicated Democrats all over the country organized parties of this kind; over the years they mushroomed into a gigantic charity drive known as the "March of

Dimes." Washington's birthday in February was observed by the Washington supper at the Presbyterian Church and a masquerade ball at the town hall. Always held on weekends, such events provided some indoor entertainment for the skiers who came from the city to stay at the Maplehurst. These city slickers, in turn, provided entertainment for the natives by crashing the supper and ball in ski apparel.

A Zoning Commission of five members was approved at town meeting, but they were not allowed an expense appropriation. Their charge was to report back in 1936 with recommendations for boundaries and regulations for zoning districts. Further business at town meeting included the appropriation of $1,400 to tar and complete construction on the Gregg Lake road from Clinton Corner to the lake. The completion of Route 31, now referred to as the North Branch Road, was finally accomplished in 1935, but not without a special town meeting in July, when the final financial plans were approved.

Antrim's resistance to the New Deal was evidenced by an editorial denouncing the Social Security plan, which was nevertheless passed by Congress in August. The welfare situation was deemed serious, since the recipients seemed to be satisfied to go job-less and let the government support them. A return to the institution of poorhouses was suggested as a saving to the tax-paying public. Both the power and telephone companies reduced their rates to ease the cost of living, but still the economic state caused changes in the lifestyles of some families. An entire group of young men left town in November in hope of finding work in Florida, while other local homes became havens for out-of-work relatives from other states.

In spite of the hardships of winter and the depression, spring and summer were happy, productive seasons. On April 27 the Mt. Crotched Encampment observed the 116th anniversary of Odd Fellowship in America. An afternoon parade of Patriarchs Militant, sixty men in the uniform of the organization, was led by the Bugle and Drum Corps, and George Nylander on horseback. A turkey supper for 169 was followed by an entertainment at the town hall, with performances by out-of-town artists.

Police Chief George Nylander made the news again when he confronted a band of gypsies on Main Street and told them to "beat it." Not a common occurrence, the sight of these oddly-dressed strangers was enough to start rumors running through town of kidnapping, theft, and more unspeakable crimes—unspeakable because no one really knew what gypsies were supposed to do anyway.

The Fourth of July celebration had a new feature in the evening—an amateur show. This was inspired by the popularity of the Major Bowes Amateur Hour on radio. Young and old with all kinds of talent were enticed to perform by the promise of money prizes. A stage was constructed at the ball grounds and equipped with a powerful audio system. While singers predominated, other performers tap-danced or played guitars. This novel form of entertainment was repeated during the year and, in fact, has remained popular, with variation, to the present day.

An old-fashioned entertainment was provided in August by the Rebekahs when they put on a minstrel show to top off their summer fair. Pre-publicity announced that the show would contain local *clean* jokes. In one of these jokes an endman told of meeting Everett Davis (who was known for getting the most out of a dollar) at Niagara Falls.

> *Endman: What are you doing here?*
> *Everett: I'm on my honeymoon.*
> *Endman: Well, I don't see Ethel anywhere.*
> *Everett: Oh, she stayed home—she's been here before.*

The road through North Branch Village was straightened at Barrett Corner in May. When the Franklin Pierce Highway was built in 1930 this little stretch of road winding between the dwelling houses had not been altered. Imagine the traffic between Keene and Concord suddenly coming upon the picturesque curve between Ed Grant's and George Barrett's house. The danger of driving up onto the wide verandah of Barrett's big brick house (now David's Restaurant) was considerably lessened by this improvement, although it detracted from the beauty of the area.

Earl Cutter was appointed the new postmaster, a position he held for nearly forty years. It is interesting to note that the post office was open every week night until 7:45 p.m. during the Christmas season, and three hours on Christmas day.

Another local boy who made good was William Congreve, Jr. In March he was appointed head of the municipal bond department of Stroud and Company of Philadelphia and New York. Previously, Billy had served in a similar capacity on the staff of Governor Pinchot of Pennsylvania, who gained national recognition by negotiating the settlement of a coal strike in 1923.

There was a revived interest in quilt-making this year. Although now highly regarded as a folk art, the practice had waned considerably during the first part of the twentieth century, with the colorful and interesting products giving way to pastel-colored woolen blankets. But in 1935 people were concerned with getting the most possible use out of everything, hence the revival. The Women's Relief Corps had regularly scheduled "Patchwork Parties" in addition to their business meetings.

Chain letters appeared in local mailboxes for the first time this year. By sending a dime to the first person on a list of names, and copies of the letter to five friends, one was assured that he was not only contributing to the "World Remedy for Depression," but would become wealthy in a matter of weeks.

The high school has always been the source of great interest in any small town, with its activities providing much in the line of entertainment, not to mention controversies regarding finances and the quality of education. Antrim at this time had good reason to be proud of its school. Under the leadership of Headmaster Thomas Chaffee, the academically-inclined pupils were receiving a superior education. For several years AHS graduates had gone on to outstanding achievement in such colleges as Brown, Middlebury, Dartmouth, Yale, and Mount Holyoke. In 1935 the local physics team took first place in the state scholarship competition, and not for the first time. Innovations made in the fall term included forming the first student council, and the introduction of contract work in English and the sciences. The first high school girls' basketball team was organized under scholastic rules, and intramural sports were held every Friday afternoon (during school time!) at the ball grounds. Some of this must have seemed revolutionary at the time and, indeed, even today contract teaching is considered a modern device, associated with individualized learning.

But the weakness in this fine program is obvious. Students with no interest in higher education were given short shrift, with very few courses offered as incentive to stay in school, so as a result there were many dropouts. There were still no classes in home economics or shop, and that year in School Meeting a commercial course was voted down.

March saw the last regular Sunday service in the Methodist church. The number of church families was small, and the financial burden was great. For a few years afterward, an annual meeting was held, but gradually the members joined other local churches. Finally the building was sold. As long as the Methodist church flourished in Antrim, it had the reputation of being the center of many "good times."

Passenger service had been cut to one daily train each way between Concord and Peterborough, and in November a short-lived bus service between the two towns was discontinued. This meant that people were relying more and more on the automobile as a reliable and flexible mode of transportation from Antrim to anywhere. As an independent way to get around, it worked very well for about seven years, until World War II brought much automobile travel to a screeching halt.

Christmas was observed throughout the community in traditional ways, and the lighted community tree on the Baptist church triangle was joined by more house and store decorations than ever—a sure sign that things were looking up.

Wanted: One or More Arks

1936   A major upset occurred at town meeting 1936 when Archie Perkins defeated Elmer Merrill for the position of road agent, 188-179. Elmer had served the town in this capacity for many years and, although he had been the object of one man's criticism in 1933, had proven himself well able to carry out the duties of this most demanding of town offices. But the majority ruled, and for nearly ten years Archie showed the town that he was worthy of their trust. In 1945 Elmer proved again that "you can't keep a good man down," by being duly elected to and holding the position of road agent for many more years.

Archie received his baptism under fire very shortly after town meeting. The area was devastated by the worst spring flood in many years. When the rain and melting snow first caused the water to overflow its natural barriers *The Antrim Reporter* said there was no serious damage, and people were somewhat relieved to think that they had escaped the dangers they remembered from two years earlier. A week later, however, the rains came again, and brought far worse conditions than anyone had ever imagined could happen in Antrim. It was cut off from every other town for several days, and although it was possible to go to Bennington by rowboat, the boat would have to be dragged over high spots. All bridges became unsafe, and the new North Branch road that had been so many years in the making was badly damaged. Telegraph and telephone wires were down, although it was possible to make local calls. Neither the mail trains nor the bread trucks could get through, and school closed for *two* days! As would be expected, the homes at the foot of Depot Street were the most endangered. At the Colby farm (now Tenney's) it was necessary to go from the house to the barn by rowboat, and at the next house Maggie Shea's hens all drowned.

Of course the water receded as rapidly as it had risen, and soon life was proceeding as usual, but not without many scars to remind people of a few harrowing days. Repair to roads and bridges was still going on at the close of the year. Fortunately, no serious harm to human life resulted, but the fact that in May the state appropriated two million dollars for flood damage indicates the seriousness of the situation.

The Boston and Maine Railroad considered the flood damage the last straw, and announced in August that passenger service in and out of Antrim would not be restored. This announcement was not particularly upsetting to the citizens, as they had already learned to cope with the declining service over the last few years. In July the Whitney Bus Company of Hillsboro had petitioned to run buses between Concord and Peterborough. The advantage to Antrim was that the bus came right through the center of town, eliminating the need of taxi service from the depot.

Now that the country seemed to be pulling out of the depression people began to spend money. If you bought a new car, it made the paper. Summer traffic through the town was heavier than ever before, and one Sunday afternoon between five and six o'clock someone on Concord Street counted 124 passing cars.

There was another disaster in March—the Waumbek fire. It was discovered at three o'clock in the morning and Alice Cuddihy, one of the owners, had to drive (scantily clad, according to *The Antrim Reporter*) all the way down the lake road to Alfred Holt's (now Richard Davis's) to call Central to notify the fire department. The building was a total loss, valued at $8,000-$10,000. This large summer inn on the shores of Gregg Lake was of Victorian design, with a mansard roof and a large porch. It had started out as a bowling alley until around 1912 John Cuddihy bought it and converted it to an inn. The Cuddihys did rebuild after the fire, but summer boarding houses were on the wane, as people began to show a preference for renting small cottages on the lake.

It was this summer that Camp Birchmere opened for its first season. Although the facilities were the same as had been used by Greggmere, the management and campers were all new. These girls came from Westchester County, New York.

In September the water in Gregg Lake was unusually low, revealing rocks that had never been seen before, and prompting a lady from Boston (who had previously enjoyed camping on Gregg Lake, considering it a beauteous spot) to write a letter to *The Antrim Reporter* denouncing the lake as a quagmire brought about by the demands of the local mills. A rebuttal by Mrs. Rachel Caughey of the Center put the problem into perspective; with her special way of getting at true values, she stressed that the water (of Gregg Lake and Great Brook) provided a living for the town. Later, Elton Ellis, for many years a summer resident of White Birch Point, wrote the paper stressing that the drought of 1936 was the worst ever, but no worse at Gregg Lake than anywhere else. He insisted that the water was not unhealthful, and still fine for bathing on *his* side of the lake.

The stone wall bounding the northern section of the Maplewood Cemetery was built in April by Caughey & Pratt, contractors. This firm, headed by G.H. Caughey and H.B. Pratt, was responsible for some fine construction in Antrim and surrounding towns for the better part of two decades. The quality of craftsmanship can still be observed in such places as the bridge in Bennington village, the stone walls at the Verney farm in Bennington, Nubanusit Park in Peterborough, and the North Branch cemetery, as well as dams and buildings. Some of the stone workers were Italians whose ancestors had brought with them these artisan skills.

The bandstand on Concord Street was moved to the ball grounds in August. It had already shown signs of old age, and the broken lattice work around the bottom provided good places for games of hide and seek. The removal did not do it any good, and eventually it succumbed to the rough treatment of weather and overactive children. During the first part of the decade, however, it had provided a fine showcase for George Warren and the Antrim Band.

The total assessment of the town in 1936 was $1,121,104. This included 69 horses and 226 cows.

In June the first eighth grade graduation was held at the Presbyterian Church. Although the twenty-six graduates (from the North Branch, Center and Village schools) were seated on the stage in the vestry, the partition was opened to include the sanctuary for seating the unexpectedly large audience.

On the Fourth of July Henry Cutter finally won the three-mile race, after having come in second each of the three prior years.

A violent storm followed an unusually hot spell in July. Trees were uprooted, antennae knocked down, and gardens damaged. On this night the town also lost a valuable citizen, Hiram Eldredge, the editor of *The Antrim Reporter*. He had been at work as usual that day, and after taking his regular afternoon break with the other men who worked in the vicinity of the Barrett block (now Jackson's), he was suddenly taken ill, and died a few hours later. He had served the community as town clerk and school board member, and had been an active member of the IOOF and the Methodist church. As motor vehicle examiner he administered the driver's tests in his deep soothing voice, giving the nervous drivers assurance. Stopping and starting again on Depot Street hill had dire possibilities, but Mr. Eldredge never exhibited alarm. Since 1892 he had provided a weekly record of life in Antrim, which has been an invaluable resource to the writers of this book, and an immeasurable contribution to the town.

It was also this year that—according to the paper—everyone went to Peterborough to see the movie, *Country Doctor*, featuring the Dionne quintuplets. These babies had captured hearts all over the world, and Antrim was worldly in this respect.

Governor Francis Murphy attended the fifth annual flower show, and Prince Alexi Toumanoff of Hancock, an exile of the Russian Revolution, spoke at the Woman's Club guest night.

Site of the Saturday Night Serenade

In November the Presbyterians held a public reception for their new minister, William McNair Kittredge, and his wife. Also in November was the annual Armistice Ball, sponsored by the Legion. The state commander came to lead the grand march, which was followed by an impressive sounding of "Taps" at eleven o'clock. Music for dancing was furnished by ZaZa Ludwig and his orchestra, who operated out of the Manchester area. Any Legion post in the state that was able to sign up this band for any of their dances considered itself lucky, for ZaZa knew how to turn an ordinary dance into an unforgettable party. He made a point of getting to know all the local officers and wives by their personalities so that he could call them by name from the bandstand and make reference to something personal that had meaning for all the in-crowd. It is ironic that this man who had such a gift for entertainment and brought pleasure into so many lives had the need to take his own life a couple of decades later.

Time Marches On

1937 The year 1937 had very little unusual weather of any kind, but it proved to be only the lull before the greatest storm of all time which came the next year. But without such knowledge the town welcomed the absence of extreme cold, blizzards, floods, and droughts as a well deserved hiatus. The only local disaster that could be attributed to weather conditions occurred in September, when lightning struck Charlie White's huge barn in East Antrim, causing an $11,000 loss

It was a year of unusual sickness, however. In addition to the usual childhood epidemics and appendicitis there were cases of scarlet fever and diphtheria. It was not unusual for deaths from pneumonia to occur in this decade before the widespread use of miracle drugs came about. The annual chicken pie supper at the Presbyterian church on Washington's birthday had to be canceled because of illness, and only very dire circumstances have ever caused the cancellation of this event throughout the years. The Washington Masquerade Ball was carried out, and in spite of the physical condition of many residents it was deemed a success.

There were several innovations in the entertainment field that year, including dancing parties and recitals, for and by the pupils of Isobel MacGangler, popularly known as "Miss Mac." This energetic lady, although not a resident, held forth in the town hall with weekly lessons in tap and ballroom dancing, and large numbers of children (with and without talent) from Antrim and surrounding towns flocked to her classes. Some were undoubtedly being pushed by ambitious mothers, as the miracle of Shirley Temple's success was still a source of inspiration. Be that as it may, Miss Mac's pupils offered something refreshingly new in local entertainment.

"Jimmie and Dick," a singing cowboy duo heard daily over radio station WEEI in Boston, appeared for the first time on the Antrim Town Hall stage in conjunction with a local amateur show. In their several appearances during the next few years, they always drew a large and enthusiastic audience.

One of the most extensive and expensive improvements since the beginning of the depression was voted at town meeting, when $10,000 was approved to lay new water pipes along Main Street, from Elm Street to Aiken Street. This was achieved in June, efficiently and expertly, and included installation of larger hydrants. Other town improvements approved were the rebuilding of the Concord Street sidewalk and hard-surfacing of the East Antrim Road (now Elm Avenue) from Route 202 to Charlie White's farm.

At the annual school meeting it was decided to sell the East Antrim school at auction. Of more importance to the education of the community was the acceptance, after years of denial, of a commercial course in the high school. Opponents said a high school should not be a vocational training ground, and that students of this age still needed to be exposed to the basic mental training found in the classics: Latin, algebra, physics, and other subjects of this nature. Since the institution of the commercial course, however, it is doubtful that anyone has been able to find any fault with the program. In addition to the bookkeeping and stenography that allowed many to take a responsible position upon graduation from high school, typing was to prove an indispensable skill for those going on to college.

New business ventures flourished this year. The general store, changing names and management frequently during the decade, became known as Coolidge and Raleigh, a part of the Red and White chain. In Clinton two new stores opened: Edwards' General Store, with restaurant, at the bridge over Great Brook (now the summer residence of the Gregorys), and the Log Cabin at the Butterfield farm. Edwards' store was open year-round, and changed hands several times until it ceased being a commercial venture and finally became a family home. It had been not only a convenience for people in that area, but a popular meeting place. The Log Cabin was open only during the summer, and featured home-made ice cream, a product of the Guernsey herd kept by Byron Butterfield.

The Public Service Company of New Hampshire took over the section of the town hall block that had been inhabited previously by Sadie Lane and her Notions, and remodeled it into a display room. This company also gave free demonstrations in cooking on electric stoves, held in March at the Baptist church. How far we had come since the days of 1932! Not only could we afford to heat our homes comfortably, but now we all had the prerogative of cooking over electric burners.

The biggest change in town of a commercial venture—because it altered the appearance of the very center of the Village—was construction of the Texaco filling station on Concord Street, where the bandstand had been. The field was leveled, and four maple trees were taken down which, combined with the nature of the building itself, made this busy corner take on a modern, almost urban look. Sidewalk engineers of all ages had something to keep them interested for several weeks. The franchise was purchased by two young men from Peterborough, Wallace "Pete" Flood and Lawrence "Tink" Carll. Pete later served the town as chief of police and as selectman.

A Men's Club was formed in October with forty members and the Reverend Ralph H. Tibbals as president. The Boy Scouts were trying to interest parents in starting a Cub Scout Pack. As enthusiasm grew for new organizations, some of the older ones began to show signs of needing a rest. The Garden Club was content to have its Flower Show in the Baptist church vestry instead of the town hall, and the Legion did not promote as many activities on the Fourth of July as formerly. There was a vesper service on the Fourth on Meeting House hill, attracting 200, sparked perhaps by the 160th birthday of the town.

A new dimension was added to the combined church observances of Easter and Christmas. It was the custom to have a choir concert in the evening for both of these festivities, but this year the addition of sanctuary plays enhanced both occasions. Easter night the fine play, *Thy Kingdom Come*, was presented at the Presbyterian church, with Byron Butterfield, Ross Roberts, and Archie Swett playing the parts of three Roman soldiers who had second thoughts about the crucifixion. On Christmas Sunday night at the Baptist church the congregation saw the performances, "Childe Jesus," and, "Jeanette Isabella," two musical plays. This effective introduction of drama was brought about by Mrs. Elizabeth Felker, the public school music teacher and organist at the Baptist church.

Two venerable townsfolk died within two weeks' time. Mrs. Elizabeth Buckminster at ninety-six was the town's oldest citizen. She was the daughter of the Reverend William Hurlin. Edward Thompson, ninety-one, was the holder of the coveted Boston Post gold-headed cane, given by that newspaper to the oldest man in all communities. (Notice that it was *not* given to the oldest citizen!) In addition to having edited the *Antrim Home News* during the 1880s, Ed Thompson was also an inventor, as noted earlier in this chronology.

The winter months of 1938 brought some -30° weather, but this did not deter the citizens from going to the town hall to hear Jimmy and Dick, who appeared no fewer than three times that season. At one performance which featured local amateurs the winner was young Dick Noyes of Peterborough, who shortly thereafter launched a professional career as one of the red-headed boys in the original cast of *Life with Father,* one of Broadway's longest running plays.

Bowling enthusiasts went to Keene one night a week during the winter where the two teams of "Wisell's Whizzers" and "Clitz's Ritzes" engaged in stiff competition. In addition to these diversions, people were attending the annuals: the Senior Class play, Washington Birthday dinner and ball, and FDR's birthday card party, not to mention staying home and listening to Edgar Bergen and Charlie McCarthy on Sunday night radio.

Five articles in the town warrant asked for appropriations to hard-surface streets and roads in the Village, East Antrim, and North Branch, and all motions were passed. The largest amount raised during town meeting that year was $4,000 to publish a revised History of Antrim (one wonders what historical events were to undergo change) in one or two volumes. Nothing appeared in print until nearly thirty years later when the Tibbals *Genealogy* was published in one volume.

The precinct was awarded $6,200 for relaying cast iron pipe in two parts of the Village: one, a section of North Main Street, and two, an area encompassing the southern end of Highland Avenue and nearby sections of Pleasant and High Streets.

At the school meeting it was voted to hire a part-time nurse for $100 a year. This article had been voted down in the past. All of these improvements prompted the East Antrim correspondent to report,

This neighborhood was well represented at town meeting—and did the people vote away the money! We'll say!

A much-needed community calendar was instituted in May, posted on the bulletin board by the town hall, and published weekly in *The Antrim Reporter*. Groups who contributed announcements of their activities to this clearing-house included the churches and their subsidiary organizations; the Garden Club; Mt. Crotched Encampment; the IOOF and the Rebekahs; the American Legion, its Auxiliary and the Sons of the Legion; the Grange; the DAR; the Boy Scouts; the Rod and Gun Club; the Woman's Club; the Women's Relief Corps; the WCTU; the North Branch Ladies Home Circle; organizational boards such as the selectmen, school board, and cemetery associations; and the Chamber of Commerce and Men's Civic Club. The last group, one of the newest to be formed, was probably responsible for the promotion of the Community Calendar since the members were still riding high on a crest of enthusiasm which resulted in numerous activities during the year. Unfortunately, the project was short-lived, and the calendar was discontinued a year later.

The churches took part in the international World Day of Prayer, a custom which has prevailed ever since. But the church event which far out-shone all others in 1938 was the Presbyterian sesquicentennial observance of the founding of the church in Antrim. The three-day affair was opened on July 31 at 6:45 p.m. by tolling the Paul Revere bell 150 times. The bell, bought in 1816 for $400, is said to weigh 1,208 pounds. This dramatic opening was followed by a story pageant at eight o'clock in the church. Other activities during the following days included a song service on Meeting House Hill, a supper served by the ladies of the Baptist church, and a tea in the Presbyterian ladies' parlor, when a plate belonging to Polly Aiken was on display.

Town changes were more institutional than physical. Dr. John Doyle, a general practitioner, opened his office next to the library, just two houses below Dr. Guy Tibbetts, who had been Antrim's only doctor for many years. *The Antrim Reporter* was leased to Warren Tourtellot of Baldwinsville, Massachusetts, and Vic Dahl, who had carried on the work of the newspaper since the death of Mr. Eldredge, went elsewhere to work. This move deprived the Boy Scouts of a much-admired leader.

Smithholm at the Branch indulged in some considerable building expansion in the spring, and Butcher's store became a teen-age hangout with the institution of a new soda fountain, booths, and a juke-box. Walt Butcher also boasted that he had the only neon sign in town.

With the Great Depression finally a thing of the past people suddenly became aware that the clouds of war not only had been gathering in other parts of the world, but were reaching alarming proportions. In February, the West Hillsboro County Minister's Association adopted a resolution to be sent to President Roosevelt concerning opposition to war with Japan. In part it said, "We have no quarrel with the Japanese people, and we are confident that we have nothing to fear from them," and was signed by the Reverend Tibbals of the Baptist church, and the Reverend John W. Logan of the Center Congregational church, officers of the organization.

In March, the Legion and Auxiliary took part in a statewide mobilization test. The evening call came at seven o'clock, and by 7:25 thirty-one members were ready for duty, as were Dr. Tibbetts, Nurse Mary Griffin, and the Boy Scouts, who happened to be meeting in the fire house at that time.

No one could have guessed that this mobilization training might be put to use for a much different purpose than a sudden invasion by a foreign power, and the records don't show whether the training was used to advantage the following September.

Stormy Weather

On late Saturday afternoon, September 17, it started to rain in a nice autumnal way, and continued off and on through Sunday and Monday. By Tuesday, however, it was evident that the water was rising rapidly, and threatened to compete with the flood of 1936 in damage. On Wednesday it was still raining, school was closed, and the water was over the roads connecting Antrim with other towns. Without warning a ferocious hurricane struck the area late in the afternoon. To those who have never witnessed such a storm it is impossible to explain the feeling of panic and helplessness that everyone experienced. But in a few hours the wind had subsided, leaving a stunned and battered community. This first-hand account from the issue of September 22 (a few days late in actual appearance) of *The Antrim Reporter* tells it as it really was:

HURRICANE AND FLOOD RAISE HAVOC IN ANTRIM
COMMUNICATION CUT OFF FROM OUTSIDE WORLD:
ALL ROADS WERE CLOSED
Rising flood waters and a howling hurricane that far surpassed any storm in the history of this town, completely isolated Antrim from the outside world for two days and nights. Flood water far above the mark

The Big Blow . . . 1938 hurricane

of the flood of '36, washed out some roads and covered others to such an extent that they were impassable. When the hurricane struck, trees and light and telephone poles were uprooted and thrown about like match sticks and when the storm had passed a network of interwoven tree trunks, branches, poles and wires completely blocked every road in town.

The force of the hurricane at its height was unbelievable, huge trees toppled like ten-pins, buildings were crushed like egg shells, and boards, slates, roof and branches were tossed about as if thrown by gigantic hands. Sheets of tin from roofs were scaled through the air with enough force to decapitate a person and daylight found these sheets of metal blown to incredible distances and in some instances hung in tree tops forty feet above the ground.

Because of the impassable roads, it was impossible to receive food supplies until Friday and there was a shortage of bread and the meat supply ran low. Fortunately, the water supply was all right at all times. Mail service was cut off and there were no newspapers available, which, with the loss of radio and telephone communication left Antrim without contact with any other community. As in all cases of this kind, rumors ran wildly about, but as is also usually true, most of them proved to be greatly exaggerated or absolutely false.

Practically every able bodied man and boy in Antrim went to work to clear the streets of debris left by the storm and by Thursday noon, nearly every street was passable. A path the width of an automobile was first chopped clear and later the whole road was cleared. Washouts in the road were filled wherever possible and by Friday morning it was possible to drive to Keene and Hillsboro through North Branch. Although passable now, these roads will not be in the best of condition for quite some time.

Miraculously no one was seriously hurt, and the bright sunshine on Thursday morning found everyone out viewing the carnage, eager for news, and happy to be alive. Aesthetically the greatest damage to the town was the loss of the maple trees along Main Street.

On Tuesday, as the river was rapidly rising, Lester and Edith Hill brought their brand new daughter, Alice May, home from the hospital in Concord. They just made it before the West Henniker bridge became impassable. Imagine their consternation on Wednesday afternoon when the powerful winds blew the chimney off their house on Concord Street. Assuming that this made using the stove impossible, they had no way to heat the baby's bottle, and in those days no one would dream of giving a 12-day-old baby cold milk. So Edith, although frightened into near panic by the sight of the swaying trees in the school yard crossed the street, followed pioneer instincts and heated the bottle over the flame from a candle.

Barbara Butterfield, a student at Keene Normal School, became frightened by the news of the flood and decided the best place for her was home in Antrim. She hitched a ride to the corner of Routes 9 and 31, where the family picked her up and brought her home to the Butterfield farm. No sooner was she home than the hurricane struck. In 1970, a stranger drove into the yard at the farm, and asked the owner, Byron Butterfield, if he had a red-headed daughter. Byron answered, "No, but I have a red-headed sister who's young enough to be my daughter." "Well," said the stranger, "during the hurricane in 1938 I gave a ride to a girl with red hair who was coming from Keene Normal to this farm. I dropped her off at the corner of Route 31, and I just wondered if she got home all right." So firmly implanted in people's minds were the events of the day that a man's conscience was pricked 32 years later!

On Friday (school was back in session) an airplane flew over and dropped newspapers, giving Antrim its first real information about what had happened to the rest of New England. Local merchant Ben Butterfield drove to Bennington via High Street, past the Highlands and A.J. Pierce's home (both now owned by the Verney family) and left his car on the west side of the much-damaged bridge in the middle of Bennington. As the river had now subsided he was able to walk across to the east side where he borrowed a car and drove to Wilton, bringing back bread to a town that was far from starving, but certainly discommoded in its eating habits.

Although many citizens suffered financial loss in the devastation of buildings and standing timber, they felt almost lucky when they learned that Peterborough had been struck not only by flood and hurricane, but by a disastrous fire which wiped out much of lower Main Street. Some local citizens had unfortunately been stranded there at the time of the storm.

On September 29 *The Antrim Reporter* carried this announcement:

TOWN APPRECIATES WORK OF VOLUNTEERS

The Board of Selectmen, on behalf of the citizens, wish to sincerely thank all those who so generously offered their services on Thursday morning in the work of clearing away the debris caused by the hurricane of Wednesday evening. Your work is greatly appreciated.

The town is anxious to reimburse these men for their services and, as the Road Agent has not kept any record of those who did volunteer, if they will get in touch with Mr. Perkins he will see that they are compensated for their work.

James I. Patterson
Alfred G. Holt
Hugh M. Graham, Selectmen

Now that the initial clearing away had been accomplished, the town along with the rest of the state, turned to the more serious job of salvaging timber. Governor Murphy urged owners not to dispose of their timber until a practical plan could be worked out with the federal government, yet take great precaution against fires.

After a short time, the word came through that woodlot owners must take care of fallen and leaning timber immediately if they wished any money from it, and that federally financed Civilian Conservation Corps workers would be available. Subsequently, logging companies from Maine sent men into the area to assist with the work, and the men boarded in different places around Antrim. The work kept them here for the better part of a year. Obviously, this sudden importation of so many men, some of them single, aroused some excitement among the local girls.

The federal government, after several months of assessing the disaster and means of recovery, agreed to pay land owners four dollars an acre (up to 15 acres) for slash disposal. This consisted of burning stumps and the judicious scattering of small brush necessary to eliminate the danger of forest fires. A similarity must have been noted between this solution to our problem and that which involved paying midwest farmers for not harvesting their crops.

In the wake of the disaster the Legion announced an Emergency Mobilization call of six short blasts on the fire whistle, to be repeated in fifteen minutes. Upon hearing it all members should report to the Legion Hall. The Washington Bicentennial Committee offered to replace some of the trees on Main Street, using money left from the activities in 1932.

By the beginning of 1939 the timber salvage operation was in full swing. Steele Pond and Pierce Lake were used for storage, and access to the latter was through the property of Warren Wheeler (now Charles Rabideau's) where the logs rolling down the hill into the lake were described as an impressive sight. Bridge repair went on throughout the year; some of the more seriously damaged ones were the Estey bridge at North Branch, and the West Street and Concord Street bridges.

Although town water was reported to have been unsullied by the flood, several cases of typhoid fever required hospitalization in the following months. This may have been mere coincidence, as there was an unusual amount of sickness during the winter. Pneumonia caused a number of deaths.

The coming of spring gave everyone the usual lift. Turning their backs on the aftermath of the hurricane and a winter of severe illness, the people began looking for new forms of enjoyment. The big thing this year was the World's Fair in New York, and many fortunate local citizens spent a few days there. The trylon and perisphere symbol was seen in every imaginable manifestation, including a recipe for dessert.

The second annual High School Junior Prom was moderately successful, but was overshadowed by a Field Day in which the Junior and Senior High Schools of Hancock, Bennington, and Hillsboro competed with Antrim in track events. The resignation of Headmaster Chaffee was received with mixed emotions. He had accomplished the two things for which he had been appointed fourteen years ago: the raising of academic standards and the establishment of rigid discipline. But no one man can be all things, and families of students who dropped out of school because they felt it was meaningless and unbearable were quick to blame the headmaster for deficiencies that were not entirely his fault. Mr. and Mrs. Chaffee were honored at a reception held at the Baptist church by their many friends for their contributions to school and church.

After Dr. Doyle opened his office (the preceding year) Dr. Guy Tibbetts took a much deserved rest, spending the winter in Florida. Upon his return, however, he announced that he would be unable to resume his practice, and six weeks later, on June 2, he died. The community felt the loss deeply, knowing that the citizens had been fortunate to be served for so many years by so skilled and dedicated a doctor. A graduate of Tufts Medical School, he served in the Army Medical Corps during World War I, and was one of a thousand American doctors loaned to the British government. In December, 1918, he was decorated with the Distinguished Service Cross at Buckingham Palace by King George V. Following the war he began practice in Bennington, but after a few years he opened his office on Main Street in Antrim, across from the general store, where he remained until his death. A military funeral was held at the Baptist church, and businesses and schools were closed to allow everyone to attend. This man who had gone about his work so quietly had endeared himself to all.

This spring the Boy Scouts were rejuvenated under the expert leadership of William Holleran, who came from Berlin, New Hampshire. Later in the year the Girl Scouts reorganized, and for the first time in five years had an active troop.

An unusually dry spring and summer prompted the precinct officials to make regulations restricting the use of water from April 15 to November 1. To add to the problem the woods were still far from clean of hurricane debris, making the danger of fire a real threat. A fire did break out early one morning at the Rob Munhall farm over East. There was an auction planned there for that day, and although the barn burned flat and smouldered all day, the house and furnishings were saved, and the auction went on as scheduled.

Fair enthusiasts were happy when it was announced that the Hopkinton Fair would be held as usual, despite extensive hurricane damage. Antrim was represented at the annual Craftsmen's Fair at the University of New Hampshire by Arthur Cunningham, who set up a miniature shop in the field house and demonstrated making his specialty, three-legged fireplace stools. He paid tribute to the League of New Hampshire Arts and Crafts for encouraging artisans like himself to work with their hands, and providing a marketplace for their products.

In August a new doctor opened his office in the Maplehurst Inn, but by October he was in the hospital with a nervous breakdown. Dr. John Doyle, however, had made a successful breakthrough into the community, and he was soon joined by Dr. Montfort Haslam. Although not working together in the way of today's doctors, as Dr. Haslam's office was on the corner of Grove and Main Streets, they nevertheless combined their efforts to become a satisfactory replacement for Dr. Tibbetts. The opening of the "Havarest" convalescent home late in the year gave the town an extra measure of health security. Located in the V between North Main Street and Clinton Road, the home was operated by Mildred Mallory, R.N.

The Pirates of Penzance was presented September 1 at the town hall for the benefit of the Senior Class to an audience of four hundred. Advertised as the Community Gilbert and Sullivan Company of Antrim, the cast and crew of nearly fifty were summer and year-round residents of Antrim and surrounding towns and unfortunately this was the one and only performance under this title. Much of the success was due to the enthusiasm of director Richard K. Winslow, a senior at Wesleyan University, who was carrying on a family tradition of organizing and promoting musical activities in Antrim.

With a new headmaster, William Ramsden, the High School enjoyed new experiences, not the least of which was a more relaxed atmosphere. The annual picnic at Mescilbrooks shore at Gregg Lake was bigger and better than ever, and was followed a few weeks later by an Outing Club steak roast on Holt's Hill. Movies were used frequently for educational purposes, and guest speakers were invited for assemblies. One of the most dynamic of these was the Reverend William Turkington, who was conducting a series of meetings at the Baptist church. Evangelical in style, his singing and trumpet playing and familiarity with teenage slanguage and concerns nearly brought down the old schoolhouse.

With a few new dwelling houses going up around town, and enough available work to bring in several new citizens, the decade which had imposed hardship on the town came to an end, leaving people in an optimistic frame of mind. Despite the warning signals from Europe, the forties promised to be a time of prosperity for Antrim.

WAR AND PEACE

ALTHOUGH THE SHADOW of a world at war hung over Antrim and the country in general at the start of the fourth decade of the twentieth century, life went along serenely enough. The airplanes which were to play a major role for the first time in any war were more and more in evidence, and the young granddaughter of James Ashford, Carolyn Forehand, received her pilot's license at age sixteen in February, 1940. The far reaching social legislation of the Roosevelt administration surfaced in Antrim in the same month when food stamps were issued to those in need.

At the local level, the Antrim Outing Club held a winter carnival on Holt's Hill. The skating events had to be canceled because of the poor condition of the ice, but the skiing was good in March, and the downhill racing and slalom runs were enjoyed without benefit of such effete aids as rope tows and T bars. As usual, the affair was topped off with a bounteous supper at the Presbyterian church, followed by a carnival ball.

At town meeting, it was voted to name the old road leading from the present Mescilbrooks farm to Rablin's, Whiton Road, in honor of Dr. Whiton, who built the original part of his house (now known as the Bass farm) in 1812.

In April, the census taker came in for his customary share of criticism. There was much indignation over the scope of the questions to be asked, the general feeling being that the details were far too intimate, and some people even went so far as to wonder if "the United States was still a democracy?" Rugged individualists, they resented any sign of governmental paternalism, and later in the year, as the presidential election approached, John B. Jameson, a lifelong Democrat, shifted his allegiance to Wendell Willkie, noting "with growing apprehension the continued encroachment of the government on the rights of states and individuals."

On the other hand, there were signs that children were about to become less rugged. For the first time, the school board sought transportation for the students of the village and North Branch schools. Since then, busing has become an accepted necessity in these rural areas and is not a subject of controversy. Today, school prayers have been banned by the Supreme Court, but in 1940 the townspeople rejoiced when the court upheld a ruling that school children should pledge allegiance to the flag of the United States.

The country was slowly recovering from the Great Depression which had haunted it for a decade, but there were some lingering effects as late as 1940. The town voted to enlist the aid of the Work Progress Administration, Roosevelt's answer to unemployment, in the preparation of a tax map of the town. It also granted a four percent discount to all who paid their taxes within thirty days. It then nullified these austerity measures by authorizing a profligate $500 for police and public health protection in anticipation of the increased problems that might arise if war were declared.

In October there was cause to worry. One hundred and three Antrim men registered for the draft under the new Selective Service Act. The next month saw the re-election of Roosevelt for an unprecedented third term, much to the annoyance of the majority of Antrim voters, who preferred Wendell Willkie. They did manage to defeat a motion to allow the sale of liquor in the town.

At the close of the year, a most unusual phenomenon occurred in the form of two earthquakes within five days. The first was felt on December 20; four days later, the second shock was more severe, knocking canned goods from the shelves.

Then came 1941, a year when Antrim in common with other towns *1941* all over the country held its breath, waiting for the sword of Damocles to fall on its head. As nothing of the sort happened early in the year, it went about business as usual, holding the town meeting in March, and agreeing to purchase a stretch of shore land at Gregg Lake for no more than one hundred dollars to be used for a public beach. For twenty or more years, this was the only town beach, but it has since been replaced by the more adequate beach farther up the road.

Two notable and disastrous fires occurred in the late spring of 1941. In March, the Colby homestead (now Tenney's) on Depot Street was gutted by fire. All the members of the Chamberlain family then occupying the house escaped safely, but one son, Lyman, returned in an effort to save some of the household goods, and was trapped by the flames. He died only a few days before he was to have been inducted into the army.

On June 10, the Waumbek Inn at Gregg Lake caught fire and was destroyed. An earlier building on the same site had burned in 1936. The firemen battled herocially to prevent the high winds from spreading the fire to nearby woods, already dangerously dry. One guest at the Inn was killed by the blaze.

Over the years, public transportation in and out of Antrim had been dependent chiefly on the railroad, which Antrimites felt had badly let them down. Now a new bus service, Granite Stages, announced that it would run three trips a day from Peterborough to Hillsboro via Antrim. With gas and tire rationing imminent, this service proved to be a godsend as long as it lasted.

In December the whole country received the shock it had long been dreading: a declaration of war, precipitated by the attack on Pearl Harbor. At once, preparations began for the defense of the town. First aid classes were started under the direction of Dr. John Doyle and some of the local nurses. The air raid alarm signal was to be fourteen blasts of the siren, twice in succession, repeated every thirty minutes. An air raid wardens' school commenced at the town hall. Whatever was to come, Antrim wanted to be ready.

The Home Front

1942   Early in January, 1942, a Red Cross roll call in Antrim showed one hundred and seventy-two members. (The total population of the town including children was in the vicinity of eleven hundred.) One hundred and forty-nine persons attended the air raid wardens' school. Those who eventually were appointed wardens were fingerprinted for purposes of identification in case of a catastrophe. An inventory of cots available in the town was made, in case Antrim might have to house refugees from bombed cities some day. A tire rationing board, including Antrim and fourteen other towns, was set up in Peterborough.

Antrim High School seniors gave up their cherished class trip to

Washington, D.C., and decided to donate funds already accumulated for the trip to some worthy war cause. The presidential proclamation decreeing war time for the whole country was accepted without a murmur, unlike daylight saving time, which was thought of as arbitrary meddling with the natural rhythm of the sun. Even the news that the state legislature was about to levy a head tax on all adults produced no shock waves. The crisis of the war had united the town and the country.

The Antrim Garage was forced out of business by the war after operating twenty-seven years. Once again, fuel for home heating was in short supply, and owners of wood lots, particularly those whose lots still had trees felled by the 1938 hurricane, were urged to register them with the county agent. Many houses heated by coal or oil were converted back to wood.

It was a cold winter. Even the forsythia refused to bloom. Junius Hanchett at the Center, who had over a hundred forsythia bushes in his yard, explained that the buds were unable to endure the −20° temperatures of the frigid months of January and February.

In March, the old Silk Mill on Grove Street was sold by H.E. Wilson to a Mr. O'Leary of Lambeth Products, Inc. This mill was formerly used by Harold Kelsea, whose son built Mr. Wilson's house (now H. Stuart Hills'), the big granite foundation slabs coming from the old Federated Church in East Antrim. The pews from the church were broken up and used to make the panelling in the Silk Mill.

Despite the war, the custom of celebrating May Day was observed. Few of today's children may know about May baskets, but in 1942 children were still lovingly making them and delivering them to the homes of their favorite people. The accepted practice was to sneak onto the porch, hang the basket on the doorknob, ring the bell, and then run and hide. Anonymity was sometimes nullified by a signed note hidden in the basket.

The excitement of May Day for the children was exceeded only by the excitement of the first blackout test for the adults on May 9. Since the fire siren signal could not be heard at the Branch, the bell at Smithholm (now David's Inn) was rung for two minutes to alert the neighborhood. Air raid wardens made their appointed rounds, checking for any infractions, and everyone wondered if a real raid would ever happen.

By late May, sugar and gas rationing were in full force. In June, the rubber shortage having become acute, everyone was asked to turn in all scrap rubber to the nearest filling station. Piles of rubber items, including inner tubes, rubber boots, rubber floor mats, raincoats, bathing caps, jar rubbers, hot water bottles, dish drainers, sink stoppers, rubber heels, and rubber gloves accumulated as the patriotic townspeople responded to the call.

By late fall in 1942, the news was concerned almost exclusively with the war, which at that time was not going well for the United States. The only exception to this preoccupation was the satisfaction felt around town on hearing that a former Antrim man, Arthur N. Harriman (father of Mrs. Ralph Whittemore) had been elected mayor of New Bedford, Massachusetts, an office he was to hold for four terms. Otherwise there were few bright spots. Fuel rationing was instituted in October. The J.P. Nazers had five sons in the service to worry about. In December, the town service flag was dedicated with forty-six stars. Everyone prayed for the safety of "the boys."

In addition to air raid wardens, there were many other volunteers, some of whom put in long hours as airplane spotters. The first spotting post, established in 1942, was in the field above G.H. Caughey's (now Donatello's), managed jointly by Theodore Caughey, Gertrude Thornton, and Guy Clark under the sponsorship of the American Legion. Initially, Mr. Caughey's telephone was used through a window in his house, but eventually a shelter was built, containing its own phone and a wood stove for warmth. History does not record the sighting of any enemy planes, but one night the spotters were treated to the spectacle of a lovely double rainbow.

1943   During 1943, the spotters were moved to a location on the ball field on West Street. Here a sumptuous shelter was built, measuring eight by ten feet, shingled on the outside, and surmounted by a glassed-in cupola. Boy Scouts arrived each morning at six to start the fire and man the post for the first two hours before school. Women took over for the daytime, and men relieved them until midnight. The post was not manned (or womanned) between the hours of midnight and six. Enemy planes courteously stayed away then as well as for the rest of the twenty-four hours.

Early in the fall of 1943, the country realized that many of the long hours put in by the spotters were in fact fruitless, and might better be spent in more productive war work. In October the watching time was cut from eighteen hours to a mere four and a half, from one in the afternoon to five thirty.

The winter of 1943 was even colder than usual, putting a great strain on the scarce supply of fuel. The Congregational Church was closed in an effort to save fuel, and Sunday services were held in members' homes. By February, the thermometer registered a record 35° to 40° below zero, and for a while the schools were closed.

October saw an event Antrim had been dreading ever since the start of the war. A memorial service was held for Paul Prescott, the first of Antrim's men to be killed in action. He had been reported as missing in June. Everyone hoped that he was merely wounded or taken prisoner, but eventually it was learned that he had died and been buried in Paris. Antrim mourned, and the name of the American Legion Post was changed to Myers-Prescott.

There was more bad news in 1944. Roger C. Hill died of wounds *1944* received in the Italian campaign. Lieutenant Albert Poor died when his plane crashed over the Caribbean. Fred Butler (Elliott) was reported missing in action over France. (Freddie was for a while a prisoner of war, but came home safely, and participated in the Korean war.)

Despite the bad personal items, the overall tide of the war had finally turned in favor of the Allies. This was good news for the home folks, and so also was the fact that Tasker's store (in Hillsboro) finally had rubbers for sale. These may have been synthetic, but at that point any kind of waterproof footwear looked good.

Even though the town was preoccupied with the war, certain aspects of life went on as usual. The Public Service Office, once located in the small building at the top of Goodell's hill (now the laundromat), was consolidated with that of Hillsboro, although the office remained in the town hall building for two more years. In the November presidential election, the town voted both Republican (and lost), and dry once again. A World War II honor roll was dedicated on Armistice Day — a temporary memorial, located on the lawn of Maplehurst Inn.

By 1945, the war was noticeably winding down, and life was return- *1945* ing to normal in Antrim. Busing of school children was becoming an accepted way of life, although it was an idea still opposed by some. At town meeting, it was voted "after much oratory" to provide transportation for the children from Clinton.

At the same meeting, the town appointed a committee to consider the feasibility of annexing Antrim to Cheshire rather than Hillsboro County. The rationale for this was that Cheshire County had fewer large cities (Keene) than Hillsboro County (Nashua and Manchester), and the county tax rate would therefore be lower. In retrospect, it seems like sound reasoning, but since the goal was never accomplished, one can only suppose it was legally impossible under state law. However, William Hurlin, Antrim's representative to the state legislature, promised to do all he could to eradicate the triplicate services inherent in the cumbersome division of government into state, county, and local rule.

Franklin Roosevelt's fourth term in office had barely begun when he died in April, 1945. Republican strongholds such as Antrim never looked with favor on his long tenure, and local papers during the last days of the war had been publishing a series of editorials and letters-to-the-editor critical of his administration, sometimes to the disgust of individual servicemen, who replied in defense of their commander-in-chief. It does seem strange, however, that there was no mention of his death in the paper at that time. In contrast to the public mourning at McKinley's assassination, there was no local public expression of grief in Antrim. What the people felt about his successor, Harry Truman, is also unrecorded.

Both VE and VJ days were celebrated, however, with special afternoon union services at the town hall, including parades featuring Girl Scouts and Brownies marching in V formation, the inevitable double header soft ball games, and free dances at the town hall in the evening. It was not as lavish and spontaneous a demonstration as the one held at the end of World War I, but the length and universality of this war no doubt made it difficult to realize that it was finally over.

Some community projects directly related to the war were still being carried on. Fourteen hundred pounds of used clothing were collected to send to the hard-hit Europeans. The newly reactivated Rod and Gun Club issued free membership cards to all servicemen. American Legion men volunteered to help wives of absent servicemen with the obstinate mechanics of furnaces and storm windows, hoping thereby to prevent many torn fingernails and mashed thumbs.

The need to prevent future wars is never more acutely felt than at the end of one that has been long and destructive. In November, students from Antrim High School attended an all-day session of the Institute of International Relations in Hancock. They heard a speaker talk about the needs of displaced persons in Europe, and about the necessity of strengthening the newborn United Nations. He particularly impressed on them the urgency of establishing an agreement to contain the use of the atom bomb.

There'll Be Some Changes Made   1946

Early in 1946, honors went to two of Antrim's young people: Charles Butterfield was notified that he was one of one hundred and forty-eight boys to receive the MacArthur Victory Garden medal for 1945, and Lois Black was named archery champion at Keene Teachers' College. Perhaps on the strength of these honors, the town felt it should do more for its teenagers, and so it voted to add home economics and manual training courses to the high school curriculum. Minimal space was found for the girls' home economics in the old high school building, but there simply was not enough room for the boys' manual training, so the old basket shop on West Street was utilized. Eventually, H.E. Wilson sold the building to the school district, and after it was no longer needed by the school, it became the home of the American Legion. Earlier, as previously noted, it had been used by Lemuel Cole for the manufacture of baskets and general carpenter work, and by this time it was already forty-five years old. Since it could not be used as it stood, the boys in the manual training class turned to with a will, and learned theory and practice simultaneously by digging the ditch for the new water main and rewiring the shop. Meanwhile, the girls, also operating in a noticeable vacuum, were given a lift when the Women's Relief Corps presented them with thirty-five dollars, proceeds of a food sale, with which to buy a set of dishes for their sparsely equipped room.

For some time, little notice had been paid to the Fourth of July, but this, the first year of peace, inspired the American Legion to sponsor a gala celebration, old style. In addition to the customary parade, baseball games, and band concert, a new wrinkle was added in the form of a beauty contest. Were all the Antrim girls bashful? Or disapproving? Every contestant was from out of town, and the home folks could take no nepotic pride in the winners.

Two Antrim authors received outside recognition in 1946. Junius Hanchett was proud of his article on "Forsythias of New Hampshire," published in the magazine *Horticulture*. Avis Turner French, a local poetess, was made a member of the National Association of Authors and Journalists, familiarly known as the Eugene Field Society, in recognition of "her outstanding contribution to contemporary literature." Her poems were read weekly over radio station WHDH, and one poem, "The Dawn," won the editor's prize from *American Bard* magazine.

At year's end there was a robbery at the James A. Tuttle Library. By urban standards, crime was minimal in Antrim; by Antrim's standards, one petty robbery (a small sum of money and the librarian's wrist watch were taken) was front page news.

1947   It was obvious in 1947 that something would have to be done fairly soon about Antrim's school situation. The days of thirteen school districts and one-room school houses within walking distance of every child's house were things of the past. Already Antrim was light years behind the metropolitan areas in the facilities she offered her children, and even the inadequate buildings she possessed were no longer large enough to support the total school population without overcrowding. Edna Humphrey and Mary Warren tried to negate one shortcoming by serving hot lunches to the children at the Odd Fellows Hall for a minimal charge, but much more action was needed.

The problem was brought up at school meeting in March, but the voters were not ready to meet the issue squarely, and resorted to the age-old non-solution of appointing a committee to study the matter. It was, all in all, a day of negative rather than positive action. Apparently in an effort to reduce taxes to an infinitesimal figure, many articles in the town warrant were dismissed. A proposal to allocate five thousand dollars for a permanent World War II memorial was defeated. No money was appropriated to heat the fire station. Residents on the White Birch Point Road hoping to have that stretch of road improved had their hopes dashed. All those allergic to poison ivy would have to take their chances suffering for another year: there would be no program of eradication of poison ivy in 1947.

The question of a zoning ordinance for Antrim brought forth bitter opposition. Nearly twenty-five years would pass before a majority of the citizens conceded the need to protect the town and direct its growth through the adoption of zoning laws. Innovations took root slowly: the seed of an idea had to be sown, given plenty of time to germinate, and cultivated with care before the plant came to fruition.

The study committee on the school problem came to the inevitable conclusion: the town desperately needed a new elementary school building, and the sooner the better. Probably nobody in town disagreed with this in theory, but in practice it would mean higher taxes and there was the rub. The article in the school warrant, "to see if the town will construct and equip a new elementary school building," was hotly debated, with the pros and cons about evenly divided. Only an impassioned plea by George Hastings, who would be ninety years young in June, saved the day, and when the vote was taken, the measure was found to have passed by exactly one "yea." The school was to be built at the end of Summer Street on land willed by George Cochran to the James A. Tuttle Library and sold by the library to the town.

Also at this town meeting it was voted to eliminate all raw sewage from being dumped into Great Brook and the Contoocook River. Up to this time, the subject of water pollution had never been acted on officially, although obviously the need had been great for years. With the passage of this ordinance, all houses and businesses were granted a five-year period to install septic tanks and leach beds.

Antrim was moving into the mainstream of modern living in other ways as well. After years of being served by small and specialized stores — the meat market, the fruit store — Antrim got her first self-service supermarket when the First National Stores built a large (for Antrim) new building (now part of Wayno's) and opened for business in February, 1948.

There was progress on the cultural front, too. The first program sponsored by the Contoocook Valley Community Concert Association (with members drawn from several towns) given in the Antrim Town Hall in February attracted an audience numbering three hundred and seventy-five. The performers were Nikolai and Joanna Grandau, playing the cello and piano respectively. Antrim also had its own music club, and a fine male quartet which was much in demand at local functions. There were even three television sets in town in 1948! Roger Hilton, Baden Crampton, and Edson Tuttle were pioneers in what would become a universal custom. Edson Tuttle, in his remodeled Center schoolhouse residence, got particularly fine reception.

An old landmark, the so-called Silk Mill, was lost in June when it was destroyed by fire. Built in 1835 by John Dunlap for the manufacture of chairs, it had had a succession of owners, and was being operated by Lambeth Products, Inc., when it burned.

In the November elections, Sherman Adams, later to be President Eisenhower's assistant, won the governorship of the state. This pleased the majority of Antrim voters, as did the fact that the question of the local sale of alcoholic beverages was voted down again, two hundred and twenty-three to one hundred and thirty-six.

1949   A dance at the Grange Hall, sponsored jointly by the Grange and the American Legion, ushered in the New Year with style. This was the first of a succession of weekly dances at the Grange. A square dance orchestra welcomed in the New Year with a fanfare of drums, and everybody joined in singing Auld Lang Syne. "Everybody" included visitors from Massachusetts, Vermont, and New York. Residents of the Center wondered whether the dance was held for the benefit of any local people. Square dances were the in-thing in 1949; Antrim High School planned a series of them to raise money for student council activities. The school also decided to branch out into the area of adult education with evening classes. Kenneth Jewett, then recently appointed Fine Arts Supervisor, announced that there would be eight one-week courses offered in stenciling, typing, furniture restoration, and rug making for a nominal fee of one dollar.

The American Legion, which worked hard for the formation of a Parent-Teachers' Association, was rewarded in February when ninety persons signed up. The timing was especially propitious, coming as it did just when the school system needed all the help it could get in effecting several major changes, including construction of the elementary school, and later the memorial gymnasium. The proposed elementary school was already in trouble. Funds previously authorized were insufficient to complete it, and a special school meeting was called in September to ask for additional money. A number of voters who were more concerned with protecting their pocketbooks than improving the quality of education managed to prevail at this meeting, and the motion was defeated, one hundred and fifteen to one hundred and five. Saddened but undaunted by this injudicious turn of events, the PTA held a fair in November, raising $364 for the purchase of basketball uniforms for high school girls' and boys' teams. Any surplus was to be put in escrow to be used for playground equipment for the elementary school which they were sure would eventually be finished. The school bus was bringing thirty-one pupils from North Branch, twenty-six from Clinton, sixteen from over East; there were nearly two hundred students in all, crowded into one building (now the school house apartments), and this could not be tolerated much longer.

On a happier note, the Antrim High School held its winter carnival on Dudley's Hill (now owned by William Abbott) in February. The town cooperated whole-heartedly in this endeavor. Both the Goodell and Abbott companies provided transportation to and from the Center. Supper was served in the Grange Hall, the food having been provided by various firms in town, plus additions from public-spirited private individuals. This was followed by a basketball game in the town hall, and a record dance.

As for 1949, it was an active year for the Antrim Garden Club, which maintained a perennial garden behind the library and kept the reading room supplied with summer bouquets. In a more ambitious project, it entered the statewide measured mile roadside beautification contest, winning the first prize, a munificent one hundred and fifty dollars. This stretch of roadside extended from the Bennington town line to the top of Goodell's Hill, and the trees and bushes planted there in 1949 still please the passer-by.

Several Antrimites made news in this year. H.Burr Eldredge, son of the former editor of *The Antrim Reporter*, was elected president of the First National Bank of Winchendon, Massachusetts. Junius Hanchett of forsythia fame published a book of poetry, *The Future of Evolution*. In May, Henry Hurlin, president of Goodell Company for twenty-six years, retired at the age of ninety-two after sixty-nine years of active service. He died two months later, honored by all who knew him. In addition to his long tenure with the Goodell Company, he had been a state representative and a deacon of the Baptist church for forty years.

Elementary School

School Days, New Style

By town meeting day in 1950, Antrim voters had reached the sensible conclusion that the new elementary school had to be finished, as much in the interest of fiscal sanity as of educational excellence. In an overwhelming vote of one hundred and forty-nine to thirty-nine, $43,000 was appropriated to complete and equip the school. Money was also authorized to install showers in the town hall where, for the lack of any other suitable space, basketball games were still being played. The aura of acquiescence vanished quickly, however, when the zoning article was considered. It was soundly defeated; its day was to be much later.

The PTA, a very vital organization in the early 1950s, had several things up its sleeve. For one, there was an obvious need for a gymnasium for school use. After the long hassle over the elementary school building, any affirmative action from the taxpayers seemed unlikely, but in the event that there might be some other way to accomplish this objective, a study committee was appointed. Another and more immediately productive project was undertaken in October, when PTA members met on a Saturday to clean up and grade the grounds at the new school. Every man able to work was urged to show up, and most of them did. The ladies under the leadership of Mrs. Ross Roberts saw that the workers were fed. Despite a rainy day, the grounds were much improved by nightfall. Expenses for a bulldozer, a power shovel, gravel, etc., came to $250, but that amount was more than covered by the $407.85 collected by the ladies. It was an interesting era: for a few years, there was a resurgence of the pioneer spirit, and what could not be paid for with cash was obtained with sweat and determination. The people of Hillsboro, where a new school proposal was producing more squabbling than action, were urged by the editor of *The Hillsboro Messenger* to follow Antrim's example and band together for the common good.

At long last, Antrim's new school seemed about to be finished. In September, the contract to do the necessary remaining work was awarded to Ellerton Edwards, who, being a local contractor as well as president of the PTA, seemed to be a good choice to do the job quickly and well.

Goodell Company's seventy-fifth anniversary was celebrated in August with an open house and souvenirs for all who attended.

The outbreak of the Korean war produced a bad case of the jitters. Although McCarthyism was still to come, suspicion was building. In no mood to be caught, Antrim reactivated the faithful band of airplane spotters in December, and appointed a civil defense committee with Captain Roy Dudley, USN Retired, as its head.

Events in January, 1951, confirmed that Antrim in particular and the country in general were indeed jittery. The speaker at the first PTA meeting of the year was Captain Dudley, who spelled out in detail all the precautions the civil defense people were taking. Medical personnel were instructed in their duties, and ready. Airplane spotters had been lined up. A committee in charge of clearing roads had been appointed. The specter of the atom bomb haunted the civil defense group.

The nearest hospital was (and still is) the Monadnock Community Hospital in Peterborough. In 1951, the Antrim Hospital Aid Society was founded for the express purpose of helping the Monadnock Hospital financially. Over the years, its Hospital Aid Fair, held annually in November, has grown both in reputation and in ability to earn money. Nowadays, a long line of eager customers waits impatiently until the doors are opened at ten o'clock. The proceeds last year (1975) were over five thousand dollars, collected in the space of three hours. Members work all year on their projects, and the quilted products, Christmas decorations, and potted plants are justly famous throughout the region.

These fairs, alas, were never advertised in *The Antrim Reporter*. That paper's official demise occurred in January, 1951, although for the previous decade only the bannerhead remained to distinguish it from *The Hillsboro Messenger*. The paper continued to be printed in Antrim for a few years after the death of Hiram Eldredge, but was taken over by the *Messenger* office in the '40s, and was never thereafter the chatty, hometown newspaper it had been under Mr. Eldredge.

He would have enjoyed reporting the events of February 16, 1951, when the elementary students spent their last day in the century-old building, which after that date would house only the high school students, until they too moved out forever. Open house at the new school was held the next day, Saturday, so that all could admire the up-to-date facilities, complete with modern lunch room.

Antrim High School students now had more room for classes but still had no adequate gymnasium. Nevertheless, using the town hall for basketball, they routinely produced teams of surprising excellence. In 1951, they went all the way to the Class C finals, losing in the end to Meredith. Bruce Cuddihy, carrying on the family tradition of athletic excellence, starred in the game, and "little" Wayno Olson (then four-feet-eleven) came in to spark the team to a rally that just fell short.

A movement toward a regional school system was beginning to gather momentum, and some Antrim people saw benefits in it. As with any new idea, it was slow to take root, and many years passed before it actually was accomplished, but a tentative move in this direction was made in 1951 when Antrim was asked to join nine other area towns to explore the possibility. Peterborough was the prime mover in this effort. With the exception of Antrim, all the other towns concerned were already sending tuition students to Peterborough. Harrisville eventually dropped out. Otherwise, the original group remained intact when regionalization finally did occur.

The local amateur theatre group, the Antrim Players, was reactivated in May, 1951. By August, they were ready to present the play, *Married Widows*, written by their own Don Madden. (This was so successful that in 1952 it played in Greenfield, Henniker, and Hopkinton as well.) Revenue from the sale of tickets was used for improvements to the town hall stage. For the first time in thirty years, Antrim revived the custom of Old Home Day, and once again the play was presented in the evening, this time free of charge.

The tragedy of the Korean war, now in its second year, was brought to Antrim when Lelon Olson, brother of Wayno, was killed in action on February 14, 1951. His body was transported to New Hampshire for burial in October. All businesses closed the afternoon of the service to honor him.

School lunches, once a matter of individual lunch pails, finally progressed from the way station at Odd Fellows Hall to a bona fide hot lunch program at the elementary school. The junior and senior domestic science classes of the high school gained practical experience by helping with the program, and all students ate their noon meal in the Summer Street building.

1952   Dinner at the Presbyterian church, served by the high school seniors, was a prominent feature of Town Meeting Day, which in the fifties was an all-day affair. Prior to town meeting in 1952, the Antrim Chamber of Commerce held its own open meeting, offering the citizens a chance to discuss and become familiar with the various articles to be taken up in the warrant. Of particular interest in this year was the question of purchasing a new tank truck for the fire department. Fear of Communist attacks, or merely an accidental crash of one of the many friendly fighter planes now flying over the area from Grenier Field, led some to argue that our fire department needed beefing up, but the voters ultimately decided against a new truck. They were also opposed to beano by two to one. Several suggestions were made relative to a permanent memorial for those who served in World War II, but nothing was agreed upon. Town meeting, the purest form of democracy, once again proved how difficult a challenge democracy really is.

In April, a new two-operator switchboard was installed in the telephone office, then located in the parlor of the house on the corner of Summer and Main Streets. The Contoocook Valley Telephone Company promised good service at reasonable rates. In retrospect, the personal accommodation offered by Jennie Dearborn, Dagmar George, and Jane Pratt, to name a few, offered many advantages that today's dial phones cannot match.

Not that "old" necessarily means "better." Without invention, there would be no progress, a fact well understood by Robert A. Caughey, one of Antrim's most inventive people. In 1952, his new one-story house just south of the Bass farm (now Kallanian's) was built exclusively with particle board, a process he developed using sawdust, shavings, special flakes and resins. It was the first house in the country to be built from what heretofore had been wasted resources. This early ecological enterprise has now grown into a country-wide business which in 1975 alone produced four and a half million tons of particle board.

That was a fact not even dreamed of as Antrim prepared to celebrate her 175th anniversary. Booklets distributed in advance listed all the events to take place during the three days of festivities. On Friday night, the Antrim Music Club arranged a concert of old time songs to follow the Little League baseball game between Antrim and Bennington. Saturday started off with a parade in the morning, a basket lunch at noon, and a speech by Norris Cotton in the afternoon. One hundred people visited the historical rooms in the library, where the DAR had an exhibit and a tea, and the evening was crowned with an old-fashioned promenade, round and square dances at the town hall. So many visitors were present that the town hall was unable to accommodate all who wanted to get in.

This pointed up the need for a community building, long a pet project of sports-minded Antrimites. The problem was how to finance it, especially as the town was still in debt from the new school building. Ellerton Edwards came forth with an attractive and promising proposition. He offered to build a ninety by sixty-foot building complete with bleachers, hardwood floor, heating plant, electrical wiring, and plumbing for $25,000, surely a bargain. Goodell's and Abbott's, through their president William Hurlin, immediately pledged twenty-five percent of the cost. A committee was formed to raise another twenty-five percent from private individuals. It was argued that if the town provided the remaining fifty percent, this would raise the tax rate a paltry $6.70 per thousand, or an average cost of twenty dollars per taxpayer. There was plenty of land available between the new school and the ball field, land already owned by the town. Hopes were high.

1953   All thoughts were centered on the new gym building in 1953. This was to be the year of an all-out effort to raise twenty-five percent of the necessary monies from the citizens of the town. A house-to-house canvass brought forth both small and large pledges. Local organizations gave according to the health of their treasuries. Banquets were held, the proceeds going to the ever-growing fund. A cardboard thermometer outside the Antrim Pharmacy measured the sums collected, and indicated the amount still to be raised. The first annual Chamber of Commerce winter bazaar was a pale success compared with the fever of excitement over the new gym.

At the town meeting in March, the vote was overwhelmingly in favor of $12,500 as the town's share for the community building. It was agreed that the sewerage filter system already serving the elementary school could also be used for the gymnasium.

Edwards & Son, acting as their own architects, drew up the plans, and by summer their crew was hard at work on the actual construction. After the building was completed, the townspeople once again contributed volunteer labor to do the unskilled work necessary to finish the structure. Carrol Nichols directed the job of sanding and varnishing the floor. Many willing amateur painters waterproofed and painted the cement blocks. The involvement and commitment was so great that when the first basketball games were played, many people otherwise totally uninterested in sports attended merely because this was "their" gym.

In October there was a gala Hallowe'en "Gym Day." Ballots, available in stores and businesses, were cast and collected to see who should be crowned Queen-of-the-Gym. The winner was Miss Betty Brown, with the runners-up serving as her attendants. The PTA donated an electric scoreboard. Practically all the town attended, and when the revenues were totaled, the gym fund had increased by $620.

As with most building projects, the eventual cost exceeded the estimates. The Edwards firm absorbed the deficit.

In January, 1954, two of Antrim's foremost senior citizens passed *1954* milestones in their lives. Hiram Johnson retired as superintendent of works in Goodell Company, a position which he held for thirty-five years. He was also in the forefront of town politics, long serving as moderator of town meeting and as precinct commissioner.

Another prominent man, George Hastings, celebrated his ninety-sixth birthday in 1954. As a young man, he taught school in Antrim, later became a member of the school board, and eventually worked as a foreman at Goodell's.

The matter of a suitable World War II memorial was finally settled at town meeting. A bronze tablet inscribed to all the veterans was purchased for $482, to be installed in the gym. It was dedicated on September 4, 1954, and henceforth has been known as the Memorial Gymnasium, a tribute not only to the participants of the war but also to the spirit and determination of an entire town.

CATCHING UP

Into the Mainstream

In order to understand some of the happenings in Antrim during this period, we should look briefly at the changes taking place in surrounding towns as well. One development was the introduction of the electronic industry. Sylvania came to Hillsboro and Electropac came to Peterborough in the early fifties. Before that, New Hampshire Ball Bearing Company had also come to Peterborough. This opened up opportunities that had not been available earlier. Sylvania needed many employees, even to the point of hiring part-time workers. This led to the employment of women during the hours that their children were in school. The third shift was also available for those who could not work in the daytime hours. Jobs were here for the asking, and only fifteen to thirty minutes away by car. Many of the smaller industries in Antrim had been phased out, leaving only Goodell Company and Abbott Company, both very stable industries, but not employing all the men and women available. The electronics industries also needed technical engineers and supervisory help. These young professionals came with young families. The result was that Antrim, instead of being agricultural and industrial, shortly became a "bedroom town."

1955
to
1960

Agriculture had been needing fewer and fewer people for some years. It was becoming harder to make a living on the rocky, sparsely producing land without the outlay of more money and manpower. The number of really productive farms had dwindled to three, then two, and finally by 1970 only one dairy farm and one market gardening plant were left. Many of the old farms which had not been worked for many years had been returned to woodlots under new ownership, with pastures grown up to juniper. Growth in some pastures was kept down by the pasturing of young stock from local herds. Others were rented to outside farmers.

One farm which for many years had been the property of Wyman K. Flint had been sold to Robert Loomis as a summer home. It was first settled in 1775 by Thomas Stewart, and at that time was on the stage route from Keene to Hillsboro. In 1956 it was sold to Monadnock Research Laboratories with Winslow B. Caughey as its president. He adapted some of the buildings to laboratories for experiments in cancer research. Also housed there was Clinton Industries, headed by Robert Caughey. Both Winslow and Robert Caughey were local young men with great ability in their respective fields. On August 28, 1957, there was an open house so the community could become acquainted with the new companies and their projects.

This was the period in which town planning had its start. A Planning and Development Commission was established in 1957 to seek new industries and to investigate town planning. The town meeting voted to have a committee appointed to investigate town zoning and to report at the next annual meeting.

The North Branch school reunion was always a well-attended affair where former pupils had a chance to reminisce and exchange stories of their school days. Perhaps fertile imaginations helped to make the stories even more interesting in the re-telling than in the original.

Several of its important residents were lost to the town during the 1955-1959 period:

Emma S. Goodell, widow of the late Governor David Goodell.

Hayward Cochrane, son of the Reverend Warren Cochrane, author of the *History of Antrim, 1777-1877.*

Everett N. Davis, for forty years R.F.D. mail carrier.

George Hastings—at 98 years he outlived his insurance policy.

Town and Gown

One of the more significant changes to take place during the period 1960-1964 was the arrival of Nathaniel Hawthorne College. When Judge Kenneth McLaughlin bought the site of the former Flint farm for the college which he was planning to establish, he named the college

1960 to 1964

Hawthorne Administration Building . . . on the old Flint estate

for Hawthorne, who knew the area well. The estate included about seven hundred acres, much of it in its natural state with wild life of various kinds. The owner's mansion became the administration building; the former houses and farm buildings were adapted for dormitories and class rooms. So that all would be ready for opening day, some students came early to help with the adaptations. The college received its charter in 1962, with Judge McLaughlin as president, and John Berrigan, treasurer. It is a non-denominational, non-profit, coeducational, four-year liberal arts college. There were one hundred freshmen and a few sophomore transfer students in 1962. William Shea was chancellor. Ralph Little, a local citizen and former sales manager for Goodrich Rubber, was director of community relations and personnel housing. The location is ideal, with plenty of room for the expansion which has followed rapidly. The North Branch River runs along the boundary. There is room for athletic activities of various kinds and it is easily accessible to both Hillsboro and Antrim without being right on the doorstep of either village. In its eighth year it had a student body of 850 with its largest freshman class totalling 310. The students came from sixteen states and six foreign countries.

There was some thought of having an aviation space program when the college started, but it was postponed. In 1965 under the leadership of Major George Gibson a flight training program began. The first year

Major Gibson agreed to fly with the students from five to nine each morning and during the same evening hours, the only time he had free from his other duties. Training was carried on from a small airport in West Deering on land which was rented. In 1967 the land was purchased from the McAllister farm and a program was begun.

The site is now a commercial airport, privately owned and certified by the state of New Hampshire. It is also licensed by the Federal Aviation Agency as a flying school and certified repair station. The flight students must be trained academically, must have soloed, have a prescribed number of flying hours and pass three Federal Aviation Agency examinations: written, oral, and flight. Then they may have a private pilot's license. For a commercial license they must have more advanced training, more flight hours, and pass a more extensive examination. They may also qualify for licensing both as commercial instrument pilots and as instructors. By 1976 there were more than 100 students training, and twenty-five student instructors had been trained.

The macadam runway is 3,600 feet long and 85 feet wide, with a grass overrun of 1,500 feet. There are fourteen operating aircraft, from trainers to a thirty-passenger plane which is often used to take students on field trips. This latter aircraft has logged almost 85,000 flying hours, which is the third highest in this agency's district. Each year the Federal Aviation Agency inspects the various flying schools to select the most outstanding maintenance man and the most outstanding flight instructor. Both of these choices in 1976 were Hawthorne men.

Back in the village, the annual winter bazaars sponsored by the Chamber of Commerce continued to draw crowds on the Washington's birthday weekend. Dinner at the Presbyterian Church followed, attended by many who remembered the dinners there many years ago when dinner was served at noon.

A life guard at Gregg Lake, financed by the town, led to more and more interest in a better swimming area and parking space there, culminating in action by the Lion's club. The space used up to this time was close to the road, just opposite a group of privately owned cottages whose owners were not enthusiastic about having parked cars on their property closing off access to their houses. The town was able to acquire a quit claim deed from Raymond J. McKay to land at the north end of the lake to be developed for a picnic area, parking lot, and town beach. Unnumbered loads of sand and fill were trucked in, a bathhouse with sanitary facilities was built, a new raft was provided and safety areas were laid out for swimmers of all grades of proficiency. This was all funded jointly by the town from federal funds and by the Lion's Club. Much of the labor was provided by volunteers from the Lion's Club and interested citizens. This project was not completed in one year, but by 1969 it was practically complete.

Swimming lessons had been given by Sally Martel during the first two weeks in July. With the additional space available, two swimming instructors certified by the Red Cross, JoAnn Jennison and Nancy Jones, were able to include more children in the program. More than one hundred children have profited from the lessons each year, some helping to instruct the smaller children.

The first two weeks in July find many mothers bringing their youngsters of all ages with swimming gear and other impedimenta to the beach to enjoy the fun and sun, some staying for picnics and games past midday. Children are not to be left for the lifeguards to "babysit," but are to have their parents with them.

Another recreational facility has been the tennis court at the Cram Grove on Jameson Avenue. Philip Baker gave instruction to those who wished it, and many pleasant days have been passed in this activity by various age groups.

The year 1963 saw the change from the old hand-cranked telephone system with the "candlestick" instrument to the dial system. The local office with an operator on duty was eliminated. The central office in Hillsboro handled all calls that required an operator, while all other calls, including long distance, could be dialed by the individual from his own phone. No longer could the operator tell you that the person you were calling, who did not answer, had just passed the office on her way to the hardware store. Many interesting tales are told of the help given by the operator when a problem developed in locating someone who was urgently needed and did not answer the phone.

Persons interested in improving the appearance of the approach to the town from the south purchased a quantity of daffodil bulbs to be planted on the bank opposite the Goodell Company plant. The next spring they made a beautiful display. The blooms were a great attraction to children, some of whom honored their mothers or their teachers with bouquets. Unfortunately, the soil was so poor that the life of the bulbs was short, but each spring finds a few brave blooms coming up through the grass.

Horseback riding staged a comeback about this time. As the

number of riding horses increased it was not uncommon to see riders, especially on the unpaved roads outside the village. Dr. Alfred Chandler's daughters, the leaders in the trend, were ready and willing to teach others the skills necessary for riding and caring for horses. Awards were won by Antrim representatives at nearby horse shows.

A 4H Club had been organized and, due to the interest of the young people in raising sheep, the group was named the 4H Clover Snippers. Several families acquired sheep for the first time. The Brzozowskis, the Healeys, and the Rabideaus brought home many ribbons from the fairs they attended each fall. The proud owners spent anxious hours during the lambing season, hoping for warm weather so the newcomers would not be chilled. Parents were also involved; they had the responsibilities when the young people were in school.

Prominent citizens who died during these years were: George Nylander, former police chief; Arthur Proctor, painter and roofer; Carl Robinson, former management executive of Goodell Company; Maurice Cutter, for many years owner of the local meat market.

Moving Along

A committee to prepare a town history that would extend the chronicle written by the Reverend Warren R. Cochrane, published in 1877, had commissioned the Reverend Ralph Tibbals to write such an account in the twenties. Much research had been done along genealogical lines by Mr. Tibbals. However, due to economic conditions and the European war, the town voted in 1940 to discontinue this activity. But in 1965 a sum of three thousand dollars was voted to bring the history up to date. After considering the problem, a committee decided to publish the genealogical material as the *Genealogical Records of Antrim, N.H., 1877-1940*. This was published in 1967 with Rose Wilkinson Poor editor. The committee included Hiram W. Johnson as chairman, plus William H. Hurlin, Byron Butterfield, Myrtie K. Brooks, Ellerton Edwards, Robert Flanders, and Mrs. Poor. *1965 to 1970*

In town meeting of 1968 the town voted to have a committee appointed to gather material for "an historical narrative of what has transpired in Antrim during the period extending from the date of the Cochrane history of 1877 to the present date." This committee was made up of Ellerton H. Edwards as chairman, with Byron G. Butterfield, Earl X. Cutter, Harold Fleming, Donald B. Madden, Beverly Tenney, and Miriam Roberts as secretary. In September, 1968, Mrs.

Tenney resigned, and Arleen P. White and Alice B. Thompson were added. Each member of the committee was assigned a period to research and report to the group later.

In October, 1967, there was an unusual visitor in town. A young, seven-hundred-pound, dark brown bull moose took a southern route on his fall stroll, arriving in Antrim and stayed over the weekend. He had a beautiful pair of antlers. He roamed around town, appearing here and there, always causing excitement since only occasionally had one of his kind favored us with a visit. Finally, he settled for Byron Butterfield's pasture within sight of the house. It was Friday when he arrived, and by Saturday he staged an "at home," attended by approximately five hundred guests, many of them equipped with cameras. Mike Chase attempted a nearer view, but managed to get back to safety when the beast challenged his presence. One bystander is reported to have called, "Do that again so I can get a picture!" By Sunday the moose had left, but was reported in Hancock and other places in the area.

A bicentennial committee was appointed in 1968 to plan for the two hundredth anniversary of the town in 1977. The following persons were appointed: Frederick Roberts, Robert Caughey, Robert Dunlap, David Hurlin, Jane Hill, Eleanor Lane, Dorothy Lang, Isabel Nichols, and Barrett Proctor.

The home of former Governor David Goodell, recently owned by Fred Proctor, was severely damaged by fire in August, 1968. It was one of the older houses in town. Ten cords of wood burned in the adjoining woodshed, causing a very hot fire. No farming had been done there for several years. Firemen were able to save the shell of the house, but the inside was nearly ruined. Later the house was sold and renovated.

A first step was taken in 1967 toward providing a system of sewage disposal for the town. This was made necessary by new regulations regarding pollution of streams. A committee made up of Robert Caughey, Earl Packard, and Charles Gilmore was appointed to initiate the possibility of joint action with Bennington and the Monadnock Paper Mills, Inc., in at least a portion of the project. The study showed very evident need of improving conditions in brooks which empty into the Contoocook River. Application was made to the Department of Housing and Urban Development for financial assistance. In 1969 HUD approved money for the engineer's final drawing for the system but then things came to a halt as there were no funds available from the federal government.

The summer of 1969 saw the beginnings of the Lobster Theatre. A group of sub-teens interested in dramatic production began working on a project of their own. They were given the use of the barn on the Robert Flanders place. The choice of name was decided by the fact that before their "first night" performance they had had lobster for dinner. The flats, flies, and curtain subsequently were adorned with the lobster motif by the staff. The house seated sixteen, and two performances were given each evening. The demand for tickets was so great that it was necessary to get one's bid in early. "Charlie Brown" and "The Matchmaker" were their first offerings, both received with great applause. Dan Hurlin was the official producer and director.

Since the height of the stage is limited, as the players grow in stature they are retired from acting and become backstage assistants!

Later in 1969 two Antrim citizens were affected by a rather bizarre happening. Two freight cars were unintentionally uncoupled from a freight train in Jaffrey, and took off on a trip of their own toward Peterborough. The track has a slight slope from Jaffrey along the Contoocook River, so the cars picked up speed as they traveled the six miles. At one crossing a car driven by Lawrence Attridge stopped just as the cars swept by, the force of air being strong enough to turn the car. The track ends in Peterborough, which did not concern the cars, but did concern the trainman who was alone on the ride. He managed to jump off just before the end of the track, but the cars continued across Main Street and crashed into three automobiles parked on the other side. One, a brand new Chrysler, was demolished; the second, a van belonging to Fred Roberts of Antrim, was smashed on one side; the third was slightly damaged. A mighty crash followed by instant darkness in the town, caused by the cars' colliding with a utility pole, brought the wild ride to an end. The trainman, approaching a nervous wreck, was treated at the Monadnock Community Hospital and released. Marguerite Roberts, who had driven the van to Peterborough, needed an alternative way to get home.

A new medical center was built by Drs. Alfred Chandler and Louis Wiederhold on Elm Street, where there was a pleasant outlook and plenty of room for parking. They had outgrown the location on Main Street. The new building has a large reception area, two examining rooms and a consulting room for each doctor, a business office, a

Medical Center

laboratory, and an X-ray center. There was also space on a lower level for other offices: in 1974 Dr. A.J. Homicz, dentist, moved in, and Dr. James Mancini, optometrist, came in 1975 to practice here part-time. The facility is a fine addition to the town.

Among the deaths during these years were:

Hiram W. Johnson, retired works manager of Goodell Company. He had been town moderator, 1924-1962; representative to the General Court, 1931-1932, and trustee of trust funds, 1954-1969. He and Mrs. Johnson had observed their fiftieth wedding anniversary in January.

Myrtie K. Brooks, a dairy farmer until 1968. She had been a member of the school board, town auditor, and had taught in Antrim, Hancock, Hillsboro, Concord, and Nashua.

Archie M. Swett, town clerk, member and treasurer of the school board, former tax collector, and former postmaster.

Frank E. Wheeler, for many years station agent at the Antrim railroad station.

George H. Caughey, engineer in the firm of Caughey & Pratt. He had built dams, bridges, and buildings in this area since the 1920s.

Ethel C. Davis, librarian of the James A. Tuttle Library for twenty-five years.

Earlier, the Monadnock Community Hospital Auxiliary Association had been formed at the hospital in Peterborough with branches in each of the towns served by the hospital. The Antrim branch started small with a Christmas sale at the home of a member. Each year they continued to raise money for the hospital with Christmas sales. It was not long before they outgrew members' living rooms and had to move to the Fellowship Hall in the Baptist Church. There came a year when the sale took over an additional room in the basement. The next move was to the Presbyterian Church where the parlor, vestry, kindergarten, and the whole educational unit were utilized. Each year the amount of money has grown, and the sale has become a widely attended event, usually held on the second Saturday in November. So far the unit has provided: a defibrillator, cardiac monitor, pulmonary testing machine, hypothermal blanket, recovery bed, six oxygen valves and flow meters, table for the operating room, electrodyne monitor with tape run-off, six cribs for the nursery, and three cribs for the pediatric department.

Coming of Age

It was 1970 when Antrim High School closed its doors as such, since the new Contoocook Valley Regional School was ready for use. The last basketball award night with banquet was held in March, and the last commencement exercises were held in the gym in June.

1970

The Civil War monument on the Baptist Church lawn was treated to a good cleaning and repair session. It had settled unevenly so that the poor soldier appeared to be tipping backward. In the base was found a box containing a list of the names of the Civil War veterans along with newspapers of the post-war period and glass negatives of early photographs.

This was a splendid year for the Little League. Antrim won its ninth straight game and the Crotched Mountain Junior League Championship. The team was coached by Bruce Cuddihy and Don Paige.

The Boston Post cane was awarded to John Caughey, at ninety-six the oldest man in town. Mr. Caughey has become an artist since he retired from active work as a builder. He did his first painting in his late eighties, learning from experience as he went along.

Because of the new school system, the Contoocook Valley cooperative, there was great interest in its effect on the tax rate. In 1970 the rate went up from $55.40 per thousand to $61.60, $50.00 of this for the school budget.

Greystone Lodge burned in November, due to the carelessness of a group from out of town. This summer hotel, constructed in 1910, had twenty rooms, and was built partly of field stone with wide porches and a rustic appearance. It was a popular spot from World War I up to the twenties. There was a golf course nearby, but not much of interest for a young clientele, so it was largely patronized by those who were content to sit and rock on the porch. Also, the wider use of cars made

Soldiers' Monument

touring possible throughout the whole region. When it burned it had not been used as a hotel for many years. It had changed hands several times, when parts of it had been removed and the rest used by the owners for their summer homes. The field stone walls are all that remain of a spot that held memories for many people.

1971   The beginning of 1971 saw the old school bell permanently mounted at the Shea athletic field. It had been silent since the former school was sold to be made into an apartment house, but had remained in the school building. It was formerly used for summoning the students in the morning, calling them in from recess, and calling them back after the lunch hour. Overly-vigorous ringing by some young men often resulted in its being turned over. This meant that it did not ring again until someone went up into the belfry to right it, which was half the fun.

John Durgin's saw mill burned one February day when the temperature was twenty below zero. The mill was located in Bennington near where the old Antrim railroad station once stood. But when the

Bennington fire department truck arrived, its pump was frozen. The fire was later brought under control by the Antrim firemen.

After thirty-six years as postmaster, Earl Cutter retired in May. With the coming of Nathaniel Hawthorne College, the post office had become the scene of greater activity, which Mr. Cutter handled with efficiency, and the removal to its larger quarters had also been carried out by him. Philip Lang, who had been working in the office, carried on until he was finally appointed postmaster the following February.

The Antrim High School class of 1911 enjoyed its sixty-year reunion at a dinner at Maplehurst Inn in June. Six of the graduates of a class of nine were present, namely: Cranston Eldredge, Clarence Elliott, William Hurlin, May Ashford McLean, Eleanor Stearns Purdy, and Ross Roberts. The class marshal, Hazel Burnham Rand, also attended.

A group of women from the Antrim Baptist Church have made a name for themselves with their quilting projects. They were in need of a different method for replenishing their treasury and hit upon quilting, a craft which has come down from our foremothers who used small pieces of material which they seamed together in various designs. They lined the resulting quilt tops and inserted a filler to add warmth, and with many tiny stitches quilted designs to hold the three thicknesses together.

It pays to advertise, and a small notice in the *Yankee Magazine* soon resulted in enough orders to keep the ladies busy for some time. Some of the orders were for new quilts, some were for just the quilting of projects already started. The beautiful old patterns for piecing were revived with many hands working on cutting the pieces, sewing them together, and getting them ready for the final touches. Designs were drawn by Mrs. Carroll Johnson; sewing was done by any of the church women who were interested in doing it.

Two hundred quilts later, the ladies had made enough money to renovate the church sanctuary. The quilters meet three days a week in the fellowship hall from ten to two o'clock. It takes 175-200 hours to quilt a full-sized quilt.

Conditions at the town dump on Depot Street did not conform to the *1972* new state laws being enacted for the disposal of solid waste. Burning dumps were to be ended by 1975 and the covering of waste was required for sanitary reasons. Once again, cooperation between Antrim and Bennington made possible a sanitary landfill of eighty-six acres in North Bennington, at a cost of $30,000, with Antrim's share $22,500. The vote in Antrim was 69-30. Since 1975, Francestown has also been included. No more is it possible for "dump pickers" to work through the refuse to pick out articles of house furnishings and clothing to improve their lot. There are not so many chances for "pot shots" at rats, either. Dump stickers are necessary for the townspeople who use the new facility.

"Earth Week" clean-up resulted in a drive for paper and can collection for recycling, sponsored by the Woman's Club. By the middle of May, over a ton of recycling material had been brought in by the school children. The Middle School library was to profit from the sale.

Each year a fishing derby for children is sponsored by the Odd Fellows: In 1972 the biggest fish were caught by Jeff Page and David Brooks. The third largest was by Jonmarie Maloney and the smallest by Ronda Clough.

John Caughey, or Uncle John as he is affectionately called, had his ninety-eighth birthday party at his home. Seventy-five guests were present.

Once again the Clover Snippers 4H Club was in the news. In April they attended the Connecticut Judging School. One of their members, Tom Rabideau, was a senior counsellor at Spruce Pond 4H Club Camp in Allentown for two weeks. Later, his sheep were winners at the Hopkinton Fair, and he was picked by the Hillsboro County 4H Clubs to attend Camp Miniwance on Lake Michigan the following summer.

The Lobster Theatre offering in July was *Alice in Wonderland* — "sixty minutes of enjoyable entertainment," a critic reported. In September it was, *Just So Stories*, an adaptation of the Kipling classic tales by D. Abbott Chrisman of Boston University, who was associated with the Ravencroft Theatre in Rindge. The critic reported:"If Rudyard Kipling was hovering in the wings, we are confident that he was pleased."

The Presbyterian Church steeple was struck by lightning on August 27. An explosion followed a bolt of lightning at 9:15 P.M. Roof slates were scattered and there was eight thousand dollars' damage, as some of the wooden structure was burned.

The Conservation Commission proposed that the following be designated scenic roads: Smith Road, Old Hancock Road, Meeting House Hill Road, Craig Road, Bridal Road, Elm Avenue, Pierce Lake Road, Liberty Farm Road, Turner Hill Road, Willard Pond Road, and Old Brimstone Corner Road.

At the four-hour 1973 town meeting, there was standing room only. The matter of the scenic roads was explained: that no trees would be cut, no stone walls moved, nor would repairs such as hard-topping be allowed. The aim was to keep the roads as natural as possible. In another vote at town meeting it was decided to have a reassessment of property in town. Also, restriction on remodeling of homes was voted, with no more than two apartments in one-family houses.

At a winter carnival sponsored by radio station WBZ of Boston to benefit muscular dystrophy, held at the Crotched Mountain ski area, the star was Nora Lee Sysyn, who stole the show. At "David's," an inn and restaurant at North Branch, she plays the piano and performs each Saturday night.

Slowly but surely it was becoming evident that the town offices needed to be expanded. Since two of the formerly rented stores in the town hall were vacant, this was a good time for expansion. The space formerly used by a drug store was remodeled to provide an office for the police and one for the secretary, with the remaining space to be used for meetings of committees, especially the planning board.

The summer of '73 was remembered by many as a time of conservation of gasoline and other petroleum products due to the actions of foreign oil producing countries. However, there was gasoline and heating oil sufficient for reasonable use. As cooler weather came in the fall, 65° temperatures in homes were the rule, and many stoves and fireplaces were back in use to supplement other fuels. Wood was abundant, but the cost of cutting and preparing it for sale brought the price up so high that many could not afford it.

Zoning in the town had been under discussion over a period of years, but had been turned down each time that it came up to vote. However, this year the planning board organized a committee to study a zoning ordinance to be presented at town meeting. There had always been the protest by land owners: "It is my land and I will do as I please with it." But the committee felt that with hearings to acquaint the public with what was planned, and why it was advisable, there would be more chance of its being approved. Many towns in southern New Hampshire had suffered for lack of zoning and Antrim hoped that it could avoid these results.

August saw the first of the hearings on the zoning ordinance. Four hearings were scheduled, with the planning board assisted by officers of the state planning office. The committee was composed of Stanley Tenney as chairman, Harold Grant, Mildred Dudley, Charles Gilmore, Richard Schacht, and William Abbott. The meeting resulted in a rewriting of the ordinance.

At an October hearing on the zoning ordinance, the "grandfather clause" was the cause of some misunderstanding, but the final explanation cleared the matter to the satisfaction of most.

Antrim High School Class of 1913 held a sixty-year reunion at the house of Mr. and Mrs. Wallace George. Four members were present: Jessie Tenney Rutherford, Mae Harris Perkins, Grace Taylor, and Wallace George.

Suddenly one morning at seven o'clock, a balloon dropped into Dr. Chandler's horse corral. The two occupants had planned to land at Nathaniel Hawthorne College, but the wind failed. The doctor's field was just the place to land. Dr. and Mrs. Chandler invited them to breakfast before they went on their way.

The town was saddened on July 31 by the deaths of Mr. and Mrs. Wilbur Molin in the crash of the airplane that they had boarded in Manchester en route to New York. The crash occurred at Logan Airport in Boston. The Molins owned and operated Country Craftsmen in Hillsboro.

The report of the federal census gave Antrim a population of 1,890 as compared with 1,121 in 1960.

The energy crisis was beginning to be felt as the heating season approached. Oil dealers stated that they had enough oil for their regular customers. Various ways of saving on both electricity and oil were published. The fifty-five mile per hour speed limit was not compulsory, but voluntary compliance was good. However, the energy shortage was such a confused issue that trust in the government was becoming eroded, and the general feeling was, "Are we being had?" Stoves were purchased by some, but they soon became scarce and high priced. The manufacture of Franklin stoves and other types was a growing business. Schools saved some energy by having a longer Christmas vacation, fewer and colder showers, and lower temperatures all around.

1974   More confusion about energy marked the beginning of 1974. Daylight Saving Time became effective in January to conserve energy. This seemed a debatable measure, and many parents complained about their children having to leave for school before light. A government edict stated that a cold house would not give you a cold.

Town meeting voted $2,500 to remodel and equip the town office, $700 for a new raft at the beach, $500 for a skating rink, and $1,500 to resurface the tennis court. The zoning ordinance was passed, 273-196, thanks to the hours of hard work on the part of the committee, plus the series of hearings which had explained the ordinance and had also advised the committee on certain changes which were duly made. The meeting also doubled its support of the Hillsboro Rescue Squad by voting $1,000, but voted against a full-time policeman.

John Caughey celebrated his one hundredth birthday. His studio on Elm Avenue near the home of his son is where he spends his time painting and receiving his friends and relatives for a friendly chat.

A fire at Nathaniel Hawthorne College destroyed the business administration and economics building early in April. This was the first fire in its twelve years, which is a good record. Antrim fire fighters were assisted by firemen from surrounding towns. The building contained classrooms, a faculty office, and dormitory space.

A special bank commission had been asked to decide whether the Peterborough Savings Bank or the Valley Bank of Hillsboro should build a branch in Antrim. The Valley Bank had planned a branch here, but was building in Henniker first. Peterborough was ready to start at once. Eventually the matter was settled in favor of Peterborough.

An interesting meeting of the Extension group was addressed by Robert Richardson of Peterborough, an authority on antique stenciling. He is the great-grandson of Moses Eaton, a stenciling artist in this area. The group visited the homes of Mrs. William Lewan, Miss Edna Ryder, Miss Barbara Ziegler, and Mrs. Francis King and Miss Evelyn Perry to see the stencils in these homes, most of which were originals by Moses Eaton. In most cases these had previously been covered by wallpaper for many years.

Women's Lib came to the Little League this year when Judy Hilliard and Brenda Beauchamp joined. Although they sat on the bench some, both were allowed to play in nearly every game, but they received no special treatment or favors — they were just two of the team.

The Tenney Farm outlet on Route 202 near the Bennington line selling "our own stuff" is run by the two sons of Mr. and Mrs. Stanley Tenney — Eric, who began the project, and Mark, who joined his brother after teaching agriculture at a high school in Vermont. They hire local young people for the garden work and sell only the best quality of their produce. The rest is fed to the farm animals. They raise calves and sheep, as well as flowers, raspberries, and strawberries. A member of the family is always at the stand when it is open. As soon as the early vegetables begin, it is a busy spot.

The Old Main Room, a musical revue, was presented by Antrim High School alumni as a part of the Old Home Day celebration. It was written by Isabel Nichols and included skits, dances, and songs about life in the high school from 1895 to 1970. There was also a children's parade with thirty entries, an auction at the Goodell Company parking lot, and a dance put on by the firemen. There had been no Old Home Day celebrations for many years, so this proved very popular.

Mr. and Mrs. Adolph Baer were given a testimonial dinner in August by the Fire Department. The Baers had given the land on which the North Branch fire station was built, and Adolph had been deputy chief for eighteen years.

Mary McGrory, political columnist who is syndicated in numerous papers in New England, has enjoyed frequent vacations in the area, staying at Maplehurst Inn. She often mentions this area and its people in her columns. She said that all it took to get Nixon to resign was for her to go on vacation. She was suddenly called back to Washington to be there for the event, after spending only twenty-three hours in Antrim. She said the publication of the Pentagon Papers, the Watergate burglary, the firing of Archibald Cox, and the resignation of Spiro Agnew all spoiled previous vacations. She warned Mr. Ford to watch his step as she was planning a cruise in October.

The championship Little League team ended the season by going to a Red Sox game in Boston. It was reported that Mark Harvey must hold the record for the most ice cream cones consumed at one game.

September, 1974, saw the beginning of a new chapter in the tale of the iron bridge which crosses the Contoocook River from Antrim into North Bennington near the David Platt farm. The bridge, built in 1893, was found to need extensive repairs. The floor boards were badly worn and unsafe, and the superstructure was extensively rusted. The state would pay for part of a new bridge, but repairs on the old one would have to be borne by the two towns. In the meantime, the bridge was closed as unsafe.

A meeting of the selectmen with representatives from Congressman James Cleveland's office, the U.S. Department of Health, Education and Welfare, the New Hampshire Highway Department and with County Commissioner Edward Lobacki was planned, but the investigation stalled. At a later meeting the voters were asked to spend

$140,000 on the bridge, the cost to be allocated on the equalized valuation of the towns. It would cost more for Antrim, while it would be used more by Bennington.

At still another hearing it was asserted that the old bridge was not repairable. Although the stone abutments were in good condition, it was not wide enough for a two lane highway. This would boost the cost to $310,000. Half of this, or $155,000, would be available from the state, while Bennington's share would be $54,560 and Antrim's $101,000. Since the voters at town meeting had said "no," the selectmen were bound by that vote.

From Antrim's point of view, the bridge matter was closed, as there were only two families who used it, and there were two other bridges across the Contoocook within two miles. The county commissioners were tired of the whole thing.

Because of a fire in the Jackson house, where one occupant was overcome by smoke and heat, the planning board requested an inspection of all multi-family buildings for fire hazards. Antrim firemen offered to clean chimneys for a donation to the fire department. This could prevent chimney fires if wood were to be used for fuel for the first time in years.

During the summer state appraisers made a complete reappraisal of the property in the town. This was for the purpose of equalizing the taxes, as the town had voted for 100 percent assessment. This raised the net valuation of the town to $25,994,997, as compared with $6,558,217 in 1973 when the taxes were based on 37 percent valuation. The major increase was on land which was assessed for its future potential value. Such land in the following year could be placed in "land use," which could lower the net valuation of the town and increase the tax rate. Naturally there were accusations of unfairness on the part of those who owned many acres of land which was undeveloped and bringing in no income, yet it was assessed for its possible use.

In December, ground was broken for the new branch of the Peterborough Savings Bank. The building was to adjoin the supermarket and be built by Wayno Olson. He would rent to the bank. Antrim is one of the bank's million dollar deposit towns, and all the services of the bank are available in Antrim. This has been a great addition to the town.

Three Antrim men were appointed to the Advisory Board by the Peterborough Savings Bank. They were Wayno Olson, Richard Edmunds, and Andrew Lane. There were also members from Bennington and Hillsboro. The Antrim office of the bank was opened in March with about 250 persons attending the "Open House." The ribbon to be cut was made of one-dollar bills taped together. It was cut between the bills!

A resurgence of the Democratic Party has come to Antrim. A general dissatisfaction with happenings in Washington, such as Watergate and the pardon of Nixon, turned many people off. This, plus dislike for Governor Meldrim Thomson, resulted in formation of the Antrim Democratic Committee with William Gold as chairman. Later, Thomas Donahue became chairman.

A bad fire on March 6 destroyed the studio of John Caughey, our local artist. It was not discovered in time to save it, which meant the loss not only of the building but all the art work of the last few years. By this time Mr. Caughey was 101 years old, but a very active and alert 101. He had built his studio at age 93, and he immediately made plans to rebuild. The Chamber of Commerce launched a drive to assist. Even the school children collected a gift of $108.12, to replenish his paints and other necessities for his work. Another of his losses was a customer file with his correspondence from across the country. He had also been granted a patent for a step stool which he had invented. This has two steps and a pole at the back to use as a support as one stands on the stool. One day in his studio he was working on this when a woman came in to look at his pictures. She became interested in the stool, and inquired about it. He demonstrated its use, and how it could be dismantled to put into a car. The result was that she bought not only a picture but also a stool. Mr. Caughey was one of seven men in the United States over 100 years old to obtain a patent.

In August the Antrim-Bennington Rescue Squad was organized. The first steps were to check into the legal aspects, form a charter, and draft by-laws. The need for emergency ambulance service was becoming more apparent. Since a recent change in the laws governing ambulances in the state, the local funeral directors had given up that part of their services. Since the Hillsboro Rescue Squad was serving this area, but the demand was greater than they could meet, interest developed in a new service for Antrim and Bennington. Hillsboro had acquired a new ambulance and offered to sell their old one to the Antrim-Bennington Squad. The moving spirits for this effort came from responsible younger citizens headed by Richard Atkinson and Marshall Beauchamp. Soon a drive for money to buy equipment was begun, and the various town organizations were contacted for contributions. Those who did not have money budgeted for such use developed activities which would produce cash. There were food sales, white elephant sales and flea markets, a raffle, house-to-house solicitation, and a walkathon-bikathon. Perhaps the most unusual project was the giant Christmas card sponsored by the Woman's Club which brought in a dollar for each signature. By early 1976 there was money enough to pay for the ambulance and for some equipment.

Twelve persons took the seventy-two hour course which qualified them to staff the ambulance. This service is manned only by volunteers who have given their time for taking the preparatory course and who give their service without pay, except for donations to the squad to pay for equipment, gasoline, and incidentals.

Politics became important in the summer of 1975. There had been an election for U.S. senator which was too close to decide. After a recount became quite involved the matter was passed to the Senate for a decision. They advised a special election, which was held in September. The Democratic candidate, John Durkin, won over the Repub-

Grandpa Caughey (Uncle John)

lican, Louis Wyman. Again, New Hampshire was once more represented in the Senate! Several Antrim residents were proud to see their names in one of Mary McGrory's columns about the election. In 1974 there were three Republicans and one Democrat representing New Hampshire in Congress; in 1975 there were three Democrats and one Republican. President Ford came to New Hampshire to bolster Mr. Wyman's campaign, stopping a short time in Peterborough. This was the first time a president had been in the area since 1912. Some of the school children from Antrim were allowed to go to Peterborough to see him. Some even shook his hand.

Edna Ryder had a birthday party on her ninetieth birthday, at which the guests were invited to view the old stenciling on the walls in her workroom. The house was built in 1827.

Deaths of important individuals during 1970-76 included:

1970-Fred Raleigh, a direct descendant of Philip Riley, Antrim's earliest settler. The name had gone through many changes.

-Clara Pratt, librarian, 1956-1965.

-Vera and Byron Butterfield in 1970 and 1971. Both had been active in town affairs.

1971-Helen Ashford, at age ninety-seven.

1972-William Hurlin, retired president of Goodell Company and Abbott Company, past president of the New Hampshire Manufacturers Association, former chairman of the New Hampshire Division of the New England Council.

-Ralph Little, chairman of the board of trustees of Nathaniel Hawthorne College.

-Dr. James Jameson, Antrim native, prominent surgeon in Concord, always interested in the town's welfare.

1973-Stanley Tenney, chairman of the zoning study, member of the study committee for the regional school, former selectman.

-Laura Chestnutt, 93, artist and horsewoman.

-Ellerton Edwards, retired contractor, former school moderator, representative to the state legislature.

1975-Gordon Sudsbury, Sr., for twenty-five years fire warden on Crotched Mountain for the New Hampshire forestry service.

1976   Early in 1976 the bicentennial committee announced its plan for the year's commemoration of the nation's bicentennial. This was to include a town bazaar to be held on April 10 in the gym, with anyone who so wished having a booth for selling craft work, refreshments, or advertising products. In the afternoon there would be a re-enactment of the call to arms which took place in Antrim at the beginning of the Revolution, the presentation of the bicentennial flag to the town by Dr. J. Duane Squires of the New Hampshire Revolution Commission, and the arrival of the Conestoga wagon which was visiting all bicentennial towns in the state. Antrim is one of the twelve towns that were incorporated during the Revolution.

The annual town meeting was divided into two parts this year. The primary election was held on February 24 for the purpose of electing delegates to the political conventions in the summer. This date had been set by the legislature in order that New Hampshire should be the first state to have a primary. Both Ronald Reagan and President Ford had been in the state making speeches and shaking hands. President Ford won the Republican contest, and James Carter the Democratic.

At the annual March town meeting the tax collector's salary was raised from $750 per year to $1,500. The town was also instructed to request from the trustees of trust funds a sum of money which had been given to the town for a flag pole by the class of 1906 of Antrim High School. This had been drawing interest for twenty years and now amounted to $101.80. As the bicentennial committee was planning to erect a flag pole at the point in front of the Baptist church, the sum was added to this fund.

The town also voted to investigate the matter of providing a new town garage, to purchase two Scott paks for the fire department, to look into collecting taxes twice yearly rather than borrowing large amounts of money in anticipation of taxes, to designate Reed Carr Road a scenic road, to appropriate $2,000 for the James A. Tuttle Library to supplement the income from trust funds, and to appropriate a sum not to exceed $700 to rebuild and paint the fences at the library. The two appropriations for the library were the first town support since the Gipson fund was received in 1938.

On April 10 the events planned by the bicentennial committee took place, making the day a busy one. In addition, the historical rooms in the library were open to the public, with refreshments served by the historical committee and volunteers.

Early in May the elementary and middle schools had their commemorative program which included the raising of the liberty pole. When it had been securely planted, Timothy Corliss shinnied to the top—while the audience watched, hardly breathing—and put a hat on top, a symbol of liberty and freedom. There were colonial craft demonstrations, folk songs, a play, "The Great Declaration," and a bicentennial menu served at the school lunch room. A time capsule had been prepared by the middle school, containing articles in general use at the present time. This was properly sealed and interred, but the place is known only to those who participated. They are sworn to secrecy to avoid risk of vandalism.

This closes our narrative of the past century. It would be a satisfaction to report that all unfinished business had been completed, tied up in a package, and put away, so that the new century could start afresh. But that is not the way the world's or a town's business is done. Always there is a continuity linking the past with the present and the future. In the case of our town of Antrim there is much to be worked on, especially in the matters of sewage disposal and tax equalization. The North Bennington bridge is still undecided; the zoning ordinance may need some changes; town planning in all areas goes on. But there is a growing group of younger citizens assuming responsibility for town activities, which is always an encouraging sign. Those winds of change noted in the beginning are still blowing—even more strongly than they were one hundred years ago—which we hope foretells good things for the future.

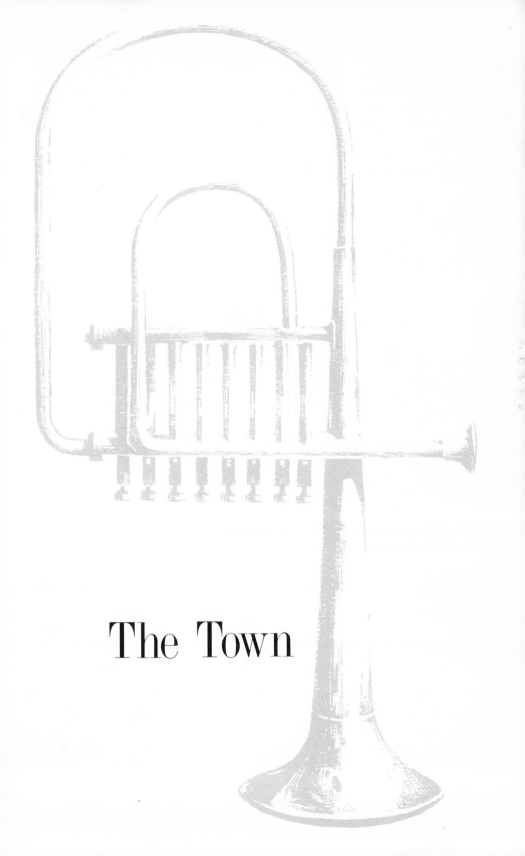

The Town

Antrim
1877-1976

a
topical history
of the last century

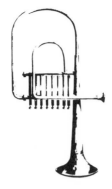

THE ARTS

IN A PRIMITIVE culture, the natural expression of art is found in practical and useful items, and our early citizens no doubt brought beauty into their lives by the creation of necessary articles. Art for art's sake would have been a frivolous waste of time. Eventually, however, Antrim overcame the obstacles of the wilderness and began to develop a sophisticated way of life. Frances Mary Steele was born here in 1839, into a world influenced greatly by the life style of Queen Victoria. Mary was a descendant of James Steele who came to the North Branch in 1780, and she grew up to become a teacher of music, painting, and English, and the head of Miss Steele's Private School for Young Women in Boston. The Victorian pattern of life dictated that a young lady would take painting lessons as a way of graciously filling up her leisure hours, but Mary Steele broke through the barrier, in the fashion of Mary Cassatt, and pursued a career. She never married, and upon her demise in 1932 a collection of her paintings of flower arrangements was presented to the Tuttle Library, where it is on display.

Laura Nulty Chestnutt came to Antrim in 1913 as the bride of Dr. Arthur A. Chestnutt. She had studied oil painting briefly in New York and continued to paint until she was in her eighties. Her earlier work includes portraits, superbly crafted, but most of the work she did in Antrim was of animals and pastoral scenes. An avid horsewoman, she used horses for many of her subjects. Although the quality of her work is unquestioned, she received little notice during her long life as an artist, but any person possessing a Laura Chestnutt painting is indeed fortunate.

John Caughey, on the other hand, has brought a modest amount of fame to the town through his work. He retired at 87 after an extended career in construction, and came to Antrim and took up oil painting. Not deterred by the disastrous fire that leveled his studio and destroyed hundreds of his pictures, he is still painting at age 102, and has an ever-growing horde of fans. The larger part of his work is made up of landscapes and still-lifes.

An established water-color artist, Edith Baker, claimed Antrim as her home and source of inspiration for nearly twenty years, coming here in the 1940s. Around the same time Ruby Allen, a retired art teacher, organized the Antrim Art Club. Many living-room walls are now adorned with paintings done by her students.

The League of New Hampshire Craftsmen is outstanding among similar organizations throughout the country for the support given its members and its growth and development over the last forty years. The quality of work accepted for sale at the eight centers is of exceptionally high standard. A charter member of the League was Helen Munroe, a potter. In 1932 she was the only teacher of pottery employed by the League, teaching classes at the University of New Hampshire. At an annual Craftsmen's Fair in Hancock she met her husband-to-be, Carroll Johnson, and after assuming the role of wife and mother in Antrim, her career in pottery gradually faded.

Arthur Cunningham, a woodworker, was an early member of the League, and generous in his praise of the organization (See Chronology, 1939). Edna Ryder came to Antrim in 1946, after a busy career in the New York State banking department, and brought her kiln with the idea of developing a hobby of ceramics. Through membership in the League the hobby became a business, and her charming small creations of lobster butter dishes and jam jars are in constant demand. She has purposely kept the business small, and never dropped the personal touch. Barbara Shea is another member of long standing, and maintains a handprinting business in her home. Her unique notepaper designs are irresistible in the market.

Poets have not flourished in Antrim in great quantity, but several are worthy of mention. The Cochrane brothers, Warren (of Town History authorship) and Clark, came here as adults, and seemingly were inspired by Antrim's rocky hills to prolific versification. Dr. Cochrane's *Poems* was published in 1908, and his younger brother produced two volumes of verse: *The Granite Hills* in 1884, and *Songs from the Hills*, in 1918.

Perley Richardson, born here in 1880, wrote poetry under the name of Potter Spaulding for many years. Many of his poems were published in *The Antrim Reporter*. Barbara Shea has had some of her poems published in children's anthologies.

Antrim's current poet laureate is Avis Turner French, who came here from Vermont when she married Malcolm French in 1923. She is a member of the American Poetry League, and a charter member of the Poetry Society of New Hampshire. Some of her impressive credits include listing in the International Who's Who in World Poetry and similar catalogues, and awards in national poetry contests. Her poems have been published in many newspapers and magazines, both at home and abroad. She has published two books of poetry: *Flickering Lights* in 1961, and *Lamplighting Memories*, circa 1970. A traditionalist in form, the beauty of her work is the warmth shown in her love of home, nature, and that lord of the hearth, the family cat.

The Mirror Cat

The mirror cat of silver gray,
Surprised me so I walked away,
But I returned as girls will do
When they have liked a mirror's view;
Then purred a song with loving grace,
And charmed the thief who wore my face.

Two of the lively arts, music and drama, have been intertwined in the life of Antrim for over a century. The various churches have been the source of many of the choral contributions, annual parades and promenades have made the appearances of instrumental groups a necessity, and each and every social and fraternal organization has fostered a dramatic group at one time or another.

William G. White came to Antrim in the last years of the nineteenth century and took an active interest in the town. He directed the Baptist Church choir and was a prime mover in organizing a choral union. He came to an untimely death in March, 1902, in an accident on the way home from church. The choral union of seventy-five members survived to present their first concert in April.

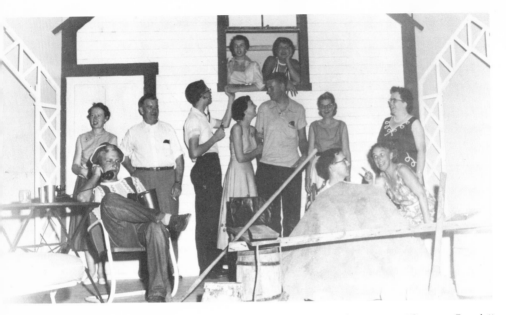

Mr. White's daughter Anna, herself an accomplished musician, married Ralph G. Winslow in 1910. He was a school music educator and composer, and following a serious illness recuperated in Antrim long enough to revive the choral union under the name of the Antrim Choral Society. They gave a concert on April 11, 1913, and the major work was the cantata, *Joan of Arc*, performed by a chorus of eighty voices, with guest and local soloists, and conducted by Mr. Winslow. The performance was attended by an audience of four hundred.

The Winslows' son, Richard, conducted his first production, *The Pirates of Penzance*, in 1939, and followed this after World War II with several other Gilbert and Sullivan operettas. During the 1960s local groups were seen and heard in two original Richard Winslow musicals, *Her Father, the King*, and *Alice-* (of Wonderland fame). This family has contributed to Antrim's choral experiences for seventy years.

Various members of the Jameson family were much in demand as singers and vocal teachers from time to time, but it was Mrs. Robert (Marie) Jameson who brought to town the skills needed for producing musical plays. She became the Presbyterian choir director, and under its auspices presented an operetta with a Chinese background, and, "The New Minister," the latter in 1917.

Other choir directors who were responsible for productions of this nature were W.A.N. Scott and Elizabeth Felker. Kenneth Jewett was director of the Monadnock chorus in the 1940s, and drew on the local choirs for a substantial part of the membership. Concerts by this group were given locally. Howard Chase, then of Bennington, was largely responsible for the organization of the Antrim Music Club, circa 1948-1953. Monthly meetings were held in the Library Hall, and annual concerts were presented by its members, both as soloists and in chorus.

Instrumental groups seem to be constantly changing membership, along with the name of the group. So it would appear that the Antrim Orchestra of 1902 might have had much the same membership as Appleton's Orchestra of 1905, with George Appleton (and his violin) as the leading musician. No social function of the era was complete without the popular renditions of this seven-member group.

Countless local musicians performed under the rubric of the Antrim Band for over fifty years, with Squires Forsaith, Morris Nay, and George Warren as three of the outstanding leaders. Always on hand for parades, they also provided many a summer evening's entertainment from the bandstand on Concord Street. On occasion the band was invited to perform in neighboring towns, both in parade and concert. While playing in Bennington one night, they treated the audience to an unusual rendition of "The Star Spangled Banner." The music was passed out, and the band commenced to play. Shortly after the opening notes it gradually became evident that all was not right. One by one the players dropped out, and the conductor peered more closely at his music, searching in vain for the cause of the dysphony. The bass drummer and one trombonist were either very brave or tone-deaf, and they completed the number in duet form. As the audience happily honked their car-horns in appreciation, it was discovered that the conductor had passed out parts from two arrangements, each in a different key! Fortunately this was the last number on the program, and the Antrim Band was able to slink home quietly and pick up the pieces of its reputation.

A flourishing theatrical group in the 1870s was the Waverly Dramatic Club. Some of the more ambitious productions were *Ten Nights in a Barroom*, and *Uncle Tom's Cabin*, starring George Cochran in the leading male roles. Fred Nay, a photographer, was stage manager and

The Antrim Players . . . "Mr. Roberts"

scenic designer for the group. Advertisements in *The Antrim Home News* offered scenery for rent by the Waverly Dramatic Club, but by 1876 the scenery was for sale, which indicates an early demise.

Now considered taboo by most communities, the minstrel show was a popular form of entertainment in Antrim. *The Belles of Blackville* was put on in 1903 for the benefit of the library. A professional actress, Rose Ethel Lapoint, directed local plays around 1913, but the person who had the most influence on local theatre was J. Lillian Larabee. Following is a history of The Antrim Players, written by Dorothy Proctor, and printed in *The Monadnock Regionnaire* in 1969:

> The Antrim Players have completed their first half century of organized work in the dramatic and musical field of entertainment.
> In a town rich with talent, the Players have maintained a steady pace of growth, graduating from the "thigh-slapping" days of "Aaron Slick from Punkin Crick" to their latest magnificent production of "The Miracle Worker."
> Retired dramatic coach in the Boston school system, Mrs. J. Lillian Larrabee arrived in Antrim prior to World War I. Realizing the town was alive with latent talent, she formed the nucleus of the original Antrim

Player Group. Her carefully-enunciated directives have passed down through succeeding generations and her influence is still felt in the battered wings of the town hall stage.

A costume room of well over 3,000 items is constantly maintained. Many of the garments, accessories, and "props" have appeared on stage at the Peterborough Players summer theatre, Keene and Manchester dramatic groups, local organizations, and the Nathaniel Hawthorne College drama department.

The Players have held membership in the New England Theatre Conference for 12 years and individual members have appeared fairly steadily in plays given by the Monadnock theatre and the Peterborough Players.

Profits realized by the Players are used to maintain the Town Hall stage, help beautify the auditorium, and provide an adequate stage lighting system. Local organizations have profited by sponsoring productions and receiving an equitable share.

Many original works have been presented by these versatile people — Donald Madden has written and produced two 3-act plays and several one act. Richard Winslow produced several original musical plays and directed many others. Isabel Nichols has written and produced many musicals for the High School Chorus.

Some members who have appeared steadily on stage for fifty years and over are Byron and Vera Butterfield and Dorothy Proctor, who also directed for thirty years. The Players are also blessed by a talented back stage crew. Art work by Barbara Shea has enhanced many a set. Wardrobe mistress Gertrude Meador has supervised miles of sturdy stitching. Philip Baker has done yeoman duty with workable, artistic scenery and sets while Priscilla and David Hurlin, a sterling acting duo, have kept a watchful eye on the costume room. Membership keeps at a fairly steady 30 in number, all of whom participate in the many activities connected with non-professional play production.

The group is now under the direction of Fred Roberts and Robert Alvin and anticipate many more years of productive pleasure in "treading the boards."

Since then the Players have given only three major productions, the most memorable of which was *Mr. Roberts*, in 1971. Directed by Dorothy Proctor, the enormous cast was headed by Bob Alvin, Fred Roberts, Barry Proctor, and Dick Ebert. Phil Baker built a battleship set that was probably seaworthy and extended many feet beyond the proscenium in all directions. Part of the meager back-stage area had to be made into a stall for the goat who was an important member of the cast. Although he performed admirably and seemed to enjoy his brief exposure to show business, he succumbed less than a week after the closing performance. An analogy might be drawn between the goat and the Antrim Players, but the many admirers of the group prefer to think of the long play-less period as a much deserved rest, and are looking forward to the time when inspiration in the form of a latter-day J. Lillian Larrabee will bring about a revival.

CEMETERIES

THERE ARE five cemeteries in Antrim, plus the family plot of the Whittemores near the Hillsboro line. Three of the old tracts are no longer used, perhaps because the churches with which they were once affiliated have long since been torn down.

The oldest burying ground in Antrim is atop Meeting House Hill, where the first meeting house stood. It is peaceful, quiet, and serene. Only traces of a few cellar holes hint of the early settlement so confidently built on the exact geographical center of the town. Here the first church, or meeting house, was raised, and the ground for the graveyard cleared. As originally laid out, the cemetery was smaller than its present size. By 1818, there was no more room in the yard, and an area about half the original size was added to the west. The log fence which defined its early limits was replaced by a stone wall around the entire perimeter, and this still stands today. In 1911, the Molly Aiken Chapter of the DAR erected the fine new gate and memorial tablets described in the chapter on military history.

For fifty years, this was the only burial place in the town. Ironically, one of the early graves on the hill was that of James Dinsmore, who was killed when he fell from the old meeting house where he was working. Many graves are not marked in any way, and as there are no records available from the early days, it is impossible to tell how many are buried there, although Dr. Cochrane estimated the number to be at least seven hundred.

One of the reasons for so many deaths in those times was the inability to control spreading epidemics once they got started. In addition to victims of disease and accident, there were those who died from plain old age, and were buried there on the hill. One of these was the Indian, Peter Waugh, said to be the last Indian living in Antrim. He died in the late spring of 1815 in his hut northwest of Gregg Pond. According to legend, he said to those around him, "I want to be buried in the white man's burying ground. I don't want to be buried by the side of the road, where the white woman's child, when it go on errand, will stop and point its finger at my grave and say 'There be old Indian buried,' and run away and be scare." His white neighbors, respecting his wish, buried him close to the north wall of the old cemetery, a little east of the middle of the wall. The legend was perpetuated by the children of the town, who for a century thereafter dared each other to stand on the Indian's grave at midnight and say, "What did you do with your life that was worth anything?" The answer, of course, was "Nothing," since the Indian could not talk.

The second cemetery in town, begun in 1826, was associated with the Center church, across the road from the parsonage (now Lewan's). It was started by Dr. Whiton, and here he was buried. It is scarcely noticeable from the road now, but a little-used path between Edna Ryder's barn and Lewan's antique shop brings one to the old iron gateway and gently sloping yard, enclosed by a stone wall and ringed with pines and maples. The tall old gravestones, mostly marble, stand close together, slanting a little here and there, making an enchanting play of light and shadow in the late afternoon sun. The marble, once white, is now weather stained and invaded by lichen, the old verses eroded by rain and hard to read:

> Stranger pause as you pass by
> As you are now, so once was I
> As I am now, so you will be
> Prepare for death and follow me.

Although North Branch never had a church building (other than the chapel on the Flint estate), it did have the third cemetery in town. This was the "Cemetery on the Plain," established in the northern section of Antrim in 1826, the same year the Center yard was begun. The Antrim North Branch Cemetery Association was incorporated in 1864, and is still in existence today. Unfortunately, the early records were all lost in the disastrous North Branch fire of 1888. This cemetery and Maplewood (the last of the five to be built) are the only two in use at the present time. The North Branch cemetery was enlarged by the purchase of an acre of land from Mrs. Elizabeth Van Hennik, and the beautiful stone wall which surrounds it was the work of the firm of Caughey & Pratt.

A fourth cemetery, started the year after the Center yard, was the one in East Antrim in connection with the Federated Church. Since the church served families from North Bennington and West Deering as well as the community in East Antrim, not all the plots there belong to native Antrimites. It has been long unused, and here one may see the archaic use of the expression "relict of," referring to a widow buried next to her husband.

About 1829, the town voted "saxons" to oversee the care of the Center, East, and North Branch cemeteries. These men were appointed to their positions annually for the next half century, the responsibility subsequently being borne by the individual cemetery associations.

The last, and now the most frequently used burial ground in Antrim, is the Maplewood cemetery, located on Route 202 just north of the village. It was established in 1862, by which time South Village, so called, was becoming the most densely populated of any area in Antrim. The land, once a "dry, poor sheep pasture," was bought by Mark and Levi Woodbury at the suggestion of J.W. Christie. The Woodburys fitted it for use and sold lots for remuneration. By a coincidence, Mr. Christie, who envisioned the land as a cemetery, was one of the first to be buried there.

The long rows of maple trees in the old (south) portion of Maplewood, planted a century ago, are now, in their maturity, a glorious and breath-taking sight in September. This original section once had a fountain installed in 1877 through the interested efforts of Mrs. Anna Woodbury, who paid half the total cost of four hundred dollars. The fountain was removed in 1947, and in 1931 the old gate which originally guarded the entrance was done away with, the opening enlarged, and a chain installed. Originally, too, there was a hearse house, but it was taken down in 1890.

The pond at the far end of this old portion of Maplewood is spring fed, and dates from 1897 when a dam was constructed to collect the water. The dam was rebuilt in 1915 by G.H. Caughey, and the small body of water with its water lilies and its beautiful "June pink" is now a summer idyl. Water from this pond is pumped to storage tanks at the top of the hill for general use.

The educated eye can tell at a glance that the oldest part of Maplewood is nearly a century younger than the Meeting House cemetery, for instance. There are no simple slate headstones here: the final tombs of these Victorians are almost ornate enough to be classified as mausoleums. Similarly, those who died in the middle twentieth century can be identified by their polished granite monuments, proof that styles change in death as in life.

The granite tombstones are mostly to be found in the Goodell annex, a section of Maplewood lying north of the original area, added in 1936. This land was acquired by gifts from Dr. Morris Christie, Sylvanus Dow, Miss Etta Miller, the Shedd family fund, and Richard Goodell, among others. The firm of Caughey & Pratt constructed a fine stone wall, similar to the one enclosing the old part, and this section has its own gate. The young maple trees bordering the roads here will one day rival the grand old specimens along the original paths.

In 1954, the Waverly Lodge IOOF installed a permanent monument to all Odd Fellows buried in the cemetery. The Antrim Garden Club planted the rambler roses along the front stone wall, adding greatly to the beauty of the cemetery. Soldiers' graves are marked by iron flag holders, and each year the flags are replaced by the American Legion. Included in the town records are copies of all tombstone inscriptions from every cemetery in town, compiled by members of the DAR circa 1912. Although not current, this information could be of great value to anyone pursuing genealogical research.

Antrim does not forget her honored dead. Money is set aside in the town budget for the maintenance of the Meeting House, Center, and East cemeteries, since they have no private associations to care for them. The members of the DAR and the American Legion are meticulous in their attention to the graves of all fallen veterans of America's wars. And every Memorial Day sees families and friends, many with bouquets of lilacs, iris, and tulips from the ancestral gardens, gathered to remember and honor those they loved. They are the personification of Whitman's poem

When lilacs last in the dooryard bloom'd,
And the great star early dropped in the western sky in the night
I mourned, and yet shall mourn with ever-returning spring.

CHURCHES

THE FIRST SETTLERS in Antrim, Scotch-Irish Protestants, were hard working, pious, God-fearing men and women who, despite the vast amount of physical labor necessary to clear the land and sustain life in what was virtually a wilderness, nevertheless set aside Sunday as the Lord's day, and kept it holy. That they had no churches or ministers surely worried them. Occasionally a minister came from a neighboring town to conduct marriage and funeral services. The first sermon in Antrim was preached in September, 1775, in Deacon Aiken's barn. The preacher was William Davidson, of Londonderry. Probably, according to the custom then, women sat in the center of the barn, and men and boys fitted in where they could.

The concept of the separation of church and state had not yet been formulated, and for many years the townspeople voted at town meeting so many days' preaching for the year in so-and-so's house. Finally, in 1784, they decided to abandon this haphazard practice and build a centrally located church.

The geographical center of the town was fixed upon the top of what is now called Meeting House hill, and here in 1785, a meeting house — an all purpose building, used both for secular and religious purposes — was erected.

Dr. Cochrane wrote an interesting account of the building efforts. A committee was chosen to plan for the building; they voted to grant the contract to "the loest bidder," and further voted "five gallons of rum for the vendue." In addition to the rum, they voted to "provide bread and cheese and dry fish for the raising at the meeting-house & butter;" that "a meat dinner be provided for the reasing;" and also voted to provide "one dozen of wooden kans, each to hold three quarts." (The spelling is theirs.) Colonel William Gregg of Londonderry was the master builder. The timber was standing when he came, but the people went at it with such vigor that all was cut, hewed, and framed in less than three weeks. The house was raised June 28, and the people rejoiced that they even had the frame of a meeting house. Dr. Whiton, Antrim's first published historian, says — "The people were so pleased with the idea of having a meeting house that, on the Sabbath next after the raising of the frame, they met in it for worship, having a Mr. Whipple for their preacher. Nothing had been done to the house but to lay down a little loose flooring, to place a few boards on blocks for seats, and a few on the beams as a screen from the sun. In time of service there arose a violent thunderstorm, and while the little congregation were fleeing for shelter, the rain poured down copiously, wetting many to the skin."

The Center Church

A new edifice, known as the Center Church, was erected in the summer of 1826 to replace the old Meeting House. Dr. Whiton, its pastor for the first twenty-eight years, came to Antrim in 1808 at the age of twenty-three to be the town's minister. He remained here forty-five years in all. The year before he resigned, he published the first history of Antrim, thus preserving for us the details of the first century of the town's life. Our debt for this service is incalculable.

By 1880, the membership of the Center Church was two hundred and sixty-three, the largest number of any church in town. The Presbyterian affiliation of the early Scottish settlers was clearly predominant. Services were held regularly in the Center Church until 1893, when the main body of Presbyterians moved to a new church in the South Village.

It is not easy to discover the exact and true facts about this move. We do know that the residents of South Antrim, numbering some seventy families in 1880, did not look forward with pleasure to a round trip of roughly five miles, one way mostly uphill, to go to church. So the Presbyterians among them petitioned the Presbytery for permission to build a church in the village. According to hearsay, permission was denied on the basis that the population of the town was not great enough for two churches of the same denomination. The Center people did not want to leave their beautiful church, so the matter was at an impasse. In fact, there seems to have been considerable bitterness between the two factions, neither side being willing to give an inch.

No written records can be found to validate the truth of what happened next, and feelings ran so high that even today it is a subject spoken of with great reluctance. However, Center Church was demolished by dynamite. Some say that it was first declared unsafe by way of excuse. Some say that a twenty-four hour notice was given, presumably so that the communion service and other objects of value could be removed first. For a while, it is said that many of the houses in the Center had pew benches on their porches, all removed to safety during the twenty-four hour period.

At any rate, it is gone today. Of the beautiful old church on the hill, the horse shed, and the chapel added in 1875, nothing but pictures and memories remain.

The East Church

Until 1826 there had been only one church in town. At the time Center Church was being built, residents of the east part of town decided to build their own neighborhood church. Banding together, they formed themselves into a society which they called, "The First United Presbyterian Congregational Baptist Society in Antrim," surely an interdenominational title, if a bit unwieldy. An acre of land near where the East cemetery now lies (off Elm Avenue near the junction of Route 202) was purchased for one hundred dollars, and settlers in East Antrim, West Deering, and North Bennington raised $4,500 to build the church in 1826. At first, there was no official church affiliation, but in 1827 it was organized as a Congregational church, with some thirty members. After four years it was reorganized as Baptist and functioned for ten years. Thereafter, it was used only occasionally by visiting preachers of various faiths.

In 1867 the steeple was thought to be unsafe, so it was removed, and in 1873 the building was sold at auction to J.B. Woodbury & Son, who took it down. No trace of its location can be found today.

The Baptist Church

The Baptists were nomads for a long time. Their first recorded meeting was in 1805 at Joseph Eaton's house in Greenfield. There was a branch church in Hancock, and for some time Bennington, known

Baptist Church

also as Society Land, was the home of the Baptists. For ten years they met at the East church, as related above. In 1852, it was voted "to hire Woodbury's hall for one year for worship."

From 1866 to 1873, the pastor was the Reverend William Hurlin, great-grandfather of David Hurlin, now president of Goodell Company. (See chapter on Industries.) William Hurlin was instrumental in building a permanent home for the Baptists. In 1871, the site of the present church was chosen, at the junction of Main and Concord Streets. The building was erected that year at a cost of $6,200. (Coincidentally, this was the identical amount the Center Church cost, but obviously materials and labor were more expensive half a century

Congregational Church

Parades and Promenades

Presbyterian Church

later, as the Baptist church is not as imposing an edifice as the former was.) Thirty-four years later it was felt that more space was needed, so the church vestry was added for $2,873.81. The eighty-one cents is not insignificant; the money for building and remodeling all the churches came in small amounts: from the widows' mites, the sale of quilts, and the church suppers.

An amusing story is told of William's son Henry, who retained the religious practices of his father, never neglecting to say grace before a meal. Once, however, his prayer began with an unusual familiarity. Goodell Company, where he worked, had that day installed a new scientific marvel — a telephone. Doubtless it was still very much on

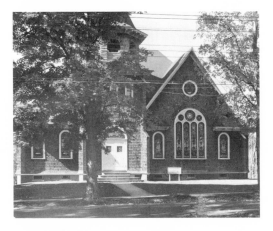

First Church of Christ, Scientist

his mind when he came home for the noon meal, sat down at the table, put his linen napkin on his lap, reverentially bowed his head, and said — "Hello."

The longest pastorate in the Baptist church was that of the Reverend Ralph Tibbals, who compiled the major part of the *Genealogical Records*, published in 1967. He ministered to his parishioners for twenty-three years, coming to Antrim in 1922. The preface to the *Genealogical Records* contains the following:

In a day when the world placed more importance on conformity, Reverend Tibbals was a champion of the freedom of the individual to think and act on honest personal conviction. He insisted on tolerance. He believed there was strength in variety of opinion, however divergent. He was ahead of his time in urging and promoting ecumenism.

Over the past one hundred years, seventeen pastors have served this church with dignity and dedication. Under their guidance, many changes and improvements have been made in the church building. In 1886 a baptistry extension was built at the north end of the auditorium, under the pulpit level. It was first used in December of that year. In 1924 a rebuilt Estey pipe organ was installed in the sanctuary. After thirty-eight years of service, it was repaired at a cost of $9,100, a sum provided by memorial gifts. In the nineteen sixties, an educational unit, pastor's study, and conference center were added at the astronomical cost of $25,000. And finally a sound system has recently been installed in the steeple, broadcasting music throughout the village.

The Methodist Church

The earliest mention of Methodists in Antrim was in 1838, when a Methodist class was formed at the Branch. The first preacher named was the Reverend Ezra Wardwell, who apparently was a circuit rider, serving several towns. By 1852, Reverend Wardwell having been succeeded by the Reverend S.S. Dudley, a church of fifty-one members was formally organized, with meetings being held sometimes at the Branch, sometimes in the East church, and sometimes in the school house at South Antrim.

During the winter of 1863-64, Dr. Cochrane reported, *new interest was awakened; through the exertions of Howard Stacey, Harold Kelsea, and Alvah Dodge, funds were raised by contributions of the citizens for the purpose of building; and on the ninth of October, 1864, a new hall was opened in South Antrim, which, with several improvements and enlargements, is now [1877] the Methodist church, and is a very neat and convenient edifice.*

This building is the one in which John Shea lives today.

When the membership outgrew this facility, a bequest from the estate of Mrs. Luke (Mary Wallace) Woodbury opened the way for the congregation to build the church now owned by the Christian Science Society. The new church was dedicated February 9, 1904, and functioned until 1935, when it became financially impossible to continue. As the church ceased its regular activities, the membership disbanded and united with other churches in the area.

The Congregational Church

When the Center Church was razed, a number of dissidents determined to retain a church in the Center, and accordingly united to form the First Congregational Church of Antrim Center. Apparently the out buildings of the old church were left standing, for on the Sunday immediately following the demolition of the church itself, this band of stalwarts began worshipping in the chapel.

Beginning with fifty-one members, the group grew to more than a hundred, and a committee was chosen to plan for the building of the stone church, which stands today just a little down the hill from the site of the old church. The report of the building committee describes their efforts:

The services of this society were begun on the nineteenth of February, 1893, and continued just two and a half years before any steps were taken to provide a permanent place of worship.

At a meeting held August 19,1895, it was voted to build a meeting house, and a committee was appointed to solicit funds for the purpose. At this meeting, Mr. James M. Gove offered to give the land for the building. Some progress was made during the next few months in securing promises of aid, and on the 24th of July, 1896, the society met and elected a building committee, and a treasurer of the building fund.

The committee was led to favor building the meeting house of field stone, the reason being that there were stones enough on the lot, and in the vicinity of it. Plans for the building. . .were furnished by H.P. Groves, architect, of Lowell, Massachusetts, the building. . .having an audience room, connected by sliding doors with a chapel. There was to be a pastor's room on the same floor, and downstairs a vestry, kitchen, and furnace rooms. The audience was to seat two hundred people. As soon as the plans were decided upon, a canvass was held, and was so successful that the committee felt warranted in commencing work in the spring of 1897; on April 21st digging the cellar was begun.

The foundation for the building was laid by Frank P. Ellenwood of Antrim; the stone walls were built by E.C. Howe of Manchester. The carpenter work was done by N.S. Coles of Bedford, Massachusetts. At every time of need there was money, sometimes from unexpected sources, but always enough. The committee decided, at some additional expense, to substitute for a plaster ceiling one of steel, which would be more durable, and make the auditorium room more attractive.

In the month of October, 1897, two events occurred of significant interest to have special mention. On Sunday the tenth, there were present at the morning service eighty-seven people. All had given for the building, many much beyond their means, but on being asked for a contribution to buy the oak pews, they responded unstintingly, and $429.00 was quickly pledged. The other event of the month occurred on the fifteenth, for on this day the bell was hung in the tower, a gift to the society from Mr. Eben Bass. It weighs, with all its fittings, 1,640 pounds. In the evening of the same day it called the people together for their mid-week prayer meeting.

It was not expected that the windows could be other than plain glass. But once again there was response when the proposal for something better was made. Hence we have the beautiful windows of opalescent glass. . .made by Spencer, Hookler and Bell of Boston, and given by different people of the congregation, the Sunday School, the Young People's Society of Christian Endeavor, and the King's Daughters. The pulpit, communion table and chair were given by interested members and friends, as were the electric light fixtures, given by Governor D.H. Goodell.

During the year 1898, the work on the building was completed, and the money to pay all bills was provided in the fall. The amount received is $5,924.35, and the amount paid out is $5,891.71. The vestry and the kitchen are not finished, nor have we a sufficient number of horse sheds. On behalf of the society, the building committee would express most hearty thanks to all who have so kindly aided in this work.

Building Committee: John Tenney
Charles Freeman Holt
Henry P. Warden

We present unto you this building, to be dedicated as a church for the service and worship of Almighty God.

The church prospered for many years. At times, the congregation reached the two hundred mark. Morning and evening services were held regularly, as well as midweek and preparatory services. Church suppers (for as little as ten cents in the early days), harvest suppers served by the best cooks in town, it was said, and strawberry festivals were not-to-be-missed events. But with the attrition of time, the attendance dwindled, and by the year 1960 the meetings were reduced to an early service during the summer only. At that time, no permanent pastor being retained, the sermons were preached by the minister of one of the town's other churches.

The Chapel at North Branch

At the entrance to the grounds of Nathaniel Hawthorne College stands a tiny chapel which for many years functioned as a non-denominational meeting house for the North Branch community. At the end of the nineteenth century, a group of religiously motivated women united to form an organization called the Ladies Circle. They sponsored an active program of religious education: a Sunday school, a youth group, and an evening preaching service, with village ministers taking turns leading the services. Support for the programs was found in free-will offerings, personal gifts, and social functions such as teas, suppers, and sales.

Many community activities took place here: old school reunions, marriages, and funerals. Though in later years its program was increasingly restricted by the social changes in the area, it nevertheless continued to function until the year 1962, when the Flint estate was purchased by Nathaniel Hawthorne College for its academic location.

The Presbyterian Church

The land on which the Presbyterian church in Antrim village stands was given by Nathan C. Jameson. The Presbyterians in the village were most enthusiastic about the new building, and even some non-Presbyterians helped with picks and shovels to excavate the cellar and make way for the foundation. The great granite stones in the foundation were hauled in and maneuvered into place by man and animal power. The architectural design was drawn by Charles W. Bolton of Philadelphia. Before any shovelful of earth was dug, $11,029 was raised and on hand when the work was begun. As the work progressed, fund raising continued, so that by the time the building was ready, there would be enough funds on hand to settle all the bills. With this in mind, though the work had been completed a short time before, the date of July 3, 1894, was set for the dedication. The church was dedicated free of debt at a total cost of $19,000.

The articles and furnishings salvaged from the Center church were installed in the new building. The Paul Revere bell was placed in the steeple; the pulpit chairs, a small spinet organ, the communion table, and some of the church pews were all brought to the new building.

In 1914, a manse was given jointly by Mrs. Nathan C. Jameson and her son-in-law, George A. Walker, in memory of his wife, Isabel Jameson Walker. In the same year, a renovated pipe organ was installed. In the 1960s, a Mr. Douglass modernized this organ and the one in the Baptist church, changing the controls from a pneumatic system to one operated by electricity. In 1955 the sanctuary was sound-proofed, a gift to the church from Mrs. Robert Jameson.

In 1957 after sixty-five years of use, the entire building needed major repairs, and at that time the sealed box placed in the cornerstone at the time of the dedication was removed, its contents updated, and it was resealed for posterity.

From 1964 to 1974, the entire basement area of the church and vestry was converted into educational facilities and classrooms, with volunteer labor and donations to cover the cost of materials. In the same way, the church kitchen was renovated for more efficient and practical use. Now the old slate roof, showing the ravages of time, is being removed area by area and replaced with asphalt shingles. The steeple, which was struck by lightning in 1972, has been repaired and reshingled. Much credit for these improvements goes to the Reverend William Clark, minister of that time, who literally was one of the laborers in the vineyard.

The church has had seventeen pastors to date. The first of these was the Reverend Warren Robert Cochrane, to whom the writers of this history are so heavily indebted. He came to Antrim in 1868, and was ordained in 1869. In 1880 he published the book from which we now draw so freely: *History of the Town of Antrim, New Hampshire, from its earliest settlement to June 27, 1877, with a brief Genealogical Record of all the Antrim families.*

The Christian Science Society

In 1949 several students of Christian Science who lived in the area around Antrim became interested in securing the use of the Methodist church building for their services. The trustees of the Methodist church were approached, offered free use of the facilities, and in 1950 fourteen members of the Society in Peterborough who lived in Antrim met and resolved to form a local Society. On September 5 of that year, an official meeting was held, and in 1951 the group applied for recognition as a branch of the First Church of Christ, Scientist in Boston, Massachusetts. In October they became officially known as the Christian Science Society, Antrim, New Hampshire.

As soon as this status was established, steps were taken to purchase the church building from the Methodist organization. With generous assistance from the Selina C. Cornish Fund, the cooperation of members and friends, and a grant from the trustees of the will of Mary Baker Eddy, the purchase was completed for the bargain price of $5,000. The Christian Science church in Antrim was dedicated free of debt in June, 1954.

The first Christian Science lecture was given in June of 1953. In January, 1954, the reading room was opened to the public. The first official practitioner of the Antrim Society was Mrs. Daisy F. Chase, who held that position until her death in 1975.

The Society maintained a full year-round program of church activities at the church building until the fall of 1970, when it was voted to hold church services only during the summer months, with services in members' homes during the remainder of the year.

St. Patrick's Church – Bennington

Since the inhabitants of Antrim were predominantly Protestant, there was no Catholic church to care for the needs of the people of that faith. We include here an account of St. Patrick's Roman Catholic Church of Bennington in recognition of its services to the Catholics of Antrim. A direct quotation from the parish records provides an interesting insight into the early beginnings:

In the early 1890s Catholic churches were few and far between. The travelling was difficult and slow. . .Mass was celebrated in homes, chiefly in farm homes, and only several times a year. About twenty Catholic families living in Antrim, Bennington, Greenfield, and Hancock, with a

strong desire for a church of their own, sought the help of Father David W.
Fitzgerald, then pastor of St. Mary's church in Hillsboro, who had been
looking after their spiritual needs.

After much debate about a suitable location, the town of Bennington was
finally selected as being the most centrally located, and a small rocky knoll
on the southeast side of the village was purchased from George Brown for
$100. Additional land was donated by Peter Hansle, making up the present
lot.

In 1895 construction was started with volunteer help, donations, and
borrowed money. John King, local carpenter and builder, and himself a
non-Catholic, was hired to head the crew. Saint Brenner was one of the
names considered, but the Irish voted for Patrick. The church was finally
dedicated by Bishop Bradley in 1896 under the patronage of Saint Patrick.

The early years of the church were not easy ones. The cost of construction
and furnishings, excluding donations, was $3,500. Heating was a major
problem. Heavy clothes and cold feet were always in style. There was no
basement, and wood was used as fuel. Horse sheds were provided for the
comfort of the horses, many of them having travelled from neighboring
towns. The sheds were later removed to provide parking space for more
modern travel.

The first Mass was celebrated by Father Fitzgerald in October, 1895, at which time he also assumed the duties of the Mission. He traveled on horseback, and his constant companion was a thoroughbred greyhound. In 1901 the Reverend Joseph Corcoran succeeded as pastor of the little Mission, which was heavily in debt. He was a master of discipline, and insisted, "If you want it and have it, you must pay for it." A lawn party was held, and the proceeds of this affair, an incredible $1,300, were sufficient to pay off the original debt of the church.

Colonel Arthur J. Pierce, although not a Catholic himself, was one of the great benefactors of the parish. He had the altar redesigned to accommodate a portrait, "The Madonna of the Chair," which he had sent from Europe, and gave the sanctuary furniture, including two china Holy Water fonts from Rome, and the steeple bell in memory of his wife, Sally Crocker Barr Pierce.

Over the years, many changes have been made in the physical aspect of the church. A new entrance has been added; a parish hall has been developed in the basement of the building; new pews, altar rail, and the Confessional all have been given in memory of loved ones. A rectory has been built across the street from the church. When the first resident pastor arrived in June of 1936, the congregation consisted of one hundred and twenty-three families living in Antrim, Bennington, Francestown, Greenfield, and Hancock. Now the church has an average of one hundred and fifty in attendance in the winter, and a summer peak of five hundred families.

The oldtime sectarian spirit is gradually giving way to the modern spirit of ecumenism. Ministers and priests sermonize in each others' churches, congregations sing each others' hymns, and tolerance and respect continue to grow. The ethic of the Reverend Ralph Tibbals may yet be fulfilled.

INDUSTRIES

INDUSTRIAL ACTIVITY in Antrim began in a very small way,
reached its zenith in the late 1800s and the early 1900s, and has been
declining ever since. Where there were once ten manufactures in
North Branch, and as many as twenty-two at one time or another
along Great Brook, today the single remaining plant of any size is
Goodell Company. One small operation, the Antrim Reel Shop, is the
only other factory offering local employment.

The rise and fall of industry in Antrim is interesting to consider. The
first mills produced essentials for the earliest settlers—grain and
lumber—utilizing power from the two natural resources Antrim was
blessed with: the North Branch River and the Great Brook. Just below
the lake which bears his name, Samuel Gregg built a small dam across
Great Brook and started a combination saw and grist mill in 1793. Even
earlier (1776) John Warren built his saw mill on the North Branch
River, and in South Village Deacon Aiken early-on put up a saw mill
for his own convenience as well as that of his neighbors. Thus the first
settlers in three sections of the town, isolated from each other because
of the lack of roads, were able to procure their essential necessities
right in the neighborhood, so to speak.

Other mills followed, each playing a vital role in maintaining the
small settlements and lightening the burden of life in the wilderness.
Fulling mills and carding shops produced cloth. Duncan's tannery
supplied leather for shoes and harnesses. Grist mills ground the grain
for bread; saw mills turned out clapboards, opening the way for more
substantial houses than the early log cabins. Specialists such as
blacksmiths and wheelwrights found plenty of work to keep them
busy.

It is likely that none of these industries initially represented full time employment for their owners. In the beginning, every man was, of necessity, a farmer, but with the coming of the industrial age, some men dreamed of escaping from an agricultural into a manufacturing environment. These were the men—the Abbotts, the Paiges, the Goodells and others—who from 1830-on established their many mills along Great Brook and at the Branch. In Clinton Village, two businesses lasted well into the middle of the twentieth century: Abbott's and Paige's.

Samuel W. Abbott came to Antrim in 1835, and with Imla Wright built the Abbott mill in 1836. The Abbott family operated a successful business on the same premises for well over a hundred years. Mr. Abbott's father, a minister with a mechanical bent, had invented a "rustic window shade," and this was one of the first products of the new factory. In addition, hat boxes and paper fans were also produced. Window shades were discontinued in 1874.

The business passed down through three generations of Abbotts, and from time to time it was deemed expedient to change products. One son, John Gano Abbott, carried on an undertaking business, and part of the building was used as a coffin warehouse. After the company began to manufacture cribs, a local pleasantry had it that "Abbott Company provides for both ends of life, but in reverse order."

The most successful phase of the business may have been after 1927, when Henry A. Hurlin, then president of Goodell Company, bought an interest in it. His sister was John G. Abbott's widow, and in this manner Antrim's two major manufacturing concerns were allied in one family. The company managed to survive both the depression and the shortage of labor and materials during the war years, and in 1947 began to manufacture and distribute the "Abbott Step-fold Playyard," perhaps their most widely known product. Business grew to the extent that it was necessary to rent more space, and finally the entire operation was moved to Keene in 1955. It was the longest continuously operating industry on Great Brook in Clinton, running for a period of one hundred and twenty-five years under the ownership of the Abbott family. The large building, sold earlier to Gates Manufacturing Company, burned to the ground in a spectacular fire in September, 1960.

The second longest running business in Clinton Village was that owned by the Paige family. The founding father was Enoch Paige, who started his business ventures when he was only twenty years old.

*Enoch Paige's Shop
. . . burned in 1910*

In short order, he acquired two mills, which he used for the production of cribs and cradles until his death in 1917. Two of his sons inherited the businesses, one factory to each son. The building that son Bert acquired was old and worn out, so he had it torn down in 1920. But son Mort continued the business at his site, although he soon changed from production of cribs and cradles to wooden reels used by the cordage trade. Under different ownership, the Antrim Reel Company is still in business, although not at the old site where the building burned in 1970, so the operation moved to Antrim village.

Generally speaking, the operation of a modern factory does not seem particularly fascinating to us today, but we find enchanting details of how things were done long ago. Perhaps we savor some subconscious satisfaction out of the comparison that seems to prove the degree of technical progress we have made. Or perhaps we cherish the stamina and perseverance of our ancestors who did things the hard way but nevertheless got them done. Austin Paige, grandson of Enoch, paints an evocative picture of the operation of the Paige mill when it was used for making cradles:

Now let us suppose you were to go into this shop in the wintertime scores of years ago. You would have to walk unless some kindhearted fellow gave you a lift in a one-horse open sleigh, and walking wasn't as easy as it is today, because the roads were rolled, not plowed. Most of the help walked several miles each way to work.
When you entered the shop, you would see groups of men clustered around the barrel stoves, with stove pipes running overhead in all directions. Some

early bird would have already lighted the kerosene lamps and kindled the fires.

When seven o'clock rolled around, several men would grab axes and proceed to chop out the dam, a necessary chore for the functioning of the water wheel, but one that no one enjoyed. Some more fortunate worker "histed" the gate, whereupon the main shafting started turning, provided a belt didn't come off.

On the bottom floor were two or three loads of round edged lumber, mostly beech, maple, and birch. The wood had been hauled in on two horse double runner sleds from a saw mill the previous day. These teams effectively ruined sledding by stopping at the top of the hill and wrapping the bridle chain around a rear runner to brake the load, thus gouging deep ruts in the road.

The lumber was sawed to different lengths on the chunking saw, and then passed on to the splitting saw. Next it went to the planer, four times through, since but one edge at a time could be planed.

The cradle itself was made on the upper floor, which meant that the wood had to be passed up there. It was wheeled under a trap door in the ceiling on a cross jack, one of the most miserable things to handle. It was a combination of a wheel barrow and a saw horse, which folded up when not in use, often pinching a finger in the process. When in use, it had the disconcerting habit of turning a somersault, dumping the load everywhere. Providing none of these catastrophes occurred, the wood was passed, a handful at a time, to a worker on the floor above.

Despite all the combustibles, fire extinguishers were merely wooden barrels, full of stagnant water, with large pails hanging on the sides. There were no blowers to get rid of the sawdust from the machines: whisk brooms were available, but the man working on the planer often looked like a large pile of shavings with a hat on.

Upstairs the cradles were cut out and processed. One man turned, by hand, all the posts (spindles) for two or three cents apiece. The rockers were sawed on a concave circular saw, producing conjunctive rockers, and eliminating the wastage frequently produced by today's bandsaws. Only one hole could be bored at a time. Sanding was done in a drum made up of a large wooden cylinder covered with carpeting, to which sandpaper was glued every night so that it might be dry by the next day. All small pieces were put in this barrel-like affair and rumbled for an hour or so.

Assembling was rather crude at that time. In place of air clamps and presses, there were Rube Goldberg contraptions worked by hand or foot levers, and glue pots heated by kerosene.

Staining and varnishing really took time. There were no spray guns, and everything was dipped in stain and hung up to dry. This took one day, and on the following day the product was dipped in varnish, which took longer to dry. The varnish was mixed with plenty of benzene, and the workers who used it were frequently 'walking on air.'

After the finish dried, the heads and foots were wrapped in bundles containing half a dozen of each, plus the sides and bottoms (either slat or wire). All merchandise was shipped knocked down. A wax coated paper separated each piece. The bundles were tied with a tarred rope which never slipped, but was hard on the man who was doing the tieing. It took several weeks to get his hands toughened up enough to stand it.

Mothers appreciated the finished product. Babies could be rocked, swung, or just left to lie and howl in a stationary crib. The swing cradle was a small crib suspended between two standards on each end, with a wooden pedal arrangement so that mother could knit and swing her offspring at the same time. As a rule, the crib was large enough to accommodate Junior for three or four years. The rocking cradle was a small crib with rockers.

Two other establishments on the upper end of Great Brook were operative in the twentieth century. One was the short-lived Antrim Creamery Corporation, incorporated in 1909 with a capital of $5,000 and eleven officers. It certainly had too little capital, and it may have had too many officers, for although the town voted the business exempt from taxes in 1910 (a practice, alas, no longer allowed), it was only in existence for seven years, although the first production of butter was enthusiastically noted in *The Antrim Reporter*, and hopes were initially high. With the great advantage of hindsight, one is inclined to wonder how the principals expected to buy the lot, erect the building, buy machinery, provide working capital, and develop sales on such a small original investment.

The Hildreth saw mill fared better. It was begun in 1871 by William Hildreth, who operated it for thirty-four years. On Hildreth's death, Paul Thayer bought it and used the lumber from the mill to build ten or more cottages on White Birch Point. From 1922 to 1948 it was owned by Caughey & Pratt, who also owned land below the mill, and were at one time seriously interested in developing the power of the four-hundred foot fall of the brook between the lake and the village. Its last working owner was Raymond McKay. Now it is privately owned and being restored—not as a working mill, but for its historical value.

Another area on Great Brook utilized for industrial purposes was that in South Village. During its most active period there were nine factories along this stretch of the brook in addition to the eighteenth century mills mentioned earlier. These put out a great diversity of products: hoes, shovels, shingles, clapboards, patent leather, excelsior, woolen goods, sewing silk, paper boxes, harnesses for weaving machines, and powder kegs, as well as the various wares produced by Goodell Company.

David Harvey Goodell was Antrim's foremost entrepreneur. For the past century, he and his successors have employed the greatest number of workers of any business in town. After Abbott Company moved to Keene, Antrim was for all intents and purposes a one factory town, although a number of Antrimites worked in Bennington at the paper mill. Until the advent of New Hampshire Ball Bearing in Peterborough and the Sylvania plant in Hillsboro, Goodell's offered the only factory employment within easy commuting distance. It is not hard to imagine, then, what exceptional power D.H. Goodell and the Goodell Company had in the town of Antrim. In view of this, the industry he founded deserves an important place in this narrative.

David Goodell started his business career in 1857 as treasurer of the Antrim Shovel Company, at that time owned by Treadwell & Company of Boston. The factory stood where the cutlery shop now stands. Shovels were made here until 1863, when the patent, together with the tools and machinery, were sold and the business moved out of town. Goodell, having invented and patented (in 1864) the "Lightning Apple-parer," formed the D.H. Goodell Company in partnership with George R. Carter of Treadwell, using the old shovel building for production. The apple parer was an immediate success: in 1866, Goodell, acting as his own salesman, sold 2,000 dozen in three weeks. The future looked bright.

Unfortunately, Treadwell & Company failed in 1870, and Goodell, having co-signed notes with his partner Carter, was legally responsible and implicated in the failure. It is said that after he paid back his part of the debt he never again signed a business note. Under the bankruptcy laws, the factory building was sold at auction—to D.H. Goodell, who was in no mood to surrender. From then on, there was no way to go but up.

Having purchased the right to manufacture the "Cahoon Seed-sower" in 1868, he continued the production of apple parers and seed sowers until 1875, when the present Goodell Company was formed. This new firm expanded its business by buying the entire operation of

Wood's Cutlery Company of nearby Bennington. To accommodate the additional machinery of the Bennington firm, an addition two stories high and seventy feet long was put up at once on the south end of the Antrim factory. Another large addition in 1879 brought the entrance up to the main street.

David Harvey Goodell was a man of remarkable energy and perseverance, always adding improvements to his business. In 1885, he installed a telephone between his office and the railroad station, possibly the first telephone in Antrim. As early as 1887, he had fire sprinklers installed in the factory with the water being stored in a forty-five hundred gallon tank on the highest building. He also put in a boiler to heat the buildings.

The business both prospered and increased, and in 1891 the company added a new structure south of the original building, some two or three hundred feet down the brook. There, handles of bone and wood were made for the cutlery items. By this time they were turning out a number of products: more than one hundred different styles of cutlery, as well as great quantities of apple parers, potato parers, cherry stoners, and seed sowers. But there was just not enough water power in Antrim to handle it all, so the company purchased the old Wood's factory building in Bennington and moved a portion of the cutlery business there. At that time, about eighty workers were employed in Bennington, and 175 in Antrim.

In a further innovative move, Goodell decided to light his buildings with electricity. Lamp light was not adequate, especially for the safe use of such rapidly moving machines as the polishing and grinding wheels. But at that time there were no public utility companies to furnish electricity. So Goodell bought the old saw mill in Bennington in 1894, removed the mill building, installed a new water wheel of large capacity and an electric dynamo sufficient to furnish fourteen hundred lights. Wires were strung between Antrim and Bennington and the factories were lighted by electricity. Later the lines were extended along the main streets of Antrim, furnishing forty-five street lights, as well as lights in some private buildings. The next year, a new and substantial dam was built—higher than the old one and thus producing more power. But by 1909, even this source was inadequate, so the company built a dam on the North Branch river just below North Branch village. Steel work gave this dam an eighty-five foot drop, and a penstock ran to the station where an eight-hundred horsepower electric dynamo provided energy enough for Goodell Company and for anyone else desiring it.

Governor Goodell died in 1915, and his son Richard became president of the company. In 1922, all the cutlery manufacturing operations were moved from Bennington and consolidated in Antrim. The Bennington land, water rights, and physical plant were sold to the Monadnock Paper mill of that town. For some time it had been evident that to produce and promote the sale of electric energy properly and economically much greater financial assets were required than were available to the company. In 1916 all the generating equipment was sold and eventually diverted to the rapidly expanding Public Service Company of New Hampshire.

Richard Goodell retired in 1923, after selling his interest in Goodell Company to Henry A. Hurlin, long a member of the administrative team of both Goodells. During his presidency, the company made a very successful line of plastic handled tableware, sold in large volumes in five and ten cent stores across the nation. In WWII, when there was a shortage of steel for household cutlery, the company made butcher cutlery, mostly for the armed services. Since then, this line of merchandise has been continued, including such items as heavy butcher cutlery, putty knives, and scrapers.

Henry Hurlin died in 1949 at the age of ninety-three, never having really retired. His son William succeeded him as president of the company, and in 1960 William's son David followed as president. During this time, the business was consolidated in the buildings

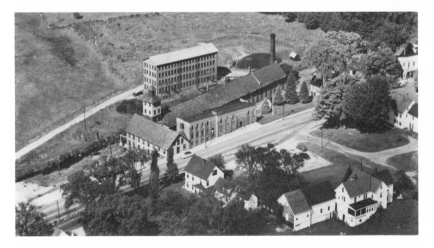

Goodell Company from the air

north of High Street, and the other buildings were sold. Profit sharing and a liberal health and accident program at company expense were introduced. Later an aggressive program involving substantial investment in new machinery, plant renovation, and sales promotion was begun.

A century ago, the company began with the manufacture of the "White Mountain Apple-parer." If any proof were needed of its worth, it is sufficient to note that it is still being produced and sold today. It is a sturdy and utilitarian machine, but it is not today's product that brings a gleam to the eye of the collector. When an auctioneer holds up an apple parer made in the nineteenth century, marked Goodell Company, Antrim, then bidding begins in earnest.

Other Goodell Company items have value to the collector. Not long ago, a lady in Minnesota wrote to say that she had bought an old set of bone handled knives made in Antrim, and would appreciate information concerning them. We live in a vast country, but even a small town may be known halfway across the continent because of the product of one of its factories.

The fifty-five years after Gregg witnessed great activity on Great Brook as industry harnessed the stream. Cochrane states, "It (Great Brook) is fed by springs; it does not dry up like other streams. From the pond to the river, the water is now used fourteen times, and might be used much more. It is the life of the town." But it was no pastoral idyl for the mill owners, and there was a definite shortage of water, particularly in late summer, or when leaks in the dams drained mill ponds at night and the shops downstream were forced to wait until later in the morning for their ponds to fill. Sometimes Gregg or his successors failed to open the gate early enough to have the ponds filled by sunrise. Clearly, some method of regulation was needed.

Ezra Hyde, if not the originator, was certainly an early proponent of an idea to cure the mill owners' problems. He suggested that a company be formed to control the stream for the good of all members who joined. He had come to Antrim in 1840, erected a dwelling (now Martin Nichols') on the road to the river (later called Depot Street) and was active in several businesses in the South Village, none of them particularly prosperous. Dr. Cochrane describes him as a "stirring, enterprising man, and his business here was prosperous until the 'hard times' of that day compelled him to stop." One gets the impression that Hyde was a promoter with good ideas, but possibly without the tenacity to bring his excellent concepts to fruition. Nevertheless, he cannot be faulted for his work in connection with the Clinton and South Antrim Water Company.

On February 20, 1847, fourteen owners of mill sites on Great Brook bonded themselves to Ezra Hyde to purchase the water privilege at the outlet of Gregg Lake, each man being assessed his proportionate share of the cost. They agreed that

said company shall keep a good and sufficient dam at the outlet of Gregg Pond, so as to raise the water therein to an iron bolt on a stone north of the flume or dam at said outlet, at all seasons, and shall cause to be drawn daily and every day except Sunday three square feet of water, to be measured as it passes on a board or plank through the flume or to be drawn from the dam at Thompson's mill, so called, if the dam at the mill is sufficiently tight to hold all the water, and shall cause the gate to be hoisted at sunrise every morning and kept up the same twelve hours each and every day, Sundays excepted, and no more so long as there is a sufficient quantity of water in said pond to supply said quantity, and when there is not sufficient, to draw what will run the same number of hours, Sundays excepted.

Our forefathers were long winded!!

An interesting sidelight is that the primary purpose of the iron bolt was to gauge the height of the water, and by June first, to assure that the meadows at the north and west ends of the pond were drained so that the hay might be cut. This regulation was important, and carefully enforced.

The first session of the new company was held at Abbott's shop on March 6, 1847, and the officers chosen. Subsequent meetings produced some changes in regulations, and some reports of financial crises. In 1848, it was voted to have the gate opened one hour before sunrise when the time was less than twelve hours between sunrise and sunset. In 1849, all bills were paid with a surplus of $12.53 in the treasury, but in 1854, there was only 34c on hand, and no way to pay for repairs to the dam the previous season. In 1876, William Hildreth was chosen to solicit money to pay for widening the canal. He raised sixty-nine dollars in contributions. In 1880, D.H. Goodell offered to pay half of all existing debts and half of the expense of hoisting the gate, provided the other shareholders raised the rest of the money. E.Z. Hastings solicited three dollars on each share to take care of that matter. Again in 1881, D.H. Goodell agreed to pay for the ensuing year "as much as all the other shareholders." The year before, he had expended $443.12 in rebuilding the dam and excavating the canal.

In the following years, one after another of the shareholders of the water company shifted their power source from water to electricity. About 1955, Raymond McKay, then owner of the Hildreth site, became the last shareholder in the Clinton and South Village Water Company, and its sole owner. In 1965, the Antrim Precinct purchased his equity, and it now owns the dam and all the water privileges. This transfer of ownership marked the end of the line for an organization which had been in existence for one hundred and twelve years.

In its heyday, it contributed mightily to the economic well being of the town. Dr. Cochrane lists twenty-two different mills on Great Brook. At one time or another, the owners of most of them were members of the water company. The names of the original investors are on record and, with few exceptions, it is possible to locate their mill sites. Descendants of some are currently members of our community. To be sure, their mills were not large and, judging from the area of their ponds, probably did not develop more than twenty horsepower, but they are a lasting testimony to the Yankee enterprise and ingenuity of our forefathers.

The late Paul F. Paige, a native of Antrim who never lost his love for the town, wrote:

Great Brook has always been an inspiration to me. I skated on it, swam in it, and from it I learned about commerce and industry. I doubt if there are many streams of its size and length that have done a better job, or meant more to a community.

I knew and admired the men whose mills used it for power, and the men whose livelihoods depended upon it. It took no government loan to harness it, no Corps of Army Engineers to survey it, or specify where mills were to be built. Its faithfulness over many generations has meant much. It is one of the oldest things in town, yet one of the youngest, for tomorrow it will flow as fresh and strong as it ever did before a white man threw a dam across it.

The early ventures on both North Branch River and Great Brook were modest. The area of the mill ponds indicated slight power and small plants. The written record also reveals very humble beginnings. Typical were Daniel Parkhurst with a force of six men, Harold Kelsea with sixteen in his silk mill, and Robbins and Flint in 1839 with annual sales of $3,000. Also in keeping with the times was a lease for thirty-five years, James Aiken, Jr., to Seth Hadley in 1804, of "a certain mill site" for ten dollars and a promise "to deliver annually five hundred feet of good merchantable boards." It is more than likely that many were part-time projects to fill in between seasons on the farm.

Fire was an ever-present danger. As late as 1927, Abbott Company heated its woodshop with stoves. Particularly in the early shops, insurance was suspect and seldom purchased. The concept of shared risk through incorporation was little used. Cost accounting was a nebulous theory. Postal or passenger service was by stage. Goods were delivered and shipped by wagon freight. When the railroad came in 1878 the nearest station was in Bennington, not Antrim.

All these factors made small business ventures precarious. But the most salient point is that neither Antrim nor any other small town, however remote from the mainstream, could escape the inevitable thrust of big business. Giant corporations with their great concentrations of capital eventually made life untenable for the little man who operated on a shoestring. And so it is that Antrim lost most of her industries, and became primarily a bedroom town. It may be that in the future her people will decide to broaden their tax base and lure some modern industries within her borders. Or it may be that her people, prizing their non-polluted air, their relatively clear streams, and their quiet woodlands, will be content to live here and commute elsewhere to work. But they will always remember those pioneers of industry here, who produced what they had to for their own existence, and had a little left over to sell.

LIBRARIES

W HEN ANTRIM was first settled, the people were a hard working, hardy breed. They were of Scotch Irish heritage, loyal Presbyterians with a love of knowledge. So it was not surprising that before many years had passed, an interest in establishing a library took form. The Social Library was one of the earliest attempts, begun before the incorporation of the town in 1777. The books that were gathered together were largely theology, history, and philosophy, which were probably loaned or given by residents or friends. This venture did not last very long, and one can imagine that people who had worked outside from dawn to dusk, and had only candle light or the light from a fireplace by which to read, soon began to nod and were obliged to put the reading aside until a later time. Later, a juvenile library was begun under the care of Dr. Whiton. When Sunday School libraries were formed, the juvenile books were sold at auction, bringing in more than they cost.

Interest in these attempts waned during the first half of the 1800s until February, 1866, when the Antrim Library Association was formed. Each member paid ten dollars, and there were nine subscribers, to wit: Mrs. Mark Woodbury, Morris Christie, Artemus Brown, Eben Bass, James W. Perkins, N.W.C. Jameson, Mark J.W. Foster, J.E. Vose, and Reed P. Whittemore. The townspeople could use the library by paying a dollar and a half per year. The books were housed in what is now the small front dining room at the Maplehurst Inn. Later the several hundred volumes were moved to a small room on the second floor of the building now owned by Charles Jackson. At the town meeting in 1892, $150 was appropriated and the town voted to accept the provisions of an act of the legislature for establishment of free libraries. In January, 1893, the Antrim Free Library was opened. When the town hall was built in 1894, the books were once again moved to what was the original selectmen's room, as this was more accessible to the public. With Miss Sarah Adams as librarian, and with a small financial grant from the town, the library was able to acquire more books and to become more active.

Miss Adams had recently graduated from high school, so was quite young, but she soon became very capable in selecting books and readying them for circulation to the public. She was something of a practical joker. One Saturday a child came to the library with a note from a gentleman who needed something appropriate for Sunday reading. The gentleman received a copy of the New Testament in Greek! The library in the care of "Sadie," as she was affectionately called, continued in the town building until 1908, when the James A. Tuttle Library was accepted by the town.

James A. Tuttle was born in Antrim in 1841, lived all his life here, and died in 1905. He left his residual estate to the town of Antrim for the purchase of a site for, and the building and maintenance of, the James A. Tuttle Library. The estate included the farm as well as other investments. A building committee was appointed, consisting of Ephraim Simonds, David H. Goodell, Fred C. Parmenter, Charles Abbott, and George Lowe. Mr. Goodell gave the land on which the library now stands to the town. The committee was then faced with the problem of either selling or renting the Tuttle farm, cutting the grass, picking the apples, and keeping the buildings in repair. It was finally sold to J. Elro Perkins for $6,200 in June of 1912.

The James A. Tuttle Library

Meanwhile, information was sent to various architects who might be interested in planning a suitable building. The plans submitted by Edwin R. Clarke of Lowell were selected, and the work began. The building was completed in 1908 and was turned over to the selectmen on May 27, 1908. It was opened to the public on July 12, and was dedicated with proper ceremonies on August 19, 1908. Now after nearly seventy years it is still a most satisfactory building for library purposes. The first floor includes a spacious center lobby where the circulation desk is located, and where there is space for displays and the card catalogue; there is a reading room at each side — for adults on the south side, and for children on the north. Behind these is a stack room with ample space for storage of the books that are accumulating. Upstairs there are two rooms — one which has been used for meetings of various organizations, the other designated as a historical room. It was originally intended for a trustees' room, but was later used for historical material, cared for by the Molly Aiken Chapter, DAR.

Miss Adams continued as librarian in the new location. The first gift for books for the new library was a trust fund of $500 from William H. Boutelle. All the books in the John Gardner Flint library — about 2,000 volumes — were presented to the town library by Mrs. Flint and their son, Wyman Kneeland Flint. Library hours were increased — after the sale of the Tuttle farm — from 2:30 to 9 P.M., Tuesday and Saturday. The librarian was paid twenty-five cents an hour when she presented her bill. The janitor received seventy-five dollars per year. During the years to 1938, additional funds were appropriated annually by the town, ranging from $200 to $800, depending on the amount requested by the trustees.

Miss Adams retired in October, 1917, after twenty-three years of guiding the reading of the people of Antrim. She was succeeded by Mrs. Elro Perkins. At that time books were sent to North Branch and to Clinton for the use of those who could not easily come to the village. Mrs. Edward Grant at North Branch and Mrs. George Sawyer at Clinton cared for those branch libraries. This was continued for several years with indifferent success. At the death of George Alfred Cochran in 1923, the Cochran field at the end of Summer Street was willed to the library. This field had been used for Victory gardens during World War I. It was sold to the town for twenty-five dollars when the new elementary school was built in 1948. In 1924 a rather sad note appears in the record: "No new books were bought in 1924 because the money was used for repairs." That year there was an $800 appropriation, but the building needed a new heating system which took precedence over books. Mrs. Perkins resigned in 1931, and was succeeded by Mrs. Ethel Davis, who served until 1957, a total of twenty-five years.

A real windfall came to the library in 1938 from the estate of Emma Whittemore Gipson of Greenfield, whose family had originally come from Antrim. Her estate was to be divided equally between Antrim, Hancock, and Bennington, to be used for the maintenance of the public libraries in these towns. Antrim's share was $35,878. Other bequests have come from Idabelle Jameson, Mary Bass, Mrs. Guy Tibbetts, Miss Lilla Brown, and the Pratt family. Since 1938 the town appropriation has been discontinued except when unusual expense has been involved, as in the installation of a new heating system for the whole building and for the redecoration of the first-floor rooms.

During Mrs. Davis's tenure as librarian, story hours for children were conducted. Her assistant was Mrs. Fred Proctor, and between them they prepared some interesting experiences for the children.

It was during this period that the "Saga of the Moose" came to be. Two hunters from town, Ed Goodwin and Bert Paige, went up north one fall and returned with the head of a moose which they had shot. It was carefully treated and properly mounted, when both gentlemen found that neither of their wives was too enthusiastic about a moose staring at them in their comparatively small living rooms. So the library seemed to provide the extra space for enjoying the moose. It was accepted by the trustees and placed on the wall in the children's reading room, where it stayed for several years. There came a time when the room was to be redecorated, and the moose necessarily was taken down. Since it was becoming somewhat mangy and moth-eaten, it was deemed undesirable for its previous vantage point. A new owner was sought and found, and the moose had a new home for a time. Once again, a wife objected, so the poor moose went to the town dump, but not for long. It disappeared and soon was reported in a new home at a nearby Moose Lodge.

During the years when Mrs. Davis was librarian, the book collection was well cared for, being added to as finances allowed, and being circulated more widely than before. When she retired in 1957 after twenty-five years in this position, she was honored by a reception and tea at Maplehurst Inn, where she was presented with a gift of money. Through her efforts and those of her assistant, Mrs. Pratt, much had been done to bring the library up to those standards which make it one of the better small libraries in New Hampshire. On the retirement of Mrs. Davis, Mrs. Clara Pratt was made librarian.

Mrs. Pratt attended the course in Library Techniques given at the University of New Hampshire and received a certificate at the end of the course. Story hours for the children and summer reading programs were continued and the holdings increased, due to the added income from the Gipson fund. To the selection of books she gave careful attention. Book selection is a time-consuming duty, one which must be done largely outside of library hours when interruptions are less apt to interfere.

In 1954 the town appropriated $1,500 to build an archive room in the basement for storage of school records, state papers, and other reference material for which there is no room in either the library proper or in the town office. This room has shelves for books, a study table, and chairs. Here also is stored the complete file of *The Antrim Reporter*, donated by Mrs. H.W. Eldredge. The will of Miss Ethel Muzzey gave her own library to Tuttle and made a valuable addition. Included in the important holdings are some fifty town histories, mostly from nearby New Hampshire but some from more distant communities — some even in Massachusetts. These are very valuable and do not circulate for that reason, but may be used for research within the library.

Mrs. Pratt retired on January 1, 1965, after nine years as assistant to Mrs. Davis and eight years as librarian. A public reception was held to honor her, with State Librarian E.W. Allen present. Mrs. Miriam Roberts, who had been assisting her during 1964, was selected to take her place.

For a number of years there has been a growing interest throughout New Hampshire in ways of increasing the cooperation between the local libraries and the State Library. This has led to the Library Development Program which was made possible by the appropriation of funds by the United States Congress. In 1965 the trustees voted to affiliate with the State Library in this program. Through this, the local library receives an annual grant for reference books, and the services of a library consultant for help in problems which may arise. The Antrim library is in the Keene district — one of four in the state — which holds quarterly meetings in the area, attended by representatives from the member libraries. The James A. Tuttle Library was one of the first to meet the qualifications for affiliation. The district bookmobile makes quarterly visits when about three hundred books are selected to augment the local collection. The courses in library techniques are also given in each district, making it easier for librarians to attend them. Mrs. Roberts completed the eight courses in 1975 and received her certificate. She attended nearly all of the district meetings, was an officer of the District Advisory Council, and served on several committees.

A complete new heating system was installed in the library, and the first floor rooms were redecorated in the forties. More recently the main rooms have been carpeted in a cranberry red indoor-outdoor carpet, and curtains and draperies for the big windows produce a soft, pleasant light. Lighting fixtures have been replaced with fluorescent light suitable to the type of building, and a larger circulation desk consistent with the room decor has been added. In both reading rooms the walls are lined with bookcases where books suitable for use by the age group indicated are shelved. There is also a small office near the circulation desk with sink, telephone, counter space for working, and a small electric stove. A large bookcase divides the adult reading room so that there is space for study around a table in the front half; in the other, in front of the fireplace, are rocking chairs where patrons may read at their leisure. The chairs were a memorial gift by friends and relatives of Dalton Brooks.

The children's room is also divided by a bookcase so that junior high people may have a study table on one side, and younger children may have space to sit or lie on the carpet to select and sample the exciting and colorful books available on the other side. The librarian smiles briefly when a young patron announces, "I brang my book back on Saturday." Why not *brang*? If the past tense of *ring* is *rang*, why not *brang* for the past tense of *bring*? Would that the English language were that simple. These young people can be a source of much enjoyment for a librarian whose approach is one of friendliness. For example, when a child asks, "Where is the book I had last week? It is a green one," she is willing to spend some time searching for that particular green book — and if not successful she can usually find a substitute. An early pleasant library experience can often convert a child to a book lover.

During 1974 an effort was begun to convert the second floor rooms into a more inclusive historical area. Such material has been accumulating and a committee is now working on sorting, labeling, and cataloguing all the gifts that are bringing back to life the chronicles of the past.

As the year 1975 ended, the library had a total of slightly more than 10,000 volumes, even after a drastic weeding program. The circulation was increasing — 13,000 books having been circulated in 1975.

Mrs. Roberts retired on January 1, 1976, and has been succeeded by Mrs. Isabel Nichols, who is highly qualified in every way to keep the James A. Tuttle Library growing in its service to the community.

MILITARY HISTORY

SETTLED OVER two hundred years ago, Antrim has lived through nine wars in which the United States participated. Sons of Antrim have fought in all these wars except one. Beginning with World War I, daughters of Antrim have served in various branches of the military. Patriotic fervor, at least through World War II, has been intense. In modern times (1976), attitudes toward war are changing, so perhaps some of these accounts will seem naive and chauvinistic, but it is important to remember that for the first one hundred years of Antrim's existence, all the wars were fought on American soil for the preservation of this country. The justification for World War I was that it would "make the world safe for democracy," and the direct attack on America by the Japanese in World War II made it easy to arouse the people to back the war. Only the Korean and Vietnam wars have been hard to sell. So it is natural that the early conflicts in American history seemed almost romantic to people in Antrim and elsewhere, and the involvement of the civilian population greater then than it has been recently.

In many ways, it is amazing that our earliest settlers were even aware of the Revolution. However miraculous it seems, they heard the news of the battle of Lexington almost at once. Some men were still in the process of clearing their land. Some were heads of struggling little families, dependent for food and protection. Yet, "Every man," said Dr. Cochrane, "marched for Lexington at the first sound of battle, except John Gordon, and . . . he soon enlisted for the whole war. There was not a man in Antrim that did not respond to his country's call." They only got as far as Tyngsboro, where they were met by General

Stark, who informed them they were not needed, and told them to return home and plant their corn, holding themselves ready to march again at a moment's notice.

Once home, they organized themselves into a company, choosing John Duncan captain, Thomas Nichols lieutenant, and James Dickey ensign. They met to drill, and as soon as Antrim was incorporated, the town voted in town meeting to assume its share of expenses incurred in the prosecution of the war.

A New Hampshire regiment fought at Bunker Hill, and several Antrim men, including James Aiken, were members of it. In 1777, men from Antrim marched with General Stark to face Burgoyne at Bennington. William Smith, then sixty-two, insisted on going in place of his son; he returned uninjured, and lived to be eighty-five. William Boyd served in the defense of Rhode Island, and was paid five hundred dollars by the town "for his Sarvice."

In addition to supplying fighting men, Antrim did its share to help the war effort in other ways. When the people could not raise cash, they paid their tax in beef. In 1781, the proportion to be collected from Antrim was 2,791 pounds of beef, a large levy for so small a town with few head of stock. But by great effort, they paid in full.

Too, those left in town made it their business to care for the families of absent soldiers. If a man had "made a beginning" or had "pieces of chopped wood" (as the old records called it), the town saw that this work of clearing the land was continued while the soldier was away. By public vote, the logs which had been felled were burned, and the ground prepared for crops. If money was not available, then they would contribute labor.

During 1777, about one fourth of the men of Antrim were in the army. Nearly seventy-five men, all told, were in the service at one time or another during the war, of whom a number were killed in battle, and all acquitted themselves well. One of their number, Samuel Downing, was said to be the last surviving soldier of the Revolution, dying in Edinburg, New York, at the age of one hundred and five years, two months, and twenty-one days.

In 1914, the Molly Aiken Chapter of the DAR placed markers on the graves of men buried in Antrim who either fought in the Revolutionary War or signed the Association Test. (See chapter on Cochrane's history.) Eighteen are in the old cemetery on Meeting House hill; eight are in the Center cemetery; two are in Maplewood, and six at the Branch. The Chapter also erected the memorial gates at the entrance of the cemetery on Meeting House hill, one honoring the courage and fidelity of the pioneer men and women and the Revolutionary soldiers, and the other inscribed to the twenty-two "soldiers of 1776 who lie in unmarked graves."

Probably no other conflict after the Revolution inspired the same kind of patriotism, the same feeling of urgency to defend the homeland. More and more, it seemed, young men volunteered or submitted to the draft partly in a spirit of adventure, and partly in an attempt to prove themselves men. Surely that must have been the case in the War of 1812, called by New Englanders, "Mr. Madison's war." Yet forty-four men from Antrim served in this war; five died. The war dragged on for three years, never coming closer to New Hampshire soil than Lake Champlain.

In an even farther-fetched war in 1846, Antrim sent four men to fight against Mexico in a dispute over some south-western territories, and all four were killed.

One hundred and thirty-nine Antrim men, twelve more than the quota required, took part in the Civil War. Without doubt, all fought on the side of the Union troops. Twenty-seven died, either from battle wounds or disease.

Soon after the battle at Fort Sumter, President Lincoln called on New Hampshire to supply an infantry regiment for a period of three months. Enlistments then were not "for the duration," but rather for short intervals of three, six, or nine months, thus enabling the soldiers to return periodically and take care of the essential farm chores which were too demanding for the women to perform.

Less than three weeks after the first gun was fired at Sumter, Antrim men had enlisted, and Antrim townspeople had, in special town meeting, voted to assist the families of these volunteers monetarily. Substantial sums of money for those days were voted again and again, as well as bonuses for individual enlistments. Since the town did not have sufficient cash reserves, this money was "hired," and by the end of the war the town debt had reached $32,341.17. Bonds bearing six percent interest were issued in 1870 to reduce the debt, which by 1879 was down to $7,388.47.

Cochrane lists the names of all the men from Antrim who were soldiers during the Civil War. Many of them served either in the 13th or 14th New Hampshire regiments. Some of the veterans who returned formed the nucleus of the Granite State Cadets, Charles Champney being captain of the group for a while. This organization was disbanded in 1883.

The Spanish-American war of 1898 does not seem to have had a single Antrim participant, probably due to the fact that it was so remote from the area's interest, and was of such short duration.

World War I, on the other hand, saw a great resurgence of patriotism in Antrim, with all the eligible men in town registering for the draft, and eighty-five men and women participating directly in the war, either in the United States or in Europe. For the first time, four women from Antrim served as army nurses, two in the continental United States and two in France.

In the James A. Tuttle Library there is a complete record of Antrim's participation in World War I, compiled by Fred C. Parmenter, a life-long resident who died in 1928. Included are biographical sketches of every man and woman in the service, as well as lists of the civilian members of various committees appointed by the state and/or town to assist in the war effort. All the details of the report were deemed too long for inclusion here, but an excerpt from some of the narrative paragraphs may whet the reader's interest.

By way of explanation, there was appointed in each town a "Committee of Public Safety," whose duties were to take such action as seemed necessary to preserve the safety and welfare of the public. Mr. Parmenter writes,

During the winter of 1917-18 it was very difficult to procure coal, and wood was nearly as hard to get as coal. The committee took the matter of fuel under consideration, and through their efforts many owners of wood lots were persuaded to allow men to go in and chop for themselves, they paying the owners from one to two dollars per cord. Regular choppers were few and they wanted about five dollars a cord for chopping; consequently there were many men who had never chopped any wood in their lives who went into the woods and cut enough to supply their own needs. They were obliged to work under difficulties for the snow came early in December, and by the first of January there was four feet on a level in the woods, and the weather was extremely cold all winter. It was not warm enough to melt the snow on the sidewalk in the village from the twenty-eighth of November, 1917, until the eleventh of February, 1918. However, through the efforts of the committee enough fuel was procured so there was very little suffering caused by the lack of it.

The Committee of Public Safety worked closely with the Red Cross. The Antrim chapter of the Red Cross was organized April 10, 1917, by a group from the Woman's Club, the Women's Relief Corps, the Molly Aiken chapter of the DAR, and the Presbyterian, Baptist, Methodist, and Congregational churches. It started with a membership of eighty, and by late December had increased the number to five hundred and thirty-seven. Over one half the inhabitants were members. Again from Mr. Parmenter's report:

Headquarters were opened May 14th in the small hall connected with the Nathan C. Jameson house. The use of the room was given by the Jamesons. The Electric Light Company gave the electricity for lighting, and also to run a small motor for sewing. The Boy Scouts attended to the fire when heat was required. The only expense for their headquarters from May 14th to December 31st was one dollar and twenty-five cents for a lamp socket. The rooms were open six days a week, and the days frequently lasted until twelve P.M. The ladies divided the work so there should always be a force at work in the room, and many women who could not spare the time to go to the room took work to their homes. One could hardly enter a house in town without finding some one working for the Red Cross.

With so many women working all the time it required quantities of material to keep them busy, and it was the duty of the Committee of Public Safety to supply the funds. There were various methods used beside direct solicitation, and money came from unexpected sources; nearly everyone was willing to help in some way.

One method which proved very successful was an auction. We all know that an article for which one person has no use may be just what someone else wants. Acting on that idea, they asked people to contribute the things they did not want. The people responded nobly, and when the articles were collected for sale in the yard of N.C. Jameson's house, it looked like a clearance sale from some farm house where they had been collecting for one hundred years. There were many articles of very little value, but there were a few pieces valuable for their antiquity. There was one teapot which sold for twenty-two dollars. There were other things which brought good prices, and the receipts were very satisfactory.

Of the eighty-one men who served in World War I, six did not come back. When the American Legion Post #50 was organized October 13,

1919, it was named in honor of William M. Myers, who died in battle at Chateau-Thierry on July 18, 1918. On March 21, 1921, the Woman's Auxiliary unit of the American Legion was chartered, and both organizations are still active in town.

Twenty-one years after the cessation of World War I, another holocaust erupted, this one eventually global in scope, encompassing the eastern as well as the western hemisphere. As was the case in World War I, the United States was not immediately involved, but her sympathies definitely lay on the side of the Allies, and any isolationist feelings were completely erased when the Japanese attacked Pearl Harbor in December, 1941. Once again, Antrim offered up her sons and daughters in a long and costly war. A total of one hundred and twenty-four served during the four years of the war, and of these, four lost their lives in action. The name of one of the dead, Paul H. Prescott, became part of the American Legion Post name.

The war had its effects on the home front as well. What happened in Antrim was repeated in towns and cities all across the nation: this account does not claim to be unique, but is inserted to stir the memory of those who lived through those days, and to provide a description for those born later.

From the beginning of the war, there was fear of an airborne attack by the Germans, especially along the eastern seaboard. Defense against such attacks, should they come, was organized in a pyramidal structure, fanning out from regional headquarters to volunteer community groups such as air raid wardens and airplane spotters. At first, Antrimites found it hard to take this activity seriously, but as the countries of Europe were overrun and England seemed in imminent danger of invasion, German armed might seemed capable of anything, including bombing Antrim. At that point Antrim got ready, if not to defend herself, at least to cope with any emergency.

As many as sixty air raid wardens were appointed and trained in their duties. A reporting center was set up in Carroll Johnson's house, where news of an alert could be received by telephone and then passed on to the town via the fire and factory whistles. The small building at the top of Goodell's Hill (now the laundromat) was designated as first aid headquarters in case of mass casualties. Households were polled as to the number of hoses, ladders, shovels, outside faucets and other useful fire fighting apparatus they had on hand. Incendiary bombs were the most feared weapon, and each family was urged to keep buckets of sand nearby, and to familiarize itself with the optimum method of dealing with such fiendish devices as magnesium bombs (never douse with a full stream of water, which would only compound the problem).

Fortunately, no bombs fell on Antrim, so the wardens' chief activity consisted of reporting any chinks in the blackout, while the chief warden reported the absence of excitement to the state headquarters.

Airplane spotters spent equally futile hours searching the sky for Messerschmitts. A small hut was erected in the field opposite the Grange Hall from which the spotters (mostly housewives) scanned the skies on clear days through binoculars. Men who had already worked a full day at their usual occupations manned the hut in four-hour shifts at night. The night watch, being dark, involved more listening than looking. After a while, the spotting location was moved from the Center to the ball field in the village, where it remained in operation until the area was declared safe from enemy attack.

A deprivation shared by Antrim with the rest of the country during the war years was a shortage of fuel, rubber products, and certain foods. These were doled out according to need, if at all available, by a ration board appointed by the selectmen. With the supplies of raw rubber from the Pacific cut off, tires and even rubber boots were hard to come by. Petroleum products were mainly allocated to the war effort, and gas for private automobiles was severely curtailed. Home owners were urged to use wood for fuel where possible. Ration books were issued for gasoline and for some foods. Meat, butter, and sugar were in short supply. Home gardens proliferated; people who had plenty of land shared it with their neighbors, and many lawns were converted to gardens. Rumor that the butcher was to get meat on Wednesday produced long lines of people holding their ration books and their breath as they inched their way toward the counter, hoping to arrive before the meat all disappeared.

In contrast to the organized celebration at the end of World War I, VJ Day in Antrim was observed informally. People, young and old, gathered in the center of the village, but there was no parade. In lieu of band music, Carroll Johnson spent two happy hours blowing the steam whistle at Goodell's shop. The long ordeal was over.

The Korean and Vietnam wars produced no strong feeling, either pro or con, in Antrim. They were both ideological wars, neither of which posed any direct territorial threat to the United States. Antrim sent her quota of men and women to the service, but remained emotionally relatively uninvolved. Thirty-two Antrim men and one Antrim woman served their country in the Korean conflict, and one man, Lelon A. Olson, was killed in action. His name was the third incorporated in the local American Legion Post name. Forty-one men and two women went from Antrim to the service during the long years of the Vietnam war. Complete lists of all those who served in the four wars of the twentieth century, along with other pertinent information, can be found in the archives of the James A. Tuttle Library.

THE PRECINCT

THE ANTRIM Precinct is an enigma to many people. The very word "precinct" seems to conjure up a picture of the old Seventh Precinct and Tammany Hall. Nothing could be further from the truth, even though the precinct is a political subdivision of the town. Historically the reason for this subdivision is quite easily explained. In areas where the houses were reasonably close together, a kind of social consciousness began to emerge. People saw the advantage of banding together for the common good, taking concerted action on shared problems such as the need for fire protection and for an adequate water supply. In 1849, the State Legislature, acknowledging this need, passed a law allowing towns to define certain areas within the town as precincts for the purpose of setting up the necessary machinery for fire departments, and raising the money to maintain them.

The earliest record of the precinct in Antrim is noted in the town clerk's records of March 23, 1850, when a petition, signed by sixteen voters, was presented to the selectmen "to fix the boundaries of the Precinct agreeable to an act of the State Legislature of July 6, 1849, relating to the extinguishment of fires . . ." The selectmen defined the precinct as that area of South Antrim which they felt could be adequately defended by the then existing fire equipment. That equipment, which had been purchased previously but could only be supported by donations, was in poor shape, and the passage of the new law seemed like a golden opportunity; they wasted no time taking advantage of it.

As a result of this petition, the boundaries were set by the selectmen on April 20, 1850, roughly in the shape of a rectangle, bounded on the east by the Contoocook River, on the south by the Antrim-Bennington-Hancock town lines, on the west by various property lines roughly one half mile from Main Street, and on the North by the road leading to the Rogers place (now owned by Mr. Pleasants) and on the south line of the Cochran place. As time went on, some of the citizens became disenchanted (no doubt because of increased taxation) and petitioned the selectmen to be excluded from the precinct. In some instances this was allowed, and several outlying farms were disannexed.

At a meeting called by the selectmen with Thomas Poor as moderator, it was voted to adopt the village precinct: voted to adopt the 111th Chapter of the Revised Statutes to the eleventh section including the twenty-third section; voted that the clerk procure a book to keep the necessary records of the precinct and be paid for same; voted that Charles McKeen, Augustus Laws, and Hiram Eaton be a committee to call a meeting when necessary for the purpose of repairing the engine; voted that Luke Woodbury, Charles McKeen, and Mark Woodbury hold the office of Firewards; and after they had voted to hold a meeting "in this place" the third Tuesday in March, the meeting adjourned.

Apparently the voters did not want to wait until the following March, because on June 12, 1850, there was another meeting of the precinct, when $150 was appropriated to repair the engine and purchase hose, Jonathan White, Augustus Laws, and Isaac Baldwin being appointed a committee to do the actual work. On July 19 the firewards met at Luke Woodbury's office and voted that he be chairman of the firewards, and that Jonathan White hold the office of engineer with Hiram Eaton as assistant.

The voters approved the efforts of the committee to repair the engine at the meeting the following March and, since there was some money left over, instructed the firewards to procure iron axles for the engine and have it painted. Unfortunately, no records exist to tell us what this engine was or what it looked like. We can only guess that it was of a type popular in America patterned after those of English manufacture. Most of these early engines had no suction hose but pumped water directly from a tub which was kept full by means of a bucket brigade. They required from four to six men on the pump handles to maintain a good stream of water.

In 1852 it was voted to purchase another ten feet of hose with the necessary couplings. The report of the treasurer for that year lists among other expenses, "freight on hose 25c, hose and couplings

$11.35." At the same meeting the following resolution was adopted: "That the firewards be authorized to enroll a Fire Engine Company to consist of not more than eighteen members, and each member so enrolled and returned to the Treasurer of this Precinct as having done duty in said company according to such regulations as they may prescribe shall receive for each monthly meeting the sum of twenty-five cents, and ten cents per hour for additional services in case of fire, and for every absence from monthly meeting shall be fined twenty-five cents."

It might well be asked why fire hose was bought in ten-foot lengths. The reason was that fire hose of that era was made of the best oak-tanned cow hide, and ten feet was the maximum length which could be cut from one single hide. The lap seam was riveted with copper rivets, and as long as the hose was dried and oiled with neat's-foot oil to keep it pliable, it lasted quite well. One of the expenses in 1862 was $2.50 paid to Melvin D. Poor for oiling the hose! In 1858 it was voted to purchase another hundred feet of hose and twenty-four buckets for the use of the engine company. During the Civil War apparently everyone was busy with other things, for no meetings were held during the years 1864 through 1866.

Repairs on the engine began to be more frequent and costly, and by 1872 there was agitation for a new engine, but it was not until 1876 that a committee consisting of Melvin Poor, Charles Kelsea, and John Shedd was authorized to purchase an engine for a price not to exceed $1,000. They journeyed to Boston, and bought an engine for $600. This was the Brookline #1, which was reported to have taken part in fighting the great Boston fire of 1872. The committee also purchased two hundred feet of hose for $100. Their purchases were loaded and shipped by rail to Greenfield, the closest railroad depot to Antrim, for $6.50, and then the engine was hauled the rest of the way by a team of horses for $2.50.

The Brookline #1 was a two cylinder pumper, and could pump from a brook or other source of water. It required eight men to operate, with another eight men ready to take their places after a few minutes of hard pumping. The old timers must have been iron men, for the old pumpers required a minimum of four men on a side to man the brakes (pumping handles or arms), and the normal pumping speed was sixty strokes per minute, with short periods of ninety to one hundred and twenty not being uncommon. Ten minutes of this was about all a man

Firefighting in the nineteenth century . . .

could stand, and then his relief had to take his place. It was quite a trick to do this without injuring a hand or breaking an arm.

The firewards had hoped for a new fire house to house the new engine, but the article was voted down, so temporary quarters had to be found. Each year there were articles in the warrant about a suitable place to keep the engine, and each year they were voted down. The Honorable David Goodell made space under the GAR Hall for fifty dollars per year, but this was not entirely satisfactory. Finally at a special meeting in October, 1893, the precinct authorized the commissioners to buy or lease the stable and barn on the new town hall lot on such terms as they thought proper. They leased the building for a period of ninety-nine years, and converted the building into suitable quarters for the Engine and Hose Company, and later the Hook and Ladder Company.

In 1894, it was voted to purchase a new hose reel which could be hitched to the engine to carry extra hose. In 1895, a wagon was purchased to carry the ladders which had been bought from time to time, thus procuring the basic equipment for the Hook and Ladder Company.

In 1926, there were identical articles in the town warrant and the precinct warrant to see if the voters would approve the expenditure of

...and the twentieth

$5,000 to purchase a triple combination fire truck on a Reo Speed Wagon chassis. Since this would be the first mobile piece of fire equipment and would benefit all the citizens, the money was appropriated by the town. The shiny new engine arrived in due time, and passed the tests of the New Hampshire Board of Underwriters with flying colors, although the board did recommend that the hose threads and hydrants be changed to conform to the national standard. This was done two years later, and Antrim's equipment was compatible with that of the surrounding towns.

The Reo truck saw a great deal of service both inside and outside the Precinct, and was credited with saving many buildings. In the mid-thirties, the tires gave out due to the heavy over-loading of the extra equipment carried. Tires were no longer made of a size to fit the rims, but a hurried trip to the junk yard located wheels including dual wheels for which tires could be procured, and the truck was given a new lease on life. Next the bearings in the engine gave out after a hard pumping session, but the engine was rebuilt almost overnight by the Antrim Garage (Robinson & Poor, Prop.).

Obviously the Reo's days were numbered, and in 1940 the town purchased a new fire truck: a five-hundred gallon per-minute pumper on a Diamond T chassis built by the Maxim Motor Company. Now the floor of the engine house had to be shored up with steel beams to hold the weight of two fire engines. A third engine was purchased in 1956, and old Engine #1 was retired, but not for long. North Branch had started Company #2 of the fire department, and as soon as their house was ready, Engine #1 was assigned to them. This created a problem for the precinct, as the company at the Branch looked to the commissioners for guidance and assistance, but actually the commissioners had no right to operate outside the precinct. They did all they could for Company #2 in spite of rising criticism, but to avoid further conflict the commissioners felt that the time had come to relinquish control of the fire department. In 1958, with articles in both the precinct and town warrants, control of the fire department was turned over to the town to be administered by a board of fire commissioners.

Since 1958, the town has purchased several more pieces of fire equipment. Company #1 has a new pumper, replacing the Diamond T, carrying about three thousand feet of four-inch hose. Company #2 has a pumper which replaced old engine #1, and in 1976 is to have a new tank truck. All trucks are radio-equipped and carry some of the latest equipment. The fire department has come a long way since the little wooden-axled engine of long ago, which was finally sold to Melvin Poor and his brother, Albert, for ten dollars in 1881, because they could not bear to think of its falling into uncaring hands.

The fire alarm system has also changed from simple to complex. For many years, the only alarm was the church bell, first on the Methodist and then the Baptist church. Until the early thirties there was a glass fronted box on the west side of the Baptist church which contained a key to the church, so that one could get inside to ring the bell. In 1908 there was an article in the warrant to purchase a bell to be hung in the town hall tower for a fire alarm, but the article was dismissed. It was not until 1918 that a fire alarm was installed in the tower of the engine house. This was a four-inch diameter whistle operated by compressed air. This was not very reliable, and in 1921 the system was moved to the town hall tower, the whistle changed to an eight-inch chime whistle, and new tanks and a new compressor installed. In 1928, in order to operate the whistle directly from the telephone office, Angus Nolan, who worked for Caughey & Pratt, devised a system using a small electric motor, and this is still in use today.

The modern fire department is so completely different from that of the 1800s that it is hard to imagine just what it was like to be a fireman back in Civil War days. From a bucket brigade to a modern two company fire department is quite a remarkable step forward. Things were different in 1888, and North Branch residents have just about forgotten the "Great Conflagration" of May 8, when more than half of the village burned down that afternoon. Someone was sent racing to South Antrim, but that took forty-five minutes. When the Methodist bell was rung, the men turned out, hitched two horses to the engine and started for the Branch. They added a third horse at Clinton Village, and arrived at the fire just two hours after it was first discovered. Two hours was too long, and the damage was heavy in spite of some valiant work by the boys from South Antrim.

The volunteer firemen have had their problems: they have saved many buildings and they have lost some. The old saw goes, "Yep, saved the cellar hole, by gosh." Everybody wants to help at a fire, and sometimes well meaning citizens do peculiar things—bedding being carefully carried to safety while dishes are tossed out the window—sometimes even the plumbing is ripped away and saved. People under stress can be most unpredictable.

Some of the outstanding men who have served as fire chief for the precinct are Scott Emery, Morris Burnham, John Thornton, Fred Cutter, and Gordon Sudsbury, Sr. The unsung heroes of the department are the volunteers, who sleep each night with an ear open for that first blast of the whistle, who can dress in nothing flat and be at the fire station in two minutes, ready to roll because they know that the first five minutes at a fire can mean the difference between losing it or getting it under control.

The second, and now the only responsibility of the precinct, and one closely allied to fire fighting, was to get an adequate water supply to the village. In 1890 the precinct voted to investigate the possibilities of a public water system for both domestic and fire fighting purposes. A committee consisting of Samuel Robinson, George Dresser, and Charles Gardner was appointed to report at the next meeting. They secured the services of George C. Patten, a surveyor, and investigated several large springs, as well as Gregg Lake, Campbell Pond, and Whittemore's Pond in Bennington. They gave a fine report, but were asked by the voters to have definite prices for a special meeting in September. Two special meetings brought no action, and in 1892 there was no mention of a water supply. In 1893 an article again appeared in the warrant, and this time the voters were serious. They authorized a bond issue of $25,000, and approved a contract with E. Gustine & Son of Keene to lay wooden pipe to Campbell Pond. This was ratified by a second vote on July 28, 1893, and work must have started at once, for by the following March the job was completed with twenty-six hydrants in the village. The total cost was $22,214. The precinct commissioners continued to expand the water system and improve the dam at Campbell Pond. Watering troughs were installed at the ends of the lines on several streets for the convenience of passing teams. In spite of all this activity, the debt was reduced to $11,000 by 1908.

During the late twenties, some of the original wooden pipe began to deteriorate, particularly in damp places. The pipe was made of pine, in six-foot lengths, and wrapped very tightly with steel strapping. Some of the smaller pipe was made of solid stock, and bored out, but the larger sizes were made in sections much like the old wooden silos. The steel strapping tended to rust completely away occasionally, and then a bad leak would develop. Some pipe was replaced with cast iron in the village as early as 1927, and in 1931 a program was started to replace all of the original pipe, plus the three and a half miles of wooden pipe to Campbell Pond with larger, cast iron pipe. In every year, with the exception of the years during World War II when pipe was unobtainable, work went on improving the water system. Hydrants of a newer type were installed at intervals, and by 1947 most of the work had been completed, and the main line was all cast iron except for 2,400 feet of wood, purchased when cast iron was unavailable. The last wooden line was replaced in 1952, and since then all the smaller lines have been replaced with new cast iron as money has become available.

It is interesting to note that from the early twenties to the present, all the work of repairing and relaying pipe for the precinct has been done by two concerns. The first was Caughey & Pratt, which went out of business in the early forties due to the death of Henry B. Pratt, Sr. Their equipment was purchased by Ellerton H. Edwards, who had worked for the firm as foreman for several years. He continued to do the same type of work under his own name. In 1953, his son George joined him, and the firm has incorporated under the name of E.H. Edwards & Son. Often workmen from these firms have worked overtime so that everyone would have water. In the last forty years, the community has never been without water for more than a few hours at a time.

In addition to the durability of the pipe, there have been other problems for the commissioners over the years. Initially, when rights to Campbell Pond and the land around it were acquired, one of the provisions was that cows could have access to the pond for drinking water. In the early 1900s, the board of health took exception to this unsanitary procedure, and advised that the water was unsafe for human consumption. Fences were hurriedly built, but by 1922 the situation was again serious, and the precinct decided to purchase more land around the pond.

The State Board of Health intervened again in 1939 with another ultimatum: either install a chlorinator or shut down. The injunction was heeded, and the chlorinator has been in operation ever since. It is controlled by a meter in the main line, which measures the amount of water used, and determines the necessary proportion of chlorine to be added. The meter gave the commissioners their first check on the amount of water used, which in 1940 was about sixty-thousand gallons per day, with approximately two hundred and fifty customers. With three hundred and twenty-five customers in 1974, the daily consumption rose to an average of one hundred and twenty-five thousand gallons, with peaks of two hundred and forty thousand gallons.

In an effort to increase the yield from the pond, more acreage was purchased in 1960, so that now practically all the watershed is owned by the precinct. A reforestation program started many years ago has been continued, and all the old pastures are now covered with pine and spruce, increasing the available water supply. The pond can easily handle one hundred and twenty-five thousand gallons per day during periods of normal rainfall.

Still, periods of drought were a constant worry, and in 1964 the commissioners asked for an appropriation of $2,500 to hunt for a second source of water. Several test wells were drilled in various locations in the town without much success. Down to the last $300 and discouraged, the commissioners were talking with the drilling engineer when he suddenly pointed to a sandbank and said, "Let me drill there, and I'll guarantee all the water you can use." Not quite believing, but at that point willing to be shown, the commissioners obtained permission, a well was drilled, and sure enough, there was water, lots of it! Thirty acres of land were purchased from Harvey Balch, and a gravel-packed well one hundred and twenty feet deep was installed, with a well house and appropriate gear. Pipe was laid across the Contoocook River to connect with the water system at Depot Street. This source is used only when needed to augment the supply from the pond, or in case of fire, but it is comforting to know that at least one hundred and fifty extra gallons per minute are available when needed.

In addition to the major responsibilities of fighting fire and supplying water, the precinct was briefly concerned with street lighting. For a period of several years both the precinct and the town warrants carried identical articles on street lighting, but the town eventually took over. The question of installing a public sewer system was also considered by the precinct, and voted down four times between 1909 and 1920. In retrospect, this was not only shortsighted but also unfortunate, since we are now faced with the same problem at vastly higher prices.

Over the years, the precinct has been involved in some things which were not strictly precinct affairs, but seemed necessary at the time. For instance, it is the trustee of some land which abuts the pipe land—land to be used for the benefit of Troop 2, Boy Scouts of America. It also owns the water rights and dam at Gregg Lake, the generous gift of William Hurlin. This was acquired after the town fathers refused to have anything to do with it; the precinct, realizing the value not only to the village but to the whole town, decided to accept this very thoughtful gift. This was followed in 1975 by the gift of the Summer Street dam and flowage rights of Great Brook to the precinct by Goodell Company. The Great Brook is a very vital part of the fire protection of the village, and the precinct is determined to see that this source of water is maintained and cared for.

In the space of slightly more than eighty years, the precinct changed its name four times; it changed its form of government; but it always made progress. In 1850 it was the Village Precinct. In 1867 the selectmen received a petition from the voters of the South Antrim Village Precinct to call a special meeting. This is the first time the words "South Antrim" appear, but from this date until March 18, 1893, when it was voted to adopt the provisions of Chapter 53 of the public statutes, all warrants were issued in the name of South Antrim Village Precinct. Prior to the 1893 meeting, the officers consisted of a moderator, clerk, treasurer, and three firewards, all elected annually. Adoption of Chapter 53 eliminated the firewards and substituted three commissioners elected for a one-year term. The commissioners appointed the fire chief, first engineer, and assistant. Apparently the name changed also, since all warrants were issued under the unwieldy name of the South Antrim Village Fire Precinct. At the March meeting in 1927, it was voted to adopt the provisions of Chapter 57 of the statutes, which changed the term of office of the commissioners from one to three years. In March, 1932, it was voted to petition the legislature to change the name by law to Antrim Precinct. A bill was introduced, passed, and signed on March 17, 1933.

Antrim Precinct has been particularly fortunate in having many dedicated men who have left this community a little better than they found it through their untiring efforts. In addition to the men mentioned in this brief history were George E. Dresser, George E. Hastings, and Alwin E. Young, who served as clerks; Elliot W. Baker, William E. Cram, and Archie M. Swett, who had enviable records as treasurers. The Honorable David H. Goodell, with his fellow commissioners Henry Simonds and Dr. Morris Christie, negotiated the installation of the water system in 1893. George W. Hunt was a commissioner for twenty-nine years. Hiram W. Johnson was moderator for forty-five years, an almost unbeatable record. A commissioner for thirty-one years, Mr. Johnson was the innovator of many things, including the first mobile fire engine, the renewal of the water system piping which was undertaken with the assistance of his fellow commissioners Albert E. Thornton and Maurice A. Poor, the installation of the chlorination system, the purchase of more land around the pond, and the reforestation of that land. It was Mr. Johnson as town representative who introduced the bill in the state legislature which made the name Antrim Precinct official.

ROADS

I T IS HARD to visualize that two hundred years ago when Antrim was incorporated, almost the whole area making up the Township was heavily forested with huge trees, and that no roads as we know them today existed. There were some trails leading away from the Contoocook River used by the Indians in their hunting excursions through the area, and a few paths outlined by marked trees made by surveyors when laying out sections of the "Society Land." The river itself was the only tangible connecting link with Concord to the northeast, and to near the Massachusetts line to the south.

The first settlers had to pack in by horseback, many times having to cut their way through heavy underbrush and fording the streams along the way. John Duncan, the seventh settler in Antrim, was the first to arrive by ox-cart. He came here in September, 1773, from Londonderry (about forty miles away) with his belongings, his wife, and five small children. He forded the Contoocook River at a shallow place near the mouth of Clinton Brook and proceeded to the cabin he had erected on land he had cleared during two or three previous seasons. The house now owned by A.C. Pashoian on the Clinton Road is believed to be built near the exact spot where the Duncan cabin stood.

In 1777 there were twenty widely scattered settlers living in the area—ten in the vicinity of North Branch, two in East Antrim, and ten in South Antrim. Only marked paths criss-crossed the area connecting neighbor with neighbor, and transportation was limited to horseback or walking.

In 1776 the frame of the "Great Bridge" was erected over the Contoocook River where the present bridge crosses the river at the end of Depot Street, and in 1777, following incorporation, the first road was "cut and cleared" and designated as the "Leading Road." In our town records all authorized roads are entered in the books as "Recorded Roads" and the first such entry, dated September 3, 1777, covers this "Leading Road." Included here is a facsimile of a copy of the entry, made by the town clerk, as it appears in the records.

*Map of Antrim . . . a portion of the General Highway Map of
Hillsborough County prepared in 1969 by the N.H. Dept. of
Public Works in cooperation with the U.S. Dept. of Trans-
portation.*

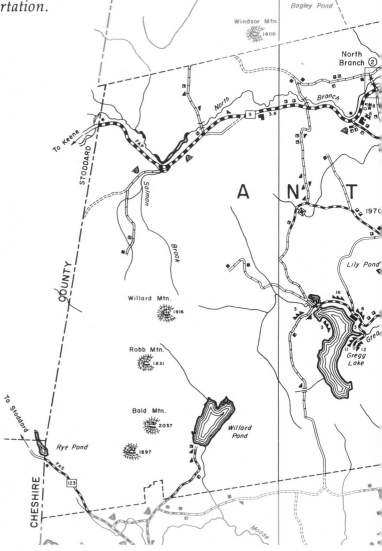

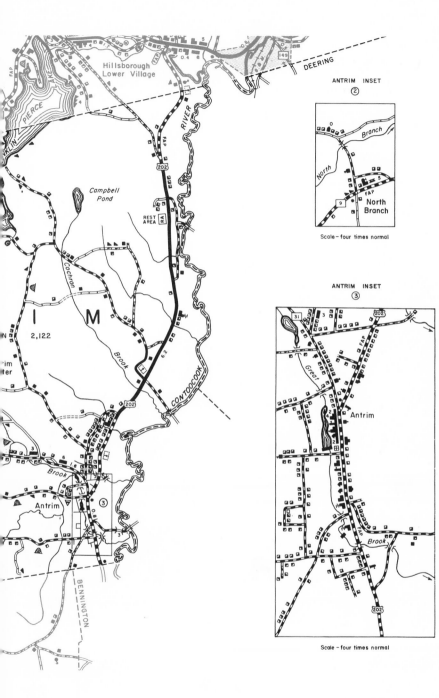

ANTRIM INSET
②

North Branch

Scale—four times normal

ANTRIM INSET
③

Antrim

Scale – four times normal

Following is an attempt to relate the landmarks contained in the original description to landmarks that exist today, so that the reader can gain a general idea of the route of this "Leading Road" through town.

Beginning at the "Great Bridge" over the Contoocook River to "James Aiken House" (near the foot of the hill on south Main Street); then northerly and a little east of our present Main Street to "Daniel McFarlands" (a little east of the intersection of Concord and Main Streets); continuing to a point a little north of the intersection of Clinton Road and Main Street; and then generally along the route of Clinton Road to "Boyd's Land" (Mescilbrooks Farm); turning there in a northwesterly direction over Whiton Road to the point where it comes out on Route 31 opposite the Bass Farm; then over Route 31 to the Grange Hall and, passing to the right of the hall, up the old road past the cemetery and site of the first Meeting House; continuing on over the hill on a road (now closed) that terminates at Route 31; over Route 31 for a very short distance and then straight north to North Branch Village, crossing Route 9 and the North Branch River Bridge near the North Branch Chapel; then easterly along the driveway in front of the administration building of Nathaniel Hawthorne College. It then proceeds easterly and to the left of the present residence of Henry Colton up over Tuttle, or English, Hill, to Route 9 near Breezy Point and thence to the Hillsborough Town line.

Most of the early roads were made without particular regard to terrain—many passing over the highest elevations for the reason that this was the first cleared land to insure good crops and was the location of the first dwellings. In laying out these roads, the objective was to open passage from neighbor to neighbor for their own convenience and not that of a long distance traveler. As a result, over sixty "Recorded Roads" were laid out in the first forty years after incorporation. No attempt is being made here to list or identify these convenience roads, but the major changes to the "Leading Road" and the location and construction of the main roads connecting Antrim with neighboring towns is referred to. Complete details of all "Recorded Roads" may be found in: (a) official town records in the town offices, (b) a special study prepared by Charles Butterfield, Byron Butterfield, and Ellerton Edwards which is on file in the historical room of the James A. Tuttle Library, and (c) a recent detailed study (1975) prepared by the Conservation Commission Committee, which is available for review in the town offices.

As previously described, the "Leading Road" went up over Meeting House Hill, coming out on Route 31 near the Dr. Robbins place. In the winter it was difficult and, at times even perilous, to travel from the south to the north part of the town, so in 1820 the town voted to build a road around the west side of the hill. This would be the present road, turning sharp left at the Grange Hall, thence along the present Route 31 to the point where the old road came down from the hill. It was completed in 1822. The road passed through land owned by Stephens Page and the following order for damages is on record:

To Mark Woodbury, Town Treasurer
Pay Stephens Page sixty two dollars, it being for damages of the new road going through his land west of the Meeting House.

Robert Gregg)
John Wallace) *Selectmen of Antrim*

Antrim - December 4, 1820.

Again referring to the "Leading Road," at a point just north of where the old road came down from the hill and joined the present Route 31, a new road was laid out in 1844, turning sharp left for a short distance thence north over Route 31 past the Pine Haven Cabins to Route 9. This then completed what is essentially the present Route 31 between Antrim and the Route 9, Keene road.

The "Courts Committee" (State of New Hampshire) laid out in 1831 what was called the new Keene Road from Hillsborough Bridge by

North Branch Village to the Stoddard line, and thence by the Box Tavern and North Nelson to Keene. From the Hillsboro line through Antrim to the Stoddard line required about six miles of road. The Town of Antrim, as well as the other towns along the route to Keene, made all possible opposition because the expense of building the road had to be borne by the individual towns—there was no such thing as State aid then. Town meetings were called; petitions were sent to the Court asking for discontinuance. Alternate plans to improve the old route from Concord to Keene through South Antrim, Hancock, and Dublin were offered. However, in the end Antrim was compelled to construct its portion of the new road at an expense of not less than four thousand dollars. The road was completed in 1834. Through the years many alterations and improvements to the road have been made, but in general it is the Route 9 we are familiar with today.

This same year (1831) the Courts Committee laid out a new road, part of the way over new ground, from Hillsborough Bridge, by Antrim South Village, to Hancock Factory Village (Bennington). Again the town strenuously opposed it, but lost out in the end. About three and one-half miles of the road was in Antrim and cost the town about two thousand dollars. This road is essentially the present route of 202 as it passes through Antrim.

The building of these two roads in the same year produced an extra financial burden of some six thousand dollars, all of which was "hired" on the credit of the town and it appears that most, if not all, of the needed funds were raised by borrowing from the local townspeople. One such note of record reads:

For value received I promise to pay Andrew C. Cochran, or order, seven hundred dollars on demand with interest annually. Antrim – October 31, 1834.

The Town of Antrim

by

Thos. McMaster, Jr.   )   *Selectmen*
Isaac Baldwin   )

On the reverse side of the note is the following notation: "Paid April 22, 1837 — $809.06." Apparently the interest was at 6% at that time.

The procedure of contracting for the building of roads at that time is interesting. When a new road was laid out, it was divided into "Lots" of varying lengths to be "Sold" at auction. A notice was posted and one such notice reads as follows:

Road at Auction

Will be sold at Public Auction on Saturday, the 25th inst. at 3 of the clock in the afternoon, the road leading from Rob't Tennants to Dimond Dodge. Sale to commence near Bob Jenank. Conditions of sale made known at the time. Antrim — June 14, 1836

Thos. McCody)

Jonathan Carr)   Selectmen of Antrim

Thos. Dunlap)

The terms of the sale as made known on June 25th read in part:

The above road will be sold in lots with the bridges included—to be built as described in the contracts hereafter specified, separate contracts for each lot—each contract shall be signed by the contractor and satisfactory security given.

A typical contract with its description of the "Lot" follows:

"Lot #3." Beginning at the termination of Lot No. 2, thence 22 rods to a stake. This lot to be made 18 ft. wide from the center of the ditches, 15 inches crowning, no rocks, roots or stumps to be within one foot of the top of the road. To be done in a workman-like manner to be acceptable of the Selectmen. To be completed by the first day of October next, to be paid in the month of November next. The undertakers to sign this obligation with a good security.

Records show that this particular lot was "Struck off" by Dave Colby at $1.25 per rod, with John McCoy as security.

In connection with the Keene Road previously mentioned, it is known that it was divided into twenty-nine lots, but no description of the lots or contracts have been found. It is also known, however, that there were sixteen successful bidders, some bidding on more than one lot. The road between Hillsborough Bridge and Hancock Factory Village was divided into ten lots.

In 1799, a company having been formed to build a turnpike from Claremont to Amherst, asked permission to pass through Antrim. At a meeting held November 18, 1799, it was voted "the town had no objection." This road cut across the northeastern edge of Antrim and was built at no cost to the town.

The Forest road passing from Charlestown, N.H., through Stoddard, Hancock, and Greenfield to Nashua was a main artery for markets to the south and east. It passed through the southwest corner of Antrim for about a mile. Antrim vigorously protested the expense

To Mark Woodbury Town Treasurer pay Stephens Page Sixty two Dollars it being for dammage of the new road going through his Land west of the Meeting house ... Selectmen of Antrim

Antrim December 4 1820

of maintaining this stretch of road as it never offered any direct benefit to the town. This is now part of State Route 123 and is maintained by the state.

The subject of laying out and maintaining Antrim roads prompts mention of what seems to have been a most peculiar situation existing in 1839. A petition was presented to the Selectmen reading as follows:

To the Selectmen of Antrim—Gentlemen:
Whereas a part of Mr. Daniel Low's barn now stands in the road, we, the undersigned request you to insert an article in the next March meeting warrant to see if the town will take any measure to move or cause to be moved, that part of said barn that now stands in the road.
Antrim—February 11, 1839.

(Signed by eleven petitioners)

The warrant for the March meeting did include as Article 13 the following—"To see if the Town will vote to take any measures to move that part of Daniel Lowe's barn that stands in the road." The town clerk's minutes of the meeting read: "Voted to dismiss the 13th article." The barn is still there! The Daniel Lowe place is now known as Mescilbrooks Farm, located on the Clinton Road.

At the first town meeting May 1, 1777, held at the home of Captain John Duncan, it was "Voted that the inhabitants shall work at Highways at the rate of half a dollar a day and find what tools the Surveyor will order them to bring." At this same meeting Maurice Lynch was elected the first "Surveyor" whose responsibility it was to oversee the building and maintenance of all town roads — probably not too different from the duties of our present elected road agent.

The following year the town was divided into three highway districts, each with its own surveyors. In 1781 there were 4; in 1782, 7; in 1800, 15; and by 1886 there were 29, each still having its own surveyor with full responsibility for the roads in his district. One such district was described as follows:

District 2. Beginning at A.A. Miller's house, running westerly by John M. Duncan's to his west line and from N.W.C. Jameson's brick house to Elijah Kimball's to the north line of the Saltmarsh farm and from Hiram Eaton's house to the corner of the road southwest of Andrew Cochran.

Volume 1, Number 2 of the *Antrim Reporter* dated October 2, 1882, contained the following news item:

If the highway surveyor in the District that leads from Antrim to Bennington was bounced twice each day, as those of us are that come over the road, we have no doubt he would cause the large stone to be removed that is in front of Chas. Gibson's. "Bart" is a good fellow, but guess he don't go that way much.

Possibly such problems as this resulted in action taken at the town meeting in 1887, when the town voted to have not more than five highway districts, and then in 1894 it was "Voted not to vote for Highway Agents by divisions," and James E. Tenney was appointed road agent for the town. The road agent is now an elected town officer who is responsible for all town roads and their maintenance.

At the 1891 Town Meeting, during the discussion of Article 5 covering the subject of appropriating money for highways, D.H. Goodell presented the following proposal:

I agree to keep the highways throughout the town of Antrim in repair from the time snow leaves them in the spring of the year 1891, till the snow comes then again, but not later than Nov. 1, 1891, to the entire satisfaction of the Board of Selectmen of Antrim, for the sum of one thousand dollars, it being understood that I shall not expend more than $25.00 for bridges, and shall not be obliged to repair roads injured by extraordinary freshets, at a greater expense than the ordinary repairs would be on the same piece of road, and that I shall have the use of the two road machines belonging to the Town without charge.

The proposal was accepted; the same proposal was in effect for the year 1892.

Also in the 1891 Town warrant, Article 11 read: "To see if the Town will vote to buy one or more Rollers for breaking out roads in the winter." The minutes of the meeting in reference to this article read: "Moved by John G. Abbott and carried by vote of the house that the Selectmen be authorized to purchase one Roller for breaking winter roads."

The January 13, 1892, issue of the *Antrim Reporter* contained the following news item:

The street snow roller which the town voted to have built at the last Town Meeting has arrived, being brought here from Francestown last Friday by Charles H. Bass' four-horse team. Its weight is 3400 pounds.

Then on January 20, 1892, the following item appeared in the *Reporter*:

The new Snow Roller was used for the first time last Friday afternoon on six inches evenfall of snow and worked to a charm, giving a wide and smooth track and quite solid. It is a great improvement over the old method. The Main road was "rolled out" from the Bennington line to the Hillsborough town line, as well as the principal thoroughfares of the village and side streets.

There is an entry in the 1892 Town Report that reads: "C.A.

Barrett—Road Roller—$55.00." It is believed that this has reference to and represents the full cost to the town of their first snow roller.

Following the complete success of the snow roller during the winter of 1892, there was a great deal of agitation for the purchase of two more, and an article appeared in the Town warrant for the March 8 meeting in 1892 to procure them. John G. Abbott prepared a statement favoring this purchase and excerpts of his statement and recommendation for the purchase of a roller called the "Monitor" follows:

To meet the requirements of a highway, a road must be wide enough to allow the meeting and passing of teams, without causing the driver to spend time and labor in making a place to turn out every time they meet a team. Consequently, most of the Towns in New Hampshire have never had a highway in winter.

A neighboring town, after such discussion, instructed the Selectmen to make inquiries and ascertain all the facts they could relative to the construction and workings of snow rollers, to the result of which was the building of the roller "Monitor."

The Monitor is built of heavy white oak plank, four inches wide; it is built in two sections, the drums being six feet in diameter and five and one-half feet wide, with a space of one foot between the drums, making the roller twelve feet wide; it runs on an arbor two and one-half inches in diameter and fitted with iron boxes; an iron scraper is attached to the back part of the machine to keep it clear.

The Monitor weighs 5500 pounds and cost to build $78.00. It usually requires four large horses to draw the roller, six horses will draw the roller over any road we have in town and people familiar with the town know we have many bad hills.

At the meeting it was voted to instruct the Selectmen to procure two more snow rollers and they were continued in use until 1926.

At the town meeting in 1926, $5,500 was appropriated for a tractor with movable tracks—plows and wings. It went into service in 1927, thus ending the nostalgic snow roller era. It is interesting to note that during the first few years of the tractor's use, the plow was held at a height so as to leave four inches of snow to provide sledding for horse drawn equipment. This provided neither good wheeling nor good sledding and, as the horse population decreased, so did the amount of snow left on the road. Eventually, with the use of salt, we attained the fine winter roads we enjoy today.

As winter roads had their problems—with snow—summer roads

had a problem too—Dust! The *Antrim Reporter* (July 3, 1912) contained the following advertisement:

> The watering cart will sprinkle the streets in town during the summer if all the families and business men on the street will pay 4 cents each day. I wish to state that the payment must be cash, not promises.
> H.W. Elliott, Antrim, N.H.

There is no record of how successful the service was. However, this problem no longer exists as all the streets and main roads are black-topped. The hard surfacing appears to have started in the 1920s and continued through the 1930s, after which all new streets and roads were so built.

By the end of the first full year after the town's incorporation, its total miles of recorded roads was probably less than eleven—the Leading Road of about six miles and the balance made up of short roads connecting neighbor with neighbor and allowing access to the Leading Road for the scattered settlers. Today there are over fifty miles of town roads and streets plus about seven miles of federal highway (Route 202) and about ten miles of state highways (Routes 31, 9, and 123), making a total of more than sixty miles of roads within the township.

The road agent is elected annually and is responsible for all maintenance of town streets and roads and the building of such new roads or streets as may be authorized by vote of the town. The total cost of such service was in excess of $60,000 in 1974. (In 1845 the total highway cost was $1000!)

The cost of building and maintaining the federal and state roads through the town is paid for by the state from funds raised by the state gasoline tax.

SCHOOLS

IN HIS *History of Antrim*, Dr. Warren Cochrane says that our Scot forefathers prized education next to religion, and had a hatred of ignorance. In this light, it does not seem unusual that the children of Deacon Aiken, as well as neighbor children, were taught in Aiken's home beginning in 1770. Their first teacher was George Bemaine, a former schoolmate of the Thomas Dilworth who authored a widely used spelling book. The only other book used was the Bible, with mathematics skimpily presented orally. At least one parent, Robert McIlvaine, wrote an arithmetic book for his children. It is now displayed in the historical rooms of the Tuttle Library. John Dinsmore was their second teacher, keeping school, as did his predecessor, only one month out of the year.

At Town Meeting in March, 1786, it was "Voted to Raise fifteen pounds for the use of a Town Scool." This money was not used for the building of a school, but probably to pay the teacher. The first schoolhouse was built in 1787 by contributions of logs and labor from the townspeople. It was located on the north side of Goodell Road, a few hundred feet from the junction with Route #202, and the site is so marked. The structure was large enough to accommodate all the children in the eastern part of town, but it was used for only ten years. By that time schoolhouses had been built at the Branch, over East, High Range (the vicinity of Reed Carr Road), and lastly in South Village, near the northeast corner of North Main and Elm Streets.

Around 1800 the town was divided into school districts, which were sub-divided according to shifts and increases in population. The peak was reached in 1852 with children attending school in fourteen districts, but shortly after this the concentration of the population in the villages prompted a gradual closing of the outlying schools.

These early schools were financed by the individual districts, although some of the revenue came from the state under the name of the Literary Fund. The bulk of the money was raised by assessing a certain rate on the taxable property in each district. Thus it was possible for the richest district to provide the most schooling in a given year. In 1832 there were twelve districts with a total of 448 students, and the entire cost of public education for the year was $564.33.

In 1886 all the districts were merged into one, with the schools known as divisions of the district. By 1909 all schools were closed except Division 1, the (south) Village; Division 2, the Center; Division 3, North Branch; and Division 4, over East. For nearly twenty-five more years school was kept continually in these four places, until in 1933 it was deemed more economical to transport the few students from over East to the Village. The Center school was the next to go, in 1940, but the North Branch held out bravely until 1946, due in no small part to the efforts of Edward Grant. Each year at School Meeting when the subject of closing the North Branch school would be brought up, Mr. Grant was fast on his feet in defense of the school to which he had contributed a large number of students over a long period of time. Upon the closing of the last of the outside schools, and with the transportation of the children to the Village, the old school building facing West Street housed all of the children of Antrim, ages 6-18, for a period of five years.

Until 1852 each district had its own "Prudential Committee," with the power to purchase school lots, build schoolhouses, and hire teachers. At the same time, by state law, there was a Superintending School Committee to visit and inspect all the district schools. The Reverend John Whiton was chairman for at least thirty-two years, but after his demise the committee more often than not consisted of one member. The Reverend Whiton's chosen profession is reflected in the section on schools in his *History of Antrim* where he remarked that teaching the children of both Protestant and Catholic families was increasingly difficult, and concluding with the rhetorical question, "If our system of popular education should ever become a *Godless* system, what must be its influence on the state of society?"

School teachers were "boarded around" in the various homes in each district, spending a week or so with each family. Miss Jennie Nesmith taught in several different schools in Antrim and Bennington between 1861 and 1894, and several years later was honored at a reunion of her former students, held at Kelsea Grove. *The Antrim Reporter* of August 26, 1903, claims that her remarks were the feature of the day.

Teachers do not 'board around' now-a-days, they do not know what they miss, the nice cream biscuits, the custard pie, and the School Ma'am cake. Now that cake, I know I've named it right, for always . . . that cake would be for first supper, almost always hot from the oven, but 'twas fine, just melting.
. . . Examination day was the dread of all young teachers . . . The row of parents and visitors, all around the room, and the 'Committeeman' asking questions — no wonder some bright boy said two 3's are 8.
. . . It was not thought the proper thing to retain the teacher a second term, she would get too well acquainted with her pupils, or they with her, therefore a change.

A far cry from today's philosophy, when a teacher may remain in the same school throughout his or her career, with the idea that familiarity breeds improvement.

The early schoolhouses were all built along the same architectural lines, with a slanting floor, and a huge fireplace at one end. The windows were very high, to discourage day-dreaming, no doubt, and the older students sat on benches, while the younger ones had small seats. Around 1842 remodeling was begun, consisting of leveling the floors, replacing the fireplaces with stoves, and supplying desks and seats which were graduated in size. By that time the school year had lengthened to two terms of eight weeks each, one in winter, and one in summer.

In 1927 Mrs. Helen Burnham wrote a paper, "Old Schools and Schoolhouses in Antrim," which is now kept in the Tuttle Library. She has done scrupulous research, and the result is an excellent history of each of the fourteen districts, including descriptions of the early buildings.

South Village was thriving in the middle 1800s, and it was necessary to divide District 1 in two, naming the new district #13. They were more popularly referred to as North and South schools, with one building on the corner of Main and Elm Streets, and a larger one on Depot Street, on the corner across from George Graham's. By 1867 these districts were reunited as #1 again, but not without opposition. The class distinction that once persisted between these two geographic areas of South Village has all but disappeared today, but it was a very real factor for many years. However, with fifty-eight students crammed into the north-end schoolhouse during the summer session of 1868, the district had to face the necessity of building an adequate structure, and after many meetings and rescinded decisions, $3,000 was appropriated to build a new school to be finished by November of 1869. It was to be in constant use for over 90 years, and is now remodeled into an apartment house, known as the "Schoolhouse Apartments." Subscriptions totaling five hundred dollars were raised to build Waverly Hall on the second floor of the building for all sorts of town gatherings until the Town Hall was built in the 1890s. Although the school report of 1870 congratulated the citizens of District 1 on the completion of their beautiful schoolhouse, the proximity to the hall was considered "a matter of deep regret."

The 1873 school report condemned the practice of fastening the teacher out on New Year's Day as foolish, and an act of rowdyism. If parents couldn't control this, the students involved should be expelled from school.

In addition to the fearsome but sometimes festive examinations held at the end of each term, other contests were often held. In 1875 District 2 at the Center entered a contest for the best common school in the area, including several towns. They won first prize, a set of Chambers' Encyclopedia, and one little girl exclaimed to her mother, "Our school won the Chamber set!" Good behavior was always worthy of commendation, and another little girl from this same school raced home one day with the advance news that her brother had won the prize for being have.

High schools were held from time to time throughout the nineteenth century, but they were private academies or tuition schools, and sometimes referred to as select schools. Sylvester Cochran held a successful academy at the Branch around 1820 in a large hall above John G. Flint's quarters, now part of Hawthorne College. Around 1830 the Antrim Publick School was held in South Village, directed by a board of trustees of prominent citizens. Sixty-five gentlemen and ladies between the ages of eleven and twenty made up the student body, several of them coming from other towns and boarding with local families. Professor James E. Vose conducted select schools at the Center, and in 1872 opened a high school at the South Village with seventy-five scholars. Although the school report commends the friends of education for establishing a permanent high school, Professor Vose left town soon afterward and the school expired.

By 1890 most schools were in session three terms each year, and the school board undertook the purchase of textbooks for the first time. Waverly Hall had been purchased and remodeled to accommodate the increasing number of students in Division 1. The main criticism made by the school board in this and many other years was too much absenteeism and tardiness, and poor attendance at end-of-term examinations, indicating a lack of parental interest.

Eventually it was decided to establish a high school in the north room of Waverly Hall, and the first term opened on September 6, 1892, with twenty-six students, and Henry J. Hall as the principal and only teacher, at a salary of sixty dollars a month. The school board members who effected this dramatic move in the town's educational system were J.F. Tenney and D.W. Cooley. From the School report of 1893: "As a prerequisite to the High School we require written examinations in the following studies: Arithmetic, Grammar, Geography, United States History, and elements of Physiology." At the end of the second term the examinations were held in English Literature, Algebra, Astronomy, and Latin. Governor Goodell made favorable closing remarks at this time, but *The Antrim Reporter* of March 8, 1893, commented: "It is possible that some things might have been done more to the tastes of a few, but on the whole it can be said the enterprise of a high school is a success."

By 1895 there were three distinct classes, and the first graduation was held on June 25 of that year, with eleven graduates.

Additional rooms were built in 1897 for $2,000 to accommodate the ever-increasing primary and grammar school population, and the third floor of this ell was outfitted to serve as a much needed laboratory for the high school.

It was common practice during these years for the school board to borrow needed money from local affluent citizens. In 1898 one friend of the school gave $100 for the purpose of hiring W.G. White to teach vocal music in each school. The option was not picked up by the board at the end of the year, and it was ten years before music was again a part of the curriculum.

The high school faculty was increased to two in 1902, leading to state accreditation. The board recommended joining a supervisory district and employing a superintendent of schools, with the state paying half the salary, and the town report of 1906 includes Superintendent H.L. Woodward's first report. The population of the town was 1,350, and there were 260 students registered in five districts. He recommended, among other things, that the elementary school should consist of eight grades, and that the ninth grade be absorbed by the high school, making a four-year high school.

By 1909 a third teacher joined the high school faculty, and there was a choice of courses to pursue: classical and scientific. Music and drawing were established in all the schools, and in 1914 home economics and agriculture were added to the high school curriculum.

North Branch needed a new building, and Mr. Flint came to the rescue in 1913 by offering to pay for a new building in exchange for the old one. For $1,200 a frame schoolhouse was built on the south side of the North Branch River. The brick building on the north side became part of the Flint estate, and was renovated. It is now part of Hawthorne College.

During the last half of the decade the home economics and agriculture classes used local homes and farms for laboratories, a practice that must have seemed enormously progressive at that time.

In 1920 the budget topped $10,000 for the first time. There was a shortage of teachers in the aftermath of the Great War, and the agricultural course was soon dropped. Local organizations added enrichment to the program, with the DAR offering history prizes to the seventh and eighth grades annually, and the Woman's Club paying for physical education and music teachers at different times during the twenties.

The trend in education seemed to be getting away from the three R's, and going toward "unnecessary frills." There is always an element of the population that opposes changes on the grounds that what was good enough for their grandfathers should be good enough for their grandchildren, but this time there seems to have been a sound basis for some concern. A number of parents of high school students felt that the program was not preparing the young people well enough for college, and besides that, discipline was getting out of hand. Pressure was put on the school board to hire a principal with a firm hand and a predilection toward academic studies, and on the strength of this Thomas Chaffee was hired in 1926 at a salary of $1,900, coming to Antrim with many years of experience.

For the next ten years the academic program in the high school grew in strength. Home economics was dropped in 1931. (For further information, see the chronology, 1935.) Music and art were strong areas of instruction under Bess Felker and Edith Messer. Philip Lang's essay on wildflower preservation won first prize in the state, and other students won regional prizes for their posters, while Mrs. Felker's orchestra engaged in state and regional concerts, and even played over the Manchester radio station. The result of the post-war baby boom was shown in the peak population of sixty-eight students in 1936, but at the same time only 56 percent of those entering high school went on to graduate.

A new superintendent for the first time in nearly twenty years advocated a sports program, a more varied curriculum, and two principals, one for the high school, and one for the elementary. This led to the installation of a commercial course in 1937, and an elementary principal in 1938. The next year saw the retirement of Mr. Chaffee, who was replaced by William Ramsden. He stayed only a short time, and was succeeded by several principals who followed this example.

World War II caused much absenteeism in the high school, as many young people were engaged in various jobs supporting the war effort. Aeronautics was added to the curriculum; several boys were in accelerated programs at the University of New Hampshire, and the population shrank to thirty students.

Following the war all the town's children were housed in one building, the Village schoolhouse, and this led to several drastic changes. Each grade needed a separate room and teacher, and the larger rooms were partitioned into small ones. Shop and home economics were added, and it was deemed economical to include the seventh and eighth grades in the high school, where a total of five

The three R's . . . the old High School

The three R's . . . the new Middle School

teachers taught thirty-one subjects. The building on West Street, now the American Legion Hall, was first leased and then purchased from H.E. Wilson to provide a shop for the boys. Physical education classes were held in the Town Hall, and hot lunches were served every noon at the Odd Fellows Hall. This necessitated a great deal of traveling during school hours, which led to some conjecture about how the children could learn anything when they were on the street all day. Complaints about the system reached a new high when Kenneth Jewett, vocal music teacher, conceived a project called "My Town — Antrim," involving all the students in the six-year high school. This project, based on the core curriculum theory, employed historical research at the library, the creation of costumes and sets, and a lot of rehearsing at the Town Hall, all of which kept the students continually on the go in full view of taxpayers for several weeks. The culmination of the project was two evening performances in November, 1948, and those who saw the show had to admit that this new-fangled kind of education must have something going for it.

There was no doubt now that if the town were to continue along the modern road to education, it had to give serious thought to building. The March, 1948, school warrant asked for $80,000 to build a new elementary school at the top of Summer Street, which would leave the old building for high school students only. The town agreed to go ahead with the school board's plans, and the land was acquired and construction got underway. But when the 1949 warrant asked for $43,000 more to complete the building, the townspeople balked. Feelings ran high, accusations were rife, but common sense ruled in the end. There was no alternative: $80,000 worth of building could not be allowed to stand unused until it deteriorated.

For many months, weekly meetings were held by the school board of Carroll Johnson, Charles Wood, and Arthur Brown, Superintendent Stewart McCormack, and the recently appointed building committee, Ben Butterfield, Bill Hurlin, and G.H. Caughey. A new proposal was presented at an August school district meeting, cutting costs by $3,000, and indicating some drastic changes to be made in the management of the construction. But it was two years before problems were sufficiently ironed out for the new school to be ready for occupancy and thus permit the high school to expand comfortably in the old building, with plenty of room for a shop.

The post-war years had seen great development in extra-curricular activities at the high school level. The DAR, Rod and Gun Club, and American Legion and its Auxiliary sponsored local students in statewide projects, most of them resulting in week-long camps or workshops. The Interscholastic Athletic League scheduled games for basketball, baseball, and softball teams, both boys' and girls'. In 1951 Antrim High School attained one of its highest points of prestige when Coach John Lawson created a basketball team that almost won the state championship. While there were to be equally fine teams in subsequent years that nearly capped the title, the team of 1950-51 had the distinction of receiving an invitation to play in the New England high school tournament at the Boston Garden. Although they lost in the first game, no one could deny that they were winners all the way. The starting five, Bruce Cuddihy, Jack Munhall, Don Dunlap, Joe White, and Barry Claflin with Dick Hartwell as swinger, always made a striking appearance when they arrived at the scene of a game. Their custom of dressing up was unheard of among high school athletes. With their green corduroy sports coats, and white shirts and ties, they had the game psychologically in their hands long before the first whistle. No doubt the spirit aroused by this team had a great deal to do with the success of the Memorial Gymnasium, which was erected in 1953.

The current expenses in the school year 1952-53 were $43,927.76, not to mention a sizeable debt on the new school. In two years' time the current budget increased a whopping 19 percent, but who worried? Industries were moving in all around Antrim, and people were better off financially than they had been for many years, with no let-down in sight.

It was time to think about improving the high school, and local representatives joined the five-town Crotched Mountain Cooperative

School Study Committee. When their report in 1958 vetoed any action at that time, it was decided nevertheless to set aside an amount in the capital reserve fund each year toward the possibility of having to build a new high school. Once burned, twice careful. A committee appointed in 1960 recommended at the next district meeting that a new building be constructed to house grades seven through twelve. It was voted affirmatively, accompanied by a lot of sentimentality about taking care of our children right here at home. In August, 1962, the new high school building was dedicated. Located at the southern end of Shea Athletic field, it became part of a complex of educational facilities. The gym, the next building south, would soon become the property of the district, and beyond that was the controversial elementary school, separated from the gym by a large playground and parking lot. Although the board members involved — Harvey Black, John Brzozowski, Edith Mulliner, and William Nay, and their accompanying building committee, Vera Butterfield, Ellen Edwards, and Stanley Tenney — worked long, hard hours, and undoubtedly encountered many obstacles, the entire project seemed to move to completion with the smoothness of maple syrup compared to the machinations involved in the completion of the elementary school a decade earlier.

In order to remain comprehensive, the high school was now forced to increase the staff by three teachers. A full range of courses was offered, including commercial, home economics, and industrial arts, as well as college preparatory subjects. Beverly Tenney enhanced the foreign language program by starting the Classical Club, associated with the national organization. Some of their colorful activities were the annual slave auction in the fall and the Roman banquet in the spring. The superintendent's report in 1963 announced, "Antrim High School now has a band," the first marching band in the history of the school. Headmaster and Coach Charles "Chick" Hamel added track to the sports curriculum, with two students placing in the top at the state meet. One of his basketball teams reached the semi-finals in state competition.

But the cost of education per pupil was very high, and total expenditures for the school year were well into the six figure bracket. A necessary addition to the elementary building increased the debt even further, and Superintendent Norman Hartfiel reported that the end was not in sight. Despite the loyal efforts made by the community to maintain a high standard of education, it was obvious that a cooperative move was necessary, and on July 1, 1968, all school property became part of the Contoocook Valley Cooperative School District, made up of nine towns. The last local class graduated on June 14, 1970, and Antrim High School came to an end, with Joseph LeBlanc as the last principal. Norman Trottier, math teacher and amateur film maker, produced a movie called, *The Death of a High School*. During the final days of the school year, the film was shown many times to small groups of students and teachers in a small, dark, all-purpose room. There was never a dry eye in the house, proving again that what the small high school may lack in educational opportunities, it more than makes up for in sentiment and fierce loyalty.

The following September saw the most dramatic school change for many decades. High school students, in fear and trepidation, lined up for the buses that would transport them to the brand new multi-million dollar high school in North Peterboro. Grades five through eight attended the old high school, newly known as the Middle School, where they were joined by grades seven and eight from Bennington. This left grades one through four with plenty of room in the elementary building. Curriculum changes were underway, also, and due to the enthusiasm of Principal Alan Page, combined with the size of the Antrim school (neither the smallest nor the largest in the district), Antrim did some pioneering in individualized education. Although teams of teachers from other parts of the state came to observe and admire, teams of parents closer to home came to censure and indict. Confusing multi-paged progress reports instead of definitive grade cards, lack of basic texts, and classes continually spilling noisily out of classrooms all contributed to criticism or misunderstanding of the program. The jury is still out: at this writing we are standing too close to the picture to be able to assess it properly.

But one thing is certain: Antrim students who have attended Con-Val High School for the past six years (more courageously each year) have contributed positively to the success of the school. The honor roll contains many local names, in all fields of endeavor. They have become class and club presidents, and succeeded in the fine and lively arts. But nowhere does the name Antrim spark as much admiration as in the field of athletics. An editorial in *The Peterborough Transcript* of June 12, 1975, contained unadulterated praise as follows:

SUCCESS FOR THE CO-OP
Congratulations to Antrim High . . . er, ConVal High . . . for the stunning performance in winning their first state Class I baseball championship.

No less than eight young athletes of the 15 carried on the squad by Coach Dick Hebert claim Antrim as their home. And this does not count the scorekeeper, Amy Webber, who is also from the same town.

The victory was a dramatic example of the success of the CV cooperative system . . . Of course none of them "made" the championship as the representative of any one community. They all played for ConVal High, but it is interesting that five of the starting nine, and eight members in all of the squad, come from only one of the nine CV towns.

So it's congratulations to the entire team, the coaching staff, and to the school system, and as one booster was heard to comment this week, "Don't let Antrim secede."

The New Hampshire Sunday News of June 8,1975, in reporting the championship game described the performances of only four ConVal Cougars, all Antrim boys: Pete Lamb, Marshall White, Doug Smith, and Craig Whitney. The fifth local player of note was Rick Cuddihy, the current contender in Antrim's athletic dynasty.

So as the world grows smaller and Antrim becomes integrated into a larger community, its citizens take no little pride in the success of the young people, knowing that the efforts to provide them with a good educational background really paid off. No history would be complete without giving credit to the teachers, too numerous to mention, from George Bemaine to the present staff, whose dedication to the needs of their students is what school is all about.

Graduation Trivia

Graduation from high school is a big moment in every student's life, causing mixed emotions as he realizes that this marks the end of childhood protection and the beginning of adult responsibilities. But in the small town the whole community gets swept up in the flurry of parties, pretty dresses, and Pomp and Circumstance. Trips to the city for new shoes and suitable gifts, decorations and rehearsals, visits from adoring grandparents and loyal alumni, all contribute to the festive occasion known as graduation week.

Some of the magic is gone now that we share our high school with eight other towns, but for seventy-six consecutive years June was more than the month of roses in Antrim.

For nearly fifty of those years the exercises were held at two-thirty, usually Friday afternoon, with a reception in the evening at the Town Hall. (The class of 1896 with some delusion of grandeur announced their reception to be held in the Opera House.) By 1907 the time of graduation (known as Commencement from 1905 on) was so firmly established that the invitation neglected to include that information. In 1943 the invitations had already been printed when the decision was made to change the time from two-thirty to seven-thirty so that announcements of the change had to be inserted.

From then on, graduation was held in the evening until 1967. That large class planned an outdoor program for the convenience of the hundreds of anticipated guests. Rehearsals were held, and stage and chairs were set up between the gym and high school in preparation for two o'clock Sunday afternoon. Sunday morning it started raining with such determination that there was no hope of salvaging the plans, and everything was moved into the gym with alacrity. The succeeding classes stuck to the two o'clock Sunday schedule, but never had the courage to try to hold graduation outside again.

The largest class was the class of 1968, with twenty-six graduates. There was a tie for the smallest class: in 1922 the two girl graduates were Evelyn Parker and Jennie Craig, and in 1926 the class was made up of Dorothy Knapp and Dorothy Barrett. The latter Dorothy often bragged about being salutatorian of her class.

It was always a matter of great community interest to learn who received the highest scholastic honors in the class, and therefore gave the valedictory and salutatory addresses, but in the middle sixties this practice was abandoned, and the welcome and farewell speeches were given by class officers or their stand-ins.

When the size of the class was manageable each graduate took part in the final exercises by presenting an essay. A lot of courage was mustered by a lot of shrinking violets in order to stand up on the Town Hall stage, dressed in uncomfortable clothes, tight shoes, and stifling cap and gown, and give a speech in front of hundreds of other people's relatives, but the pride on the faces of one's own family made it well worth the effort.

Something of the charm went out of graduation when in the early fifties the custom of having a guest speaker was introduced. Some of the speakers were fine, but the audience reaction seemed to be another time, another place: this is the night we've looked forward to for so long, and we only want to listen to our children.

Baccalaureate was another thing. The guest preachers aimed their messages at the graduates, and since their big day was still to come, the seniors had the compassion to listen attentively. For many years the whole high school took part in the baccalaureate service, marching

into the church first and forming an aisle through which the marshal led the graduates. To be chosen the marshal for the graduating class was an honor and distinction. As the decision was usually based on popularity, it would be safe to say that the class marshal was usually Mr. (or Miss, on rare occasions) Personality of the Underclass.

But for the young people themselves, the reception was perhaps the most exciting event. Many hours, both school time and after school, were spent by the seniors and willing friends transforming the Town Hall into a wonderland of color with reams of crepe paper. A measure of professional decorating was added in the late thirties when Louis "Bucky" Mallett, interior painter, offered his assistance to several classes. He not only drew a unique design for each class, but helped in carrying it out, and the results were stunning.

In the early years the girls were dressed in white, and the boys as formally as pocketbooks would allow, and the whole class lined up in front of the stage in a receiving line. Guests were ushered through, from right to left, by siblings, cousins, or close friends of the graduates who felt singularly honored to be selected for this choice position. (One long-term tradition dictated boy ushers for the afternoon, girls for the evening.) After about an hour of this, the line broke up and for the rest of the evening everyone participated in promenading around the floor, going into grand march formation for variety. The Class of 1920 became renowned for one particular thing: promenading was replaced by dancing after their reception, and so it continued until the fifties. Then the reception followed the graduation exercises, and the dance became the Senior Prom, held on another night.

Caps and gowns were introduced in 1939, with the rationalization that no one graduate would stand out from the others in his manner of dress. But fancy clothes were still needed for the dance, and now the girls' gowns could be in a variety of colors, blending with the elaborate decor of the hall.

Antrim High School's last class, 1970, broke with all tradition, and held their commencement exercises in the Hawthorne College Gymnasium. It seems to symbolize the town's general acceptance that it was time to get in step with the rest of the world and let old traditions become fond memories.

THE SESQUICENTENNIAL

ONE HUNDRED YEARS ago Antrim celebrated her centennial anniversary with day-long festivities at the Center. A thousand invitations were sent out, with preparations to feed three thousand persons — more than twice the number of permanent residents. It was an impressive venture for a small town, and the results were so successful that Dr. Cochrane devoted sixty pages of his history to it.

As the year 1927 approached, the people resolved to mark Antrim's sesquicentennial in an equally fitting manner. They began to make their plans in 1925, when at the town meeting they chose a committee "to consider together the advisability of fittingly observing the one hundred fiftieth anniversary of the incorporation of Antrim as a town."

This committee reported to the next town meeting (1926) in favor of a celebration "worthy of such an event," and suggested an historical pageant depicting the early settlement of the town. Pageants were in style then, and two members of the committee, Charles Abbott and Charles Butterfield, journeyed to Marlboro in August to view the pageant there. They were suitably impressed, and recommended that Antrim not only follow a similar course, but also that the celebration cover three days with the pageant being a prominent feature of the observance.

These recommendations were passed along to the voters at the biennial election in November, together with a suggestion that an extended committee be appointed by the moderator to continue the work of planning the details, and that the town appropriate $2,500 at the March, 1927, meeting to ensure "the grand celebration our town desires on this occasion." The voters approved the report, and the town was committed to an ambitious project.

A committee of fifteen members was duly appointed by the moderator, and these fifteen in turn named subcommittees, so that in all there finally were sixty-seven citizens at work on plans for a three-day celebration to take place August 12, 13, and 14 in 1927. One sixteenth of the population of the town eventually worked out the details of a spectacle in which one third of the town was to take part! With so many committed to the venture, success seemed assured.

Miss Leila M. Church of Rockville, Connecticut, was chosen to write the pageant; she had previously written and produced similar productions for other towns. Just before town meeting, she met with the committee for two days to discuss possible methods of treatment, and at the town meeting itself she addressed the voters, most of whom by now were enthusiastic. They readily voted the appropriation of $2,500 for expenses, and Miss Church promised to return in April to present her outline.

Late in April the theme was settled, and the various episodes blocked out. At a public meeting Miss Church read the script to the audience, who approved of everything but the title, which was to be "Men of Antrim." Even then there was some recognition of women's rights, and some thought the exclusively masculine title was a slur on the contribution of women. Curiously enough, the most vocal objection came from a man, John Fleming, who wrote "We poor boobs of men are apt to straighten our shoulders, throw out our chests, and strut around like White Leghorn roosters among a flock of hens, and think we are it. We do all the crowing, and are willing to do half the cackling when the egg is produced, but we should remember it is the good old biddy that produces the egg every time." This impassioned plea for recognition of women notwithstanding, the title stood, the interests of brevity precluding the rights of equality.

Meanwhile, the committee had also been busy. The Imperial Decorating Company of Manchester was chosen to dress up the town hall, and businessmen and private residents were urged to hire them as well. Fifteen hundred invitations were sent out to ex-residents, summer visitors, and other friends of Antrim, and the celebration began to take on the flavor of a gala Old Home Day. In addition to the pageant, which was to be presented on two successive days, plans were made for athletic contests, a school reunion, and religious services to be part of the events. There were to be two bands, one home grown and the other imported from Greenfield, Massachusetts.

As time went on, the plans became more detailed. A little flurry was caused by the false report that an admission fee of two dollars was to be charged for the pageant. This was vehemently denied: it was to be absolutely FREE. At the centennial celebration the guests were fed free of charge; this time they were to be entertained gratis. A charge of fifteen cents would be made for the souvenir program, however. Together with the revenue from the sale of advertisements, this would make the pamphlet self-supporting.

The site chosen for the pageant was the field belonging to Mrs. Julia Tenney on West Street. Admirably suited for the purpose, this large open space was set off with pines which provided natural entrances for the cast, and the gradually rising slope at the rear was a perfect backdrop. The audience had a clear view from a knoll on Elmer Merrill's land. For the evening performance, large flood lights were erected under the direction of Byron Butterfield. (Nature also provided a bright moon to enhance the setting.)

Rehearsals for the pageant started in July, the appointed leaders of each episode having enlisted the requisite number of participants. Miss Church, writer-producer-director, drilled the various groups evenings in the auditorium of the town hall. Carrying on from there, group leaders conducted their own rehearsals, perfecting and polishing the action. The ladies of the ballet, fifty strong, flitted through the woods in practice, intent and uninhibited nymphs. Properties were solicited. "Anyone having old guns, flax or spinning wheels, or old lanterns, please loan for the pageant." Horses, wagons, and a stage coach were lined up. Miss Anna Noetzel, in charge of costumes, distributed patterns and instructions for those to be made at home, and those that were too complicated for local seamstresses were sent for. Singers were rehearsed, and lines were learned. Even the skeptics who said it couldn't be done were caught up in the fever.

Preparations went on for the other events as well. Charles Prentiss, ably assisted by Alwin Young, had charge of the competitive athletic events at Shea Field, where there were prizes for the winners. Archie Swett and his committee planned the school reunion, which was to start on Friday evening and continue through the day on Saturday. Sunday was to be given over to religious services, under the chairmanship of Mrs. C. Louise Smith. Band concerts and promenades were planned to round out the festivities.

A dress rehearsal on Thursday, August 11, went off successfully, and all that remained was for the weather to cooperate. Miraculously, it did. A hard shower passed around Antrim Friday afternoon during the performance of the pageant, causing some anxiety, but it was nothing more than a threat. A few insignificant drops of rain fell on Saturday during the school reunion; however, the skies soon cleared, and the evening was beautiful. Sunday afternoon was cloudy, but the light rain which fell during the service on Meeting House Hill was not enough to dampen the spirits of the audience.

On Friday, August 12, the village was in gala dress. Main Street was resplendent in flags and bunting. A parade headed by the Antrim band marched to the athletic field for the track events. Here the youngsters worked off some excess energy and were rewarded with prizes.

At three in the afternoon, the first performance of the pageant was given. For two and a half hours, the audience watched enthralled. Some three thousand spectators attended that afternoon, and on Saturday evening the attendance was said to be in the vicinity of twelve thousand, which may have been an exaggeration. Antrim police, augmented by some extras from Hillsboro and Peterborough plus two state policemen, kept the traffic under control.

Friday evening a concert was given at the bandstand by the 419th Infantry Band of Greenfield, which also provided the music for the pageant. After this, the Antrim High School alumni met in the town hall auditorium for a pop concert and variety show; so much time was spent in joyful reunion and reminiscing that the prepared program was somewhat neglected.

On Saturday morning, transportation was provided so that old school scenes could be revisited and old memories relived. At noon a parade of several hundred former and present students formed at the high school building, led by the Antrim Band, with Norman J. Morse as drum major. The marchers, many in the costume of their student days, were grouped under banners indicating the years of their attendance. The parade wound up West Street, across Jameson Avenue, down Summer Street, along Main Street to Concord Street and the high school grounds, where a basket lunch was served.

At three o'clock, a baseball game between Antrim and Hillsboro drew a big crowd. The Antrim team, thought to be the better of the two, was narrowly defeated by a score of eight to seven. Most of the Antrim players, including their crack pitcher Al Thornton, had spent many late hours rehearsing for the pageant; otherwise, the score might have been different.

The second performance of the pageant was given under lights on Saturday evening. This was by all odds the crowning feature of the three days of celebration. It traced, in a series of tableaux, the history of Antrim from the arrival of the first settlers through the agony of World War I. Philip Riley was played by Fred C. Raleigh, a sixth generation direct descendant. As he entered on his horse, the silhouettes of the five ships which brought the pioneers to America crossed the skyline of the hill in back, as did a procession of early settlers, with their children, animals, and meager possessions. In the foreground, the fifty ladies of the Dawn Ballet performed their dance, symbolic of the dawn of the new town.

The scene which followed starred George Curtis as an Indian chief, and Mrs. Grace Hastings Whipple as an Indian maid, singing their love song so clearly that it could be distinctly heard by all the audience. They were surrounded by a chorus of Indians, some mounted and some on foot.

Suddenly a horseman (Forrest Tenney) appeared, warning Riley of the Indian uprising of 1746. At first unconvinced of danger, Riley saw in the background a trio of settlers being realistically attacked by the Indians, and agreed to leave the area.

Some twenty years later, James Aiken arrived with his small family, the second pioneer in the town. The Reverend Ralph Tibbals played the part of Aiken, Mrs. Jessie Black his wife, and Margaret Felker,

Left, "Deacon Aiken and Family"; above, "Civil War Wedding."

Frances Tibbals, Harvey Black, and Isabel Butterfield trudged along as the Aiken children. Once again, the ships (sails and masts, carried by men on the far, unseen side of the hill) scudded across the horizon.

To illustrate the skills of the early homemakers, twenty ladies with their spinning wheels gathered and spun their flax and their neighborly gossip together to the tune of familiar Scottish airs.

In the last scenes before the intermission, all the men of Antrim assembled at Aiken's house on hearing news of the battle of Lexington and, led by fife and drum, marched off to join the fight. One man, William Smith (Archie Swett), stayed behind to gather provisions for the march, and left the sorrowing women the next day. The women loaded an ox cart with provisions and knelt while Smith prayed for divine blessing before driving off.

Finally, the men having returned safely, a town meeting was held, and John Duncan (Fred Burnham) was chosen to take a petition to the legislature requesting that Antrim be incorporated as a town. This ended the first part of the pageant.

After the intermission, the action commenced with a three-part scene: seven ladies riding pillion with seven men on horseback; Captain John Duncan's household goods arriving in 1773 in the first cart seen in town; and a stage coach drawn by four white horses illustrating the mode of travel after 1801 when the turnpike was opened.

Next came a two-part dancing episode. Men in tall hats escorted women in hoop skirts toward a series of gates to the tune, "Seeing Nellie Home," followed by a colonial group representing their ancestors and dancing a stately minuet.

The Civil War wedding scene (Mr. and Mrs. Albert Thornton, the bridal couple) was attended by forty guests who witnessed the ceremony, following which the groom bade the bride farewell and joined the group of soldiers in blue who marched off to the war. The sorrowing bride was led away by her mother, and the remaining guests danced a reel.

The grand finale featured five ladies in allegorical guise: Independence, Loyalty, Humanity, Justice, and History. One hundred and eight men representing early settlers, soldiers of the Revolutionary War, the War of 1812, the grenadiers, and men who fought in the Civil War and World War I massed around them, while the ladies summed up the courage and honor of these "Men of Antrim."

The entire impressive spectacle lasted two hours and a half, and in appreciation of her efforts, Miss Church was presented with bouquets at the conclusion of each performance, and a check for four hundred dollars. Everyone thought she was worth every penny of it.

Sunday was devoted to religious services. Morning worship took place at the Presbyterian church in the village, and vespers were held on Meeting House Hill where the first church stood.

During Saturday and Sunday afternoons the library was open, with hostesses serving tea in the historical room, the public having loaned antiques for the display. Two hundred and forty-five persons signed the library's register, of whom fifteen had lived in Antrim fifty years earlier.

No doubt about it, it was an impressive and unforgettable celebration. Only a few details remained to wrap it up. The usual small town rumors circulated and were promptly denied. The sesquicentennial was NOT $1,000 in debt — actually it returned $180 to the town treasury, notwithstanding that the pageant alone cost $2,600. The surplus came from the sale of post card pictures, which netted the committee $600. Aside from the pictures and the souvenir program, the whole thing had not cost the audience one penny — it was as free as the New Hampshire air.

Flowery letters and telegrams passed from Miss Church to Antrim, and vice versa. In a letter beginning, "Dear Antrim," Miss Church thanked all who took part, with especial thanks to Mr. Whitney for his work on her "dream ships," and Miss Noetzel for her unselfish labor on the costumes. Others warranted compliments: the group in charge of the rented costumes not only saw to the fitting, but kept track of everything and collected them after the performance for return shipment; Erwin Putnam, who was the official photographer; Byron Butterfield, who was in charge of preparing the pageant field; and police Chief Nylander who, with his assistants, coped with a traffic problem of a magnitude never before seen in Antrim.

As impressive as the whole celebration was, the crowning achievement may have been the feeling of unity it promoted in the town. Working together for a common goal, with rivalries and petty jealousies put aside, all the townspeople produced an outstanding public ceremony of which they could justly be proud.

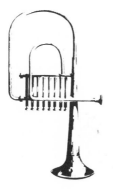

Reprise

REPRISE

THE HANDFUL of pioneers who applied for Antrim's charter in 1777 never envisioned the vast changes that were to occur in the relatively short span of two centuries. The population has increased a hundredfold. What started as a farming community was, by 1877, a thriving industrial village, and is now essentially a bedroom town. One room school houses are only a memory; the original fourteen districts of the first hundred years were finally consolidated into one educational compound, and a recent change has resulted in a school system governed by a nine-community board. The "Leading Road" has been expanded into a sixty mile long network, linking neighbor to neighbor in all parts of the town. Cars, trucks, motorcycles, and recreational vehicles speed along these highways, sometimes stopping briefly to deliver goods, or replenish supplies, or enjoy the scenery before moving on.

More and more people "from away" have chosen to stop here permanently — young families who wish to escape the city and bring up their children in a safer and more relaxed atmosphere, and older people, who choose to retire here for economic and other reasons. All have sought some degree of that stability so typical of the small New England town and perpetuated by those whose roots have long been in Antrim.

Transformation is evident from decade to decade, almost from year to year. There are fewer parades now. Today's children probably do not know what a "promenade" is — or was. For them, and for all who want to remember how Antrim grew, this book has been written.

The pattern of change we record here is both inescapable and encouraging. Growth and adaptability are necessary for survival. Yet the roots nourish the plant, and Antrim remains essentially what she always was: a community of people who live and work and play together, mindful of each other's needs, bound by a common goal. In this bicentennial year, we salute her future.

303

LIST OF ILLUSTRATIONS

INDEX

a

b

C

Campbell Pond, 42, 55, 110-11, 117, 259-60
Cannell, William B., 116
Carll, Lawrence, 148
Carr, Jonathan, 25, 271
Carter House, the, 44, 88, 102, 117
Caughey, George H., 144, 162, 184, 211, 285
Caughey, John, 185, 188, 191, 194, 202
Caughey, Rachel, 144
Caughey, Robert A., 173, 177, 182
Caughey, Theodore, 162
Caughey, Winslow, 177
Caughey's mill, 109, 112
Caughey & Pratt, 144, 184, 211-12, 258, 260
Cemeteries, Center, 210, 246; Meeting House 45, 125, 209, 246-47; Maplewood 125, 131, 144, 210-11, 246; North Branch 115, 144, 210, 246; over East 211
Chaffee, Thomas, 141, 155, 156, 282-83
Chamberlain, Lyman, 160
Champney, Charles, 248
Chandler, Alfred, 181, 183, 190
Chapin, Henry, 30
Chase, Daisy F., 223
Chase, Howard, 205
Chase, Michael, vi, 182
Cheney, Nina, 60
Chestnutt, Arthur A., 201
Chestnutt, Laura, 196, 201
Christian Science Society, 127, 217, 219, 223
Christie, Josiah W., 211
Christie, Morris, 30, 75, 212, 238, 263
Church, Leila M., 293-94, 298
Claflin, Barry, 285
Clark, Guy, 162

Clark, William, vi, 222
Cleaves, Nathan, 22
Clement, Albert, 55
Clement, Dow, 117
Clinton Industries, 177
Clinton & South Antrim Water Company, 235-36
Clinton Village, 30, 44, 45, 53, 60, 66, 119, 124, 129, 131, 164, 168, 227-28, 259, 278
Clough, Rhonda, 188
Cochlan, Michael, 16
Cochran, Andrew C., 270, 273
Cochran, George A., 77, 167, 205, 240
Cochran, Sylvester, 280
Cochrane, Clark, 202-03
Cochrane, Hayward, 177
Cochrane, Munson, 118
Cochrane, Warren R., 3, *passim* Cochrane Revisited, 30, 48, 86, 177, 181, 202-03, 209, 213, 222, 234, 236, 245, 247
Colby, Amos, 64
Colby, Dave, 271
Colby, George, 57
Cole, Lemuel D., 67, 165
Colton, Henry, 268
Congregational Church, 44, 50, 151, 163, 219-20-21
Congreve, William Jr., 140
Conservation Commission, 188, 268
Contoocook Manor, 126

d

e

Eaton, Charles, 64
Eaton, Hiram, 254, 273
Ebert, Dick, 207
Edmunds, Richard, 194
Edwards, Ellen, 286
Edwards, Ellerton, vi, 170, 174, 181, 196, 260, 268
Edwards, George, 260
Edwards & Son, 174-75, 260
Eldredge, Cranston, 187
Eldredge, H. Burr, 96, 169
Eldredge, Hiram, 31, 47, 49, 73, 118, 133, 145, 171
Electric lights, 36, 40, 41, 44, 46, 49, 113, 232, 262
Elementary school, 167-68, 170-71, 284-85-86
Ellenwood, Frank P., 220
Elliott, Clarence, 187
Elliott, Fred Butler, 163
Elliott, Henry W., 276
Ellis, Elton, 144
Emery, Scott, 259

f

Farnham, Wilbert D., 73
Federated Church, 211, 215
Felker, Elizabeth, 148, 205, 283
Felker, Margaret, 296
Felt, J.L., 25
Fire fighting, 65, 66, 253-59 *passim*
Flanders, Robert, vi, 181, 183
Fleming, Harold, 181
Fleming, John, 293
Flint, Hutchinson, 16
Flint, John G., 46, 240
Flint, Wyman K., 133, 177, 240
Flood, Wallace (Pete), 148
Forehand, Carolyn, 158
Forsaith, Squires, 205
Foster, Mark, J.W., 238
Four H, vii, 181, 188
Fourth of July, vii, 32, 40, 104, 119, 121, 125, 128-29, 133, 136, 140, 165
French, Avis Turner, 166, 203
French, Malcolm, 53, 111, 203
Fuglestad, Andrew, 121

g

h

j

k

l

m

Methodist Church, 61, 116, 127, 136, 141, 145, 218
Michael, Elizabeth, vi
Mile's boarding house, 88, 89, 90
Miller, Alfred A., 273
Miller, Etta, 211
Miltimore, James, 12
Molin, Mr. and Mrs. Wilbur, 190
Monadnock Paper Mills, vi, 113, 124, 182, 233, 320
Monadnock Research Laboratories, 177
Morse, Norman J., 37, 295
Mountain View House, the, 74
Mulliner, Edith, 286
Munhall, Jack, 285
Munhall, Rob, 156
Muzzey, Ethel, 51, 242
Myers, William M., 250

Nichols, Ethel, 130
Nichols, Isabel Butterfield, 182, 192, 244, 297
Nichols, Martin, 234
Nichols, Thomas, 246
Noetzel, Anna, 123, 294, 299
Nolan, Angus, 258
North Branch, 30, 37, 42, 46, 50, 53, 59, 66, 110, 118, 124, 131, 137, 138, 140, 149, 153, 155, 168, 227, 258, 277-78
North Branch Chapel, 124, 221, 268
North Branch fire, 33, 34, 259
North Branch Ladies Home Circle, 150, 221
North Branch river, 29, 86, 117, 177, 226, 236
North Branch school, 128, 177, 282
Nylander, George, 139, 181, 299

n

Nathaniel Hawthorne College, 177-78-79, 187, 190-91, 207, 221, 268
Natural disasters: Blizzard of '88, 33; Dark day, 14; dysentery, 16; earthquake, 159; hard winter of 1779, 13; hurricane of '38, 151-52-53; Spanish influenza, 109; spotted fever, 22; tornado 1892, 39, 1922, 115
Nay, Fred, 205
Nay, Morris, 205
Nay, William, 286
Nazer, J.P., 162
Nesmith, Jennie, 278
Nesmith, Robert, 22
Nichols, Carrol, 174
Nichols, Daniel, 23

o

Odd Fellows' Hall, 33, 40, 116, 133, 166, 172, 284
Odd Fellows Waverly Lodge, vii, 32, 139, 145, 150, 188, 212
Olson, Lelon, 172, 252
Olson, Wayno, 172, 193-94
Otterson, George, 6
Otterson, James, 6
over East, 53, 60, 124, 146-47, 149, 156, 168, 277-78

p

r

t

u

v

W

Y

Z

Parades and Promenades was produced and printed in a limited edition of 750 copies for the Antrim History Committee by Phoenix Publishing of Canaan, New Hampshire. Designed by A. L. Morris, the book was composed in Palatino and printed by Courier Printing Company in Littleton, New Hampshire.

The paper is 70# eggshell, Monadnock Caress text, furnished through the courtesy of Monadnock Paper Mills, Inc. of Bennington, New Hampshire. Jacket and endleaves are printed on 80# Astrolite text, also a Monadnock stock.

The binding in Joanna Western Mills' Arrestox book cloth was executed by New Hampshire Bindery, Inc. in Concord, New Hampshire.